W9-CYC-277

John Guare

VOLUME ONE

The War against the Kitchen Sink

Smith and Kraus *Books For Actors*

CONTEMPORARY PLAYWRIGHTS SERIES

If you require pre-publication information about upcoming Smith and Kraus books, you may receive our semi-annual catalogue, free of charge, by sending your name and address to *Smith and Kraus Catalogue, P.O. Box 127, One Main Street, Lyme, NH 03768. Or call us at (800) 895-4331, fax (603) 795-4427.*

John Guare

VOLUME ONE

The War against the Kitchen Sink

Contemporary Playwrights Series

SK

A Smith and Kraus Book

A Smith and Kraus Book
Published by Smith and Kraus, Inc.
One Main Street, PO Box 127, Lyme, NH 03768

ISBN 1-57525-031-4

Contents

The War against the Kitchen Sink
A preface by John Guare

In 1949, I wrote three plays that the neighborhood kids performed in Bobby Shlomm's garage in East Atlantic Beach on Long Island. Thanks to the photo story the local newspaper ran on the eleven-year-old playwright, my parents gave me a Royal portable typewriter for my twelfth birthday which I would need because I was now officially a playwright. And a playwright it had to be. I had seen *Annie Get Your Gun* and was really impressed by a vivid Indian ceremony that scared the hell out of me along with Ethel Merman. I had seen *Where's Charley* with Ray Bolger leading us, the audience, in a joyous singalong of the show's hit "Once In Love With Amy." *Life* magazine, my main connection to the world, showed naked girls waving from giant champagne glasses in *Gentlemen Prefer Blondes*. I got my parents to take me to that. I was going to be in the theater.

In 1950, *Life* magazine covered the opening of a new play called *The Wisteria Trees* by Joshua Logan who did musicals like *South Pacific*. He had taken a Russian play I had never heard of called *The Cherry Orchard* and changed the locale to the Deep South. I understood that move. Every week I saw remarkable actresses like Kim Stanley and Geraldine Page on our Magnavox's 12-inch screen finding brutal truths of loneliness while poised on the brink of wisteria-soaked hysteria. Human emotion could not be rendered true unless it cried out in southern accents which were not easy to come by when you're living in Jackson Heights, Queens. I got a copy of *The Cherry Orchard* out of the library and read it with a Southern accent; it was great but Logan already took it. I looked through other plays by this Chekhov guy to find the one I would set in the South, get produced on Broadway and still be fourteen. By now it was 1952 and I discovered *Three Sisters*. That was the play for me. I could understand those girls being trapped. I was trapped in being fourteen, in hating my life, in wanting life to be splendid which it was not. It was ordinary. I typed out my *Three Sisters* on that proof of my profession, my Royal portable typewriter. Every time the girls cried out for Moscow, I substituted New Orleans. Yes!

That was theater! "Get me to New Orleans!" I could hear Kim Stanley cry it out in that agonized southern voice that she used even when she played Joan of Arc being burned alive at the stake on a surrealistic CBS show called "You Are There" where every week Walter Cronkite would anchor a "live" TV pickup of an historical event.

I only got as far as the first act because typing was hard. I couldn't get to New Orleans either. But I could get to the theater. In 1952 I saw—why I wanted to see it I still don't know—Tyrone Guthrie's production of Marlowe's *Tamburlaine the Great*. *Life* must have shown pictures of it. I badgered my parents to take me. Tamburlaine stood on the stage of the Winter Garden Theater, unrolled an enormous map of the world, and strode across it. That one image so overwhelmed me that I could no longer watch TV miniatures like the original *Marty* set in living rooms like mine. I despised plays with people sitting at kitchen tables pouring their hearts out and the people in the audience oohing when the people in the play turned on the faucet and real water came out. That kitchen sink. That was what I hated most.

We had a wonderful neighbor at East Atlantic Beach named Glendon Allvine who had written a play in 1939 about the life of Gilbert and Sullivan called *Knights of Song* with a cast of 120 that was done on Broadway by Oscar Hammerstein. It may have only lasted a week but Mr. Allvine had been there. One week *is* so far ahead of never. In 1954 Glen worked in the press department at the American Shakespeare Festival in Stratford, Connecticut. I went up to visit him and saw Katherine Hepburn and Alfred Drake and Morris Carnovsky do *Much Ado About Nothing, Merchant of Venice*, Fritz Weaver do *Hamlet*, June Havoc and Hiram Sherman do *A Midsummer Night's Dream*. Not once, but over and over. Reading the plays made sense after seeing them. What I loved about Shakespeare was he used no stage directions. He didn't use a parenthesis after a character's name to instruct the actor how to say the line, *i.e., (With bitter irony.)* and then have the line be something like "Okay." Shakespeare packed the emotion into the line of dialogue. He also wrote lots of scene changes. Shakespeare says "The Sea Coast of Bohemia" and you believe it. I saw if you give audiences an honest crumb of information, they'll build it into an entire Forest of Arden.

Now it was 1957. I couldn't wait to see John Osborne's revolutionary *Look Back in Anger* which was coming to New York. The curtain went up. No! Not a kitchen sink! Where is the revolution?

For me, it didn't come till a couple of years later when Osborne's *The Entertainer* opened, starring Laurence Olivier as the down-at-the-heels comedian. The shock was Olivier played out front to me as if I was not in New York, but in the audience of a shabby theater at a cheesy English seaside resort. And it disturbed me. It was the first time I realized that the audience could play a role in the play. The audience was not a passive witness as it was in realistic, naturalistic plays, barred from the play by a brutal fourth wall.

The other clues I had been collecting started to make sense. I realized that what I loved about musicals was that no fourth wall existed. The clown acknowledged my presence by needing my laughter. Up to then I thought serious plays were the ones with no laughter and plays with lots of laughs were feathers. But *The Entertainer* was a serious play about the death of an Empire that made me roar with laughter. It had songs and girls. I loved it. I ignored *The Entertainer's* gloomy domestic bits that would alternate with the theater scenes. The kitchen sink in residence was the price to be paid for the dazzle created by Osborne and made manifest by Olivier. I looked at other plays and realized that what I loved about, say, *The Glass Menagerie* was not the emotional authenticity guaranteed by its Southerness. No. I loved the Williams play because Tom was telling me his idea of the truth. In 1957, I saw an Anouilh play called *Time Remembered* that had a full orchestra in the pit but it wasn't a musical. Vernon Duke wrote a score to accompany this play. Between the extravagance of Richard Burton's performance and the lushness of Duke's music, Anouilh's romanticism soared into a realm of lunatic poetry that touched a real pain about loss. The music lulled me into thinking I was seeing a show that was all pleasure and then suddenly took me somewhere else, some place dark. I was knocked out by Lorraine Hansberry's *A Raisin in the Sun* which began in the dreaded living room with a dreaded kitchen sink spouting water. But suddenly in the second act, in a stroke of madness, the play moved into an imagined African interior. I was inside Sidney Poitier's head. I was not simply engaged in watching these people. In one flash I understood these people. And then we were back in the kitchen. I began to expand the enemy list to include the Actor's Studio Strasberg brand of Stanislavski that sought perfection in the small detail of behavior. That was great for movies and television. But this was the stage! Let me see the great gesture delivered by the clowns that I was lucky to see: Bea Lillie, Nancy Walker, Judy Holliday, Zero Mostel. Those raunchy boisterous strippers of *Gypsy* warmed me up for Ethel Merman's blaring out her rage: "Someone tell me when is it my turn?" Bert Lahr played six different roles in S.J. Perelman's *The Beauty Part* and destroyed the idea of a single coherent human identity for once and for all. Arthur Kopit (who was my age for God's sake) wrote the outrageous *Oh Dad Poor Dad...* as directed by Jerome Robbins with a great clown named Barbara Harris. There was a remarkable play called *The Red Eye of Love* by Arnold Weinstein, *The Caretaker* by Pinter, Albee's *Zoo Story* and Beckett's *Krapp's Last Tape*. Arthur Miller? I wanted everybody in *The Crucible* to go nuts, especially John Proctor. I didn't want anybody to be spared. I wanted attention to be paid only to Tamburlaine or his mirror, the hilarious fools who thought they were Tamburlaine striding over the map of their own private world.

A remarkable critic and translator Una Ellis-Fermor wrote there were only two times in the history of the theater where the unconscious was made palpable, the Greeks and the Jacobeans.

Putting the unconscious on stage? Unlocking that? Yes, that's what I responded to in *Three Sisters*. Get me to Moscow. Get me to New Orleans. Get me some shape to the voices in my head. Show me the forces moving me. Don't show me a theater whose prime focus is only creating an illusion of surface reality, where the play is true because— look—it's a real room with real water running into the kitchen sink. Ergo it's real. Zola wrote in the preface to his classic naturalistic play *Therese Raquin* that with the new advances in theatrical scenery "No one can any longer deny the possibility of producing the reality of environment on the stage." In the second half of the nineteenth century, the discovery of electricity allowed the theater to replicate the very life of the new ticket-buying audience. The curtain could go up on a mirror of the middle-class audience's lives and for the price of a ticket, the audience could say "Yes, that is where I live. I believe what I see. So I'll believe what I hear." Zola could fill his environment with a truth. But the new audience wanted a theater that told them, not only is your life fine, after it deals with this evening's problem, say, divorce or illegitimacy, life is going to go back to being fine and we'll never say anything further to disturb you. We'll lull you and reassure you. How could we lie? Look how artfully we've replicated life. If it looks real, it is real. "But this is photography... This is the misunderstood naturalism which holds that art merely consists of drawing a piece of nature in a natural way; it is not the great naturalism which seeks out the points where the great battles are fought, which loves to see what you do not see every day, which delights in the struggle between natural forces, whether these forces are called love and hate, rebellious or social instincts, which finds the beautiful or ugly unimportant if only it is great." Strindberg wrote this in 1889, eight years after Zola.

I was learning the difference between the plays of Pinero and the plays of Shaw, the difference between Eugene O'Neill who along with Tennessee Williams showed you the consequences of illusions, as against a representative Broadway playwright such as William Inge. Great White Way Naturalism told you indeed Little Sheba might not Come Back but don't worry, we'll learn from this experience and everything will be all right. I was beginning to see that Great White Way naturalism is to reality what sentimentality is to feeling. I was beginning to learn that theater has to get into the deepest part of your dreams, has to show you a mirror you might recoil from, but also show you reality so you might know what to do with it. What's the best route to that place of our secret voices? Tennessee Williams wrote two one-act plays called *Slapstick Tragedies.* I loved that title. He showed one way to that part of our brain or our souls. The part of theater that's vaudeville.

I was in Egypt in 1965 and got a packet of clippings from my parents about the Pope's visit to New York. Imagine! The first time a pope had left Rome to travel overseas to plea for peace. My parents said you might think you're seeing the world but the world has come to us. And they wrote me all about the joy of seeing the Pope on Queens Boulevard. I started writing *The House of Blue Leaves* that day in Cairo. Yes, it would take place in the living room but that living room would have everything in it, including the kitchen sink but crammed with lots of songs and talking to the audience. If I had been in New York, I would have discounted that Papal day and sniffed at my parents' response. Being in Egypt allowed me for the first time to look into my life, into the world of my parents and realize that no life is ordinary.

Out of *The House of Blue Leaves* being read at the O'Neill Theater Center in Waterford, Connecticut, I got a fellowship to Yale in the annus mirabilis of 1966/67—a year when Robert Lowell, Jonathan Miller, Irene Worth were in residence there as were two great clowns, Ron Leibman, a fantastic Mosca in *Volpone,* and Linda Lavin who was in *Dynamite Tonight,* an hallucinatory opera by William Bolcom and Arnold Weinstein which I saw fourteen times; it never failed to move me or make me howl with laughter. It was now 1968 and during an antiwar demonstration in Times Square a policeman's horse veered around in the crowd; its head knocked me out. When I came to, I saw a giant billboard of Frank Sinatra holding a gun lit by giant search lights. The site of the political demonstration was inadvertently the site of the gala opening of a movie called *The Detective*. Beneath that billboard, a policeman was helping me up. I wrote *Cop-Out* for Ron and Linda. *Home Fires* was its curtain-raiser.

Cop-Out ran only a few days; its closing set me into such a depression that I went to the Arctic Circle to get away. Since I was in Norway, I would give Ibsen another chance. I found his last play *When We Dead Awaken*. I stayed away a number of months and came back to New York where I had success with *House of Blue Leaves* and a musical version of Shakespeare's *Two Gentlemen of Verona* starring the great Raul Julia that I wrote with Galt MacDermot and Mel Shapiro. But having what I dreamed of having only made me question where I was headed; I wrote *Rich & Famous* again for Ron and Linda. In response to some personal emotional upheaval, I finally used Norway and wrote *Marco Polo Sings a Solo,* which takes place on an iceberg at the millennium and also gave me a chance to use that map of the world. *Moon Under Miami* began life as a screenplay called *Moon Over Miami,* written in 1981 as a response to the new Reagan era to star John Belushi and be directed by Louis Malle. Was the only way to write a political play by attempting to find the equivalent of a savage political cartoon by Thomas Nast?

Well, Belushi died. The movie unraveled. A few years later, Louis said "John, do it as a play." And I did it the summer of 1987 at The Williamstown Theater Festival with a cast of great clowns, namely Nathan Lane, Lewis J. Stadlen, Julie Hagerty, Glenne Headley, James Belushi, and a staggering performer named Laurel Cronin (as Fran Farkus) who died before she could be fully appreciated. I couldn't figure out what to do with the mermaids. Yale Rep did it in 1989. I think the definition of nonnaturalistic theater is when you have to keep asking "Who the hell are the mermaids?" I could not figure out what to do with the mermaids or what was Fran's true identity until 1995 when Neel Keller directed the new *Moon* in Chicago at the Remains Theater with sublimely brutal scenery by Red Grooms. Not only did the play close, the theater closed with it. I had all ready done the Arctic Circle. I checked out timetables for Tierra del Fuego. But I didn't go.

When I was in Norway that time in 1969 reading Ibsen's last play *When We Dead Awaken* with its journey of the artist trying to scale the mountain top and leave the ordinary world behind, I began to realize that what the playwright does with the icon of naturalism, the kitchen sink, is the story of twentieth-century playwrighting. Does the playwright elect to keep that kitchen sink to soothe the audience? Does the playwright dismantle the kitchen sink and take the audience into dangerous terrain? How the playwright resolves this tension between surface reality and inner reality, how the playwright restores the theater to its true nature as a place of poetry, song, joy, a place of darkness where the bright truth is told, that war against the kitchen sink is ultimately the history of our theater.

JOHN GUARE received the Award of Merit from the American Academy of Arts and Letters for his plays *The House of Blue Leaves, Rich and Famous, Marco Polo Sings a Solo, Landscapes of the Body,* and *Bosoms and Neglect.* His play *Six Degrees of Separation,* which was later made into a movie, received the 1990 New York Drama Critics Circle Award for Best Play.

Cop-Out

NOTE ON CAST OF CHARACTERS

One actor plays all the male parts. One actress plays all the female parts.

The only scenery in the scenes between the Policeman and the Girl is a very realistic police barricade. The signs she carries will always be blank.

In the detective scenes, the scenery is, any props are, lushly stylized as in a Universal/M.G.M. film.

The link between the two worlds of the play is the movie screen at the rear of the stage.

The Policeman/Girl scenes are acted as if in a superreal documentary.

The Arrow scenes are M.G.M. dynamic, as if every character, except Arrow, has been nominated for best performance in a supporting role. Arrow, of course, is the world's toughest superstar.

COP-OUT

As the audience come into the theater, they hear a Billie Holliday sultry voice singing:

> Whodunit, my love?
> You dunit, my love,
> With a love so completely new.
> If I gun it, my love?
> Would you shun it, my love?
> But why shoot it or boot or try to toot it?
> Do you want to know why?
>
> Our love is a crime.
> A criminal I'm.
> To be always testing
> A love so arresting
> Is surely a crime.
>
> If you beat me to death with your gun
> I wouldn't blame you
> And at your trial, would I name you?
> No,
> No,
> No.
> Whodunit, my love?
> Youdunit, my love,
> And I do.

(As the house lights come down, the song is repeated, but this time sung in a very jazzy, Astrid Gilberto, breathy, bossa nova style. At the end of the song, the lights are out. In the darkness, we hear a thonking noise. Ten counts.

Lights Up on an astonished brightness all focused down on a policeman in full uniform. The rest of the stage is dark. He slaps his nightstick against the palm of his hand, making the thonking noise. Slow, steady rhythm. He glares at us as if looking for an offender, daring some offense. His brass buttons shine. His cap is pulled down to the bridge of his nose. Ten counts. Blackout.

Lights up immediately and his whole manner has changed and the stage lighting is bright and warm and jolly. His cap is pushed to the back of his head. He unbuttons his collar and smiles the broad smile of a very shy person. He's relaxed and as warm and as bright as the lights.)

THE POLICEMAN: *(To us.)* When I was a kid, my father—my *pop* played a fabulous joke on me. We walked and walked one Maytime Sunday looking for fires to go to. Up streets. Down streets. Sniffing for smoke. Ears cocked for sirens. He held my hand and we walked and walked, which was really nice as I had only learned how to a few weeks before and the sense of one step, two step was very new. He held my hand. A very crisp, pleasant, uninflammable Sunday, all in all. All quiet. All nice. Streets of empty apartment houses because the whole world had gone off to church. My father—my *pop* suddenly picked me up and whispered in my ear—this ear—a truly strange request. Would I please yell out loud as my new pink vocal cords would, would I yell out the word Lease-Po? That I was going on two and I should start speaking if I was going to walk and it would mean a lot to him, he said, if my first words were—well, he said, I hate to put words in your mouth, but it would mean an awful lot to me if your first words were—and he said it again—if your first word was Lease-Po. I looked him in the eye simultaneously learning the brand-new emotion of bewilderment. I hated not understanding. Not understanding. That's the worst thing there is. Say it, he said. I said it. No, louder, he said, jiggling me in the crook of his arm. Lease-Po.

I want to see the blue veins pop out in your pink throat. The fireworks on your first Fourth of July—remember? I shrieked out the word so loud. My first word. Lease-Po. And the breath rushed through my mouth. And he kept jiggling me, yessing me on right there on the quiet streets. Lease-Po. Lease-Po. Lease-*PolicePolicePolice-Police-Po-Po-po*—

Policemen dropped out of fire escapes. Squad cars screeched to halts. Policeman ran up out of what I thought were deserted subway stations, and policeladies appeared and pulled talcumed guns out of their navy-blue garters. We were circled. My father—my *pop* blossomed bright red with embarrassment that flowered into laughter and he waved his fingers like a gun at the temple of his head. Kid's crazy, my dad said. And his laughter filled up the quiet streets. The wife took thalidomide, my dad says. The wife took thalidomide and drank hard liquor and went to night school while she was pregnant so the kid as a consequence got born without any brain.

No, I shrieked for my second word. No no no. He told me to, I said to the circle of guns. My father pinched me tight and whispered a brand-new word: Squealer. He clapped his hand over my mouth and waved his fingers crazily and policeladies started to cry and weeping policemen patted my father on the shoulder and my father held me up and we tsktsk-tsked our way through all the blue uniforms and, over my father's bobbing shoulder, I watched all the blue capped hands waving good-bye and the sun polished their buttons and these *(Indicates billy club.)* and talcumed guns vanished back into policeladies' garters.

Now that my arms are as strong as the crook of the arms of my pop's, and now that my father is dead, on odd occasions when the streets are empty and the sun fingers these numbers on my chest, I throw back my head on the empty Sunday streets and scream out: *Leasepo!!!!!* And *I* come running... *(He pulls his cap down onto the bridge of his nose and buttons his collar. His manner is stern and tough. He resumes beating the billy club against his palm.)* I'll teach my father to make jokes.

(Count Five. Blackout. The movie screen at the rear of the stage suddenly comes to life. A strobe light behind the screen flashes at the audience. Music plays: pow-pow-pow music like the music that would play at the credits of a detective film. The actor who plays the policeman has stripped off his policeman's coat. A jaunty fedora replaces the policeman's cap. He appears behind the screen and in silhouette with the music blaring begins firing the two pistols he carries. Pow pow pow. What a fabulous shot! Lights Up on stage. The strobe stops flashing. He comes down to us—tough, cocky, cool, supercool. His guns are drawn. He searches the audience. His name is Arrow.)

ARROW: I know you're out there, Mr. Big. I'm not going to rest till you're a bloody pulp, till I destroy your Nigger/Jew/Commie/Spickie/Dike-o/Kike-o /Faggo/Russki/Zion/Mafia. Your days are numbered, Mr. Big... or my name isn't Arrow. *(Flashes his badge.)* Brett Arrow. *(He sits in a permanent-ly tilted desk chair. He puts his feet up on an imaginary desk. He takes a swig of whiskey from a flask in his pocket. He returns his guns to the holsters under each arm.)* I love being a plainclothesman. Even in the shower, you feel you got your uniform on. And the dames you meet. I mean, they don't call us dicks for nothing. *(A knock at the door. Then another knock. He stiffens. He whips into action! His guns flash out of his holsters. He leaps out of his chair.)* Not to mention the eternal danger.

(A very Old Lady enters. She is covered with blood. She stumbles blindly for-

ward. She has arm crutches that she uses with great power. She clomp-clomps blindly downstage with great pain and difficulty.)

THE OLD LADY: *(Gasping in a Mittel Europa accent.)* Arrow? Arrow?

ARROW: *(To us.)* Those crutches aren't crutches. Those crutches are rifles. She's been sent here to do dirt. To do Arrow dirt.

OLD LADY: *(Gasping.)* Arrow?

ARROW: *(Coming up behind.)* Old lady, my ass! *(And in the deftest of karate-styles he kicks the crutches out from her. She screams and falls and struggles and gropes in terror. He examines the crutch.)* You don't do dirt to Arrow.

OLD LADY: *(Her arms flailing.)* Help? Help!

ARROW: This is strange. This is a crutch.

OLD LADY: *Hellllllpppppp!!!!!!!!*

ARROW: *(Holding her arm tight behind her back.)* Okay, lady, start talking and start talking fast. Who are you? Or else my buddy in my holster will start talking for me.

OLD LADY: *(Reaches around and feels Arrow's face.)* Arrow, is that you? Is it you?

ARROW: A lot of people have said that and then tried to put a bullet in my heart.

OLD LADY: Arrow, I'm the old lady who sells newspapers on the corner, who sells flowers in the bar—

ARROW: *(Looking at her.)* Gardenia Gertie?

OLD LADY: *(Clutching.)* Help me find the murderer?

(He picks her up and plants her in his tilted-back chair. He gives her her crutches.)

ARROW: Murderer?

OLD LADY: Stockton is dead. Dead. I come home from the used gardenia warehouse and the cabbie walks me to the door like usual and I open the door and there's Stock Stock Stock Stock—

ARROW: Calm. Calm. Arrow's here.

OLD LADY: *(Gulps.)* I'm all right now. Blood—blood—Stockton in a pile. His hands outstretched by the fireplace. Eyes looking up. Broken glass. Broken furniture. My entire life gone. Love letters ripped. My shepherd's lady in bits. Everything a stew and, over it, the awful gravy of Stockton's blood. I pick up Stock Stock—

ARROW: Easy. Easy.

OLD LADY: …I'm okay now. I pick up Stockton. Is there life? I put my mouth against his. Breathe. Breathe. No steam on the mirror I hold under his nose. I—I—I—I take his tongue and place it in my mouth and bite, Arrow. Bit hard, hoping the sudden pain would bring an Easter morning, that he'd sit up and smile and everything would be the same. But the pain only forced more blood out of the slash in his throat. And the blood gushes onto my face like a lipsticked mouth saying Dead Dead and saying that one of three people did it. *(She pulls a ripped bloody sheet of paper out of her shopping bag.)* My nephew, Gib. My niece, LaRue. *(She spits at the mention of LaRue.)* My lover, William. Here are their addresses. Written in blood.

ARROW: *(Taking the paper.)* I think I can guess whose blood it is.

OLD LADY: Those unloved hate owners of love. Stockton owned all my love and they hated him because of all this money that at my death would go to Stockton. *(From her shopping bag, she takes out an enormous pile of cash.)* Take the money. Take it all.

ARROW: *(Aghast at the sum.)* ...Policemen don't take money.

OLD LADY: Take the money. Time can't be lost.

ARROW: *(Touching the money.)* We're paid for out of your tax dollar.

OLD LADY: A hundred thousand clams. Take it. There's more.

ARROW: No! *(But he takes it and gapes at it.)*

OLD LADY: I'd rather have a fool get it than one of those killers.

ARROW: Now wait—

OLD LADY: *(Struggling out of the chair.)* You're a good man. You bought gardenias from me for your lady friends and you were never too tough to have a friendly word. I'll be home watching Stockton's body. Keening over it. He won't be buried till justice is done. Help me, Arrow. You're a tough man, but a good man. I'll be home trying to glue my shepherd's lady back together. *(She starts to exit with great dignity and difficulty.)* But all the king's horses and all the king's men... *(She is at the door.)* Could you lend me three bucks for the cab ride home? *(He gives her the money. She exits. He turns jubilantly to us, waving the shopping bag full of money at us.)*

ARROW: You see this, Mr. Big. I'm going to fight you on your own ground. This money will go to the Police Athletic League to find young boys and raise them to be cops. My dream: a police force of five-year-olds, six-year-olds, so you grow into your job with a whole sense of life force and purpose. And some of the money will stay with me, so I'll never be tempted by any of your Mafia bribes, Mr. Big-Soon-To-Be-Mr.-Tiny. There's a lot of temptations being a cop and I'm proud to say I've only fallen fourteen times. I love money. It's what this country's built on. *(Starts counting it.)* Virtue is rewarded. There is a God and His badge number is A-One.

(The Strobe behind the movie screen begins flashing. The Lights Go Down on the Arrow. Blackout. The sounds of a demonstration. Lights Up: the bright clear intense warmth of reality. A girl carries a picket sign and walks in a circle that covers most of the stage. The Policeman comes on and stands in place.

He tries to give his billy club a professional swing, but it gets caught up, the leather thong of it, gets caught in his thumb. She keeps walking, not particularly involved. She gives her sign a few shakes upward. He begins thonking his club as at the beginning. When she passes by him, the second time she's passed him, she looks at him. She stops but there are other people in the circle and she must keep up the pace. Her eyes are never off him. He keeps thonking. When she passes him, she smiles.)

GIRL: I love your rhythm. *(No response. She makes one full circle. Then:)* I love the radio. *(No response. She makes one full circle. Then:)* You like the radio?

(He stops his thonking for just a split second. She makes one full circle. Then:)

GIRL: You know why I like the radio? The surprise. *(She steps out of line in front of him.)* On records, you always know— *(She catches up to her place in line and makes one full circle, then steps out of line again. Breathless:)* You always know what you're going to hear because they're your records—but the radio—I mean, the surprise—

THE POLICEMAN: Just keep walking in the circular manner prescribed by the law—

THE GIRL: *(Makes one full circle, then:)* This is some demonstration… *(Makes one full circle.)* You gonna beat up on us?

THE POLICEMAN: *(Running out of patience.)* Look, girlie. Girl Communist.

THE GIRL: I mean, it's not like we're strangers.

THE POLICEMAN: Move on!

THE GIRL: *(Coming down behind him.)* We met in Washington Square Park last spring. You beat up on me. You broke my girl friend's head? Remember? I spit on your nose. You remember? And I stepped over my girl friend's head to pull my sign back from you, but I stopped because my spit looked like a tear in your eye. Like you were crying because you had to do your duty. That was me.

THE POLICEMAN: Yeah? Well, that wasn't me. I don't do things like that.

THE GIRL: If we could just talk? Could you arrest me, so we can talk?

THE POLICEMAN: *(Very nervous.)* Do me a favor? Please get back on line.

(She falls to the ground. He looks around. He's trying to be very cool.)

THE POLICEMAN: Look, girlie, I did not become a officer—you stand up—become no officer of the—look—to get brainwashed by any Commie dope dupes like you. We was forewarned how you Commie dope dupes like to get the ear of unsuspecting patrolmen and pour in your own particular brand of poison and wash our brains till we're all like you. Well, I don't like brainwashing, so kindly arise to your feet and—and walk in the aforementioned manner.

THE GIRL: *(Looking up at him.)* Officer, I am not brainwashing, if that's what is holding up our relation—

THE POLICEMAN: Look—I became a cop to catch bank robbers. These dreams of breaking up Counterfeiter Rings. God! Delivering babies in taxis. Cats off roofs. Jeez, traffic. I even had dreams of towing all these cars away—far away. But if we wasn't here, ma'am, you see that American Legion Post across the street there, those old men frothing at the mouth with anger, they'd beat the Commie crap out of you.

THE GIRL: *(Getting up.)* I'm no Commie dope dupe.

THE POLICEMAN: You think. You think. They got you so brainwashed and sanforized. I don't see no "Made in USA" on any those signs you carrying. Jeez, you're looking at the world through rose-colored rosies.

THE GIRL: No! The world it could be lovely and tender and wonderful if only...

THE POLICEMAN: Rosy ain't the color of your specks. No, sir. Pinko. That's the color they got you seeing. Boy, would I like to straighten you out on the political realities of our time. Boy, would you be in for a shock.

(She takes her sign and makes a full circle. She stops by him.)

THE GIRL: Look, if beating up on me that time, if that's what's holding up our relationship, I mean, I forgive you. You have your job to do and I have mine and there's no reason why we can't be friends.

THE POLICEMAN: *(Nervously.)* Come on, huh?

(She kneels by him and pulls at her shoe.)

THE GIRL: I'm tying my shoe. It's no electric chair to tie your shoe. *(Pause.)* I mean, it'd be all very West Side Story, you and me.

THE POLICEMAN: Boy, would I like to open your eyes.

THE GIRL: *(Standing up.)* I'd be the PR's and you could be the Polacks. Are you a Polack? I didn't mean anything personal. It's great to be anything, you know, if you like it.

THE POLICEMAN: A cop. That's what I am. Oh boy, could I straighten you out. I got some pamphlets that could show you what enemies are trying to do to this country... they're in the back seat of the patrol car. Boy, could I open your eyes...

THE GIRL: *(A long pause.)* You could put tears in my eyes and you wouldn't even have to spit.

(They look at each other. She touches his billy club very gently. The Strobe light in the screen behind them starts to flash. The sultry voice starts to sing:

> Whodunit, my love
> Youdunit, my love
> With a love so completely new...

Blackout. The music turns into "Manhattan Serenade," that early morning, day-like-any-other-day B-movie music. Arrow appears behind the screen in silhouette. Rumpled shirt, the fedora, the double holsters. Hooked permanently onto his shoulder is his jacket hanging there. He comes Downstage. He carries the piece of paper with the names written in blood. The light comes up.)

ARROW: I'm going to try this LaRue first. One Million Park Avenue. Classy address. I wonder if Mr. Big lives here. *(Pushes an elevator button and steps in.)* Eighty-ninth floor, please. *(Steps out immediately.)*

(LaRue appears. She is gorgeous, sultry. She wears a zowie green caftan with a hood studded in diamonds. She sits in one of those super-chichi, transparent blow-up chairs. She wears large studious glasses that she occasionally takes off and licks when she's lost deep in thought. Papers are scattered all over the floor. When Arrow and she meet, when their eyes touch across the stage, a saxophone plays. He advances toward her.)

LARUE: *(Cooooool.)* Don't step on my thesis.

(He advances toward her, never taking his eyes from her. However, he does avoid every page.)

LARUE: The pages are carefully filed all over the floor.

(He steps gingerly.)

LARUE: That's it—ooops—watch—yes—yes—no—yes!

(And he stands by her. Very tough. Very cool. She sizes him up.)

LARUE: I'm doing my thesis on metaphysical poetry. *(Pause. She runs her tongue over her lips.)* You like metaphysical poetry?

ARROW: *(Flashing his badge.)* Look, lady, I'm here for a job—

LARUE: It's a lot like you and me, metaphysical poetry. You yoke together two opposites and come up with something brand new, join together two ideas that never went together before and give birth to a—

ARROW: *(Cutting her off.)* Lady, my brains are in my fist and my IQ is in my holster, so kindly dispense with the poetry shit. I am here to investigate a death. You get that? A murder. I'll advise you of your Constitutional rights—

LARUE: *(Dances seductively around him.)* You don't want to improve yourself?

ARROW: *(Taking out notebook and pencil stub; tough.)* I happen to be a student at the John Jay College of Police Science on East Twentieth Street in Manhattan, majoring at nights in Accounting, Sales Psychology and Leathercrafts—

LARUE: *(Touching him.)* Name me a poet?

ARROW: *(Lighting a cigarette.)* Look, lady—I'm here to find a murderer.

LARUE: LaRue's the name—

ARROW: You're under suspicion of that murder—

LARUE: You don't know any poets! *(Singsong:)* The cop doesn't know any poets!

ARROW: I'm here to find a murderer, not get no degree. The laugh's on you, Sweetheart Miss Big, because I am formally charging you with the death, the brutal murder of Stockton and I'd like to see you buy your way out of this, you Arto Faggo.

LARUE: Stockton?

ARROW: *(Dragging deep on the smoke.)* You said it and you did it.

LARUE: Arrow, the only Stockton I know is— *(She laughs nervously, unbelieving.)*

ARROW: Yes?

LARUE: My aunt's cat. *(Covers her mouth because she's laughing at him so hard.)*

ARROW: Your aunt's cat? *(The air is filled with the sound of hundreds of cats meowing and voices laughing at Arrow.)* Nobody laughs at Arrow.
(Strikes her hard a number of times. She falls back shocked, really hurt, then she leaps at him. She beats him. He gets her in a half nelson.)

LARUE: *(Violent.)* I want your badge number, Arrow. I'll see you get busted to the engine room of the Staten Island Ferry. Let me go—

ARROW: What do you mean? A cat—
(She glares at him. He sticks his cigarette and holds it into her neck.)

LARUE: A cat! A cat! Please stop! O God, my skin. Is that smell my skin? *(He pushes her away.)* My neck, Arrow, is *bleeding!* *(Terrified.)* You burned through the *skin*— what is your badge number? I want to know your badge number. *(She lunges at him, digging at his clothes.)* Don't you wear numbers anymore?
(While she strikes his chest, he takes a long, slow, threatening drag on his cigarette. She backs away.)

LARUE: I'll tell. I'll tell. I'll—Please, no more, Arrow. I'm calm now. See, the blood is pouring out and it's cooling the pain. All cool. Cool. The cat. Yes. You want to know about the cat. Every morning, Aunt Gertie sent out to Chicken Delight for five enormous chickens for Stockton's breakfast. And while Stockton ate, she'd pet him and coo him and rub his incredible stomach that drooped on the ground like an upside-down hump and she'd knead it like dough to aid his digestion and she'd sing and ooo Oh Stockton Oh Stockton All My Money Goes To You. To You. And he'd reach up and dig his claws into her sagging cheeks and she'd wag her yellow fingers Naughty Stockton with these tears of blood oozing down her cheeks like it's coming out of my neck and he would lick the blood off Aunt Gertie's cheeks to aid his digestion and he'd leave the house, stopping only to pee on her gardenias. No, Stockton was not one of your Pink Pussycats.

ARROW: *(Quiet; after a beat, sympathetic.)* Did you do it? Kill Stockton?

LARUE: *(Shaking her head No.)* Gib.

ARROW: *(Finger snap.)* Wait, hold it, I'm on to something. Gib is Big spelled backwards. Are you accusing your cousin?

LARUE: Arrow, I think I love you.

ARROW: Where's he hiding out?

LARUE: Check the papers. He's a playwright. His play is opening tonight. Did you hear me, Arrow?

ARROW: I'll nail him. So Mr. Big's a writer? Oh, I'll kill him. Arto Faggos, I'll get you all. *(Starts to go.)*

LARUE: *(Blocking his way so he can't leave.)* You show me a law against killing cats. Arrow, I love you.

ARROW: *(Firm; strong.)* LaRue, all I know is an old lady came to me for help and that's all I know.

(Pushes her aside. She runs after him, holding onto him.)

LARUE: Arrow, I may deal in poetry, but all I dream about is violence. Violate me in the violets in the vilest way you know. I love you, Arrow. Violently. *(She digs herself into his body. She sinks, clutching him, until she is hanging on passionately to his ankle.)* I want to become you. I want to change into you.

ARROW: *(Pushing a button.)* Don't play sweet with me, smartheart. *(He steps into the elevator, dragging her with him.)* Lobby, please.

LARUE: You really hurt me, Arrow.

(Elevator opens. He steps out, dragging her with him.)

LARUE: Arrow? Don't leave! Stay? At least till the blister forms on my wound. *Our* wound. Let me see just a little more of that police brutality?

(He grinds his foot into her hand. The Billie Holliday voice that opened the play begins singing and LaRue lip syncs to it as he grinds his foot in her hand. He exits. LaRue sings to her battered hand lovingly; lip syncs.)

LARUE:

> If you beat me to death with your gun
> I wouldn't blame you.
> And at your trial, would I name you?
> No
> No
> No

(She is on her back, her hand in the spotlight and the spot gets smaller and

smaller and the Strobe light behind the screen begins to flash and flash. Blackout.)

(The Sounds of a Demonstration take over. A police barricade is D.L. The Policeman stands at the C. end of it, beating his stick against his palm. He seems quiet, nervous. The Girl appears at the rear of the stage carrying her sign. She pushes and nudges and excuses herself through the crowd till she is at the barricade. She nudges him. He starts. Then he sees it's she. He looks out front again, beating his club, but he's very pleased and happy. She sings very quietly and not quite on key:)

THE GIRL:

> I love a cop.
>
> I love a cop.
>
> What a situation!
>
> Ain't it awful?
>
> Life is really grim.
>
> I can only say that it's unlawful
>
> What I feel for him.

(He's embarrassed and so pleased and looks around to make sure no one is watching them. She leans over the barricade, her picket sign by her side. They speak quietly and both look out front. From a distance, you wouldn't know they were together.)

THE GIRL: That song is from the life story of Fiorello LaGuardia.

THE POLICEMAN: *(Blushing.)* They named the airport after?

THE GIRL: My roommate in college—

THE POLICEMAN: You're so smart—really—

THE GIRL: No social conscience at all this girl, but, boy, she loved show tunes and that song's from "Fiorello" and it won a Pulitzer Prize. I hate show tunes. But I love that song, "I Love A Cop!" *(He shushes her.)*

THE POLICEMAN: *(Blushing.)* Come on, I'm on the duty.

THE GIRL: *(Whispers it.)* I love a cop, I love a cop. I'll whisper if from the cellars. We've known each other four months now and it's like all my life I waited for you. Maybe when I was little, you saved my life, a cop did, or maybe held me up at Coney Island when I got lost in the Easter parade. A million different reasons, but whatever they are, I always knew I'd love a cop. And you got me the abortion so easy. They treated me like a queen. You know everybody.

(He shushes her.)

THE GIRL: My own parents should've treated me as nice as that abortionist— you and the abortionist—that's the two times I been treated best in my whole life. The first nice time I ever had was our making love so tender in the patrol car on all the pamphlets that day we met four months ago and you turned on the siren and the flashing red light when I—when we *happened*—you were so tender and cars sped by the speed trap and you kissed me for every blipblipblip on the radar... you were so tender... and then the other man. He cut out the child so tender, as easy as you'd put it in. I don't like the word they have for that operation. I would like to think of it as a—yes, a premature Caesarean. We had our premature Caesar while he was still pure... *(She is at his side.)*

THE POLICEMAN: *(Very quiet...)* You're so beautiful... *(Duty calls. He beats the barricade suddenly with his club and she jumps back.)* Look behind the barricade!!!!! *(To her.)* Make believe we don't know each other.

THE GIRL: *(Back behind the barricade.)* Hi, Stranger!

THE POLICEMAN: Listen to me—I'm up for a promotion.

THE GIRL: Oh, that's wonder—

THE POLICEMAN: Don't look happy. People can see us. Don't look like I'm talking.

THE GIRL: *(Dour face.)* Oh, that's wonderful.

THE POLICEMAN: But, you see, they know I'm hanging around you. They are very suspicious down at the station house. I mean, you don't arrest anybody as many times as I've arrested you and then never book them. I mean, they're suspicious. You are a known demonstrator. Jeez, it'd be better for my career, better for me to hang around with murderers or gypsy cab drivers than consorting with known demonstrators.

THE GIRL: *(Clutching her sign.)* You want me to stop picketing? I can't do that. *(And she gives her sign a good shake upward.)*

THE POLICEMAN: *(Looking at the sign.)* Well... then... there's no other choice. To show my faith in the Force before they promote me, I will have to have—a little op-operation.

THE GIRL: Operation! Are you sick?

THE POLICEMAN: Don't look at me. It's a very simple op-oper—I got a pamphlet on it right here. Most cops has it— *(He takes the pamphlet from his coat, hangs it over his billy club and passes it to her behind his back.)* —like after, most cops *have* it like after two or three kids, you see, and it's really painless. It's like a club, a fraternity, and all the serious cops—well, ninety-five percent of the Los Angeles Police Force has them. Have them. I mean, you see the statistics right there.

THE GIRL: What kind of operation...?

THE POLICEMAN: It's really simple. They just—you see this chart—they just snip the tube that leads to the pros-prostate that fer-fer-tilizes the se-se-se. Well, it's not like you're nothing. No, it makes you even more virile because there's no knock-up fear like I knocked you up. It's just a little snip and ninety-five percent like I said of the L.A. Police—and that's the best in the country—the best force in the—Everybody knows that—and I knew I'd have the operation someday because all serious cops has it. Have it. But I didn't think it'd be this soon. Vasec-vasectomy. A pretty word, huh? I mean, I wish you hadn't had that abor-abor—I mean, we woulda had one kid you know and I really want to be a cop and they're suspicious of me hanging around with you and it's just to show faith and I feel I thrown my life away because I love you and you're *still* carrying signs and can I ever trust you and I don't know what to do do do do. *(He is trying not to cry.)*

THE GIRL: *(Dazed; touches his sleeve. Sings:)*

What a situation!

Ain't it awful?

Life is really grim.

THE POLICEMAN: I mean, ninety-five percent—L.A.—says it right here—very simple—just a snip—

(Voices of a Demonstration rise up. They are both very quiet and very lost. The Lights Fade on them. The screen appears with the flashing Strobe light. Weird color lights and Indian music plays. Arrow appears behind the screen in silhouette. He strides out cocky, tough.)

ARROW: Green Witch Village. Blaaagh. Gib's Theatre is along here somewhere. Look at them panhandlers. *(Comes down to us. A close-up.)* I'd like to take a few minutes here to tell any young sports out there between the ages of eighteen and twenty-nine, standing at least five foot two with twenty-twenty eyeballs and a hatred of evil and no previous bad stuff, I couldn't advise you about choosing this *(Flashes his badge.)* as a more better way of life. *(He watches someone go by.)* Out of the way, beads. Get a haircut. *(To us.)* With all the protesting going on today, I want to know why you don't hear nobody squawking against this country's name. America—get this—named after Amerigo Vespucci. Dago Woppo. Amerigo Vespucci, my ass. Shows you how the Mafia sunk its teeth into America right from the fourteen ninety-two.

(And one of those legless panhandlers who wheel around on dollies pushes himself up behind Arrow. Wheels wears a heavy overcoat and an old hat and scarves around his neck. We can see a little mustache and dark glasses. Arrow, trying to ignore this new arrival, to us.)

ARROW: Mr. Big, are you hiding down here in Green Witch Village?

WHEELS: Pssssst.

ARROW: Hiding here under all this dirt?

WHEELS: Hey, Meester—

ARROW: Get out of here, Wheels, or I'll push you in on a 902—

> *(Wheels looks around, then hands Arrow a large red rose with a message hanging off it.)*

WHEELS: *(Spanish Peter Lorre accent.)* Meester, buy a flower?

ARROW: There's only one old lady this gumshoe buys blossoms from—

WHEELS: *(Whisper.)* Read dee message—

ARROW: "Call me, Arrow… LaRue." LaRue????????

WHEELS: Call her.

ARROW: You got a dime?

> *(Wheels whips out a walkie-talkie. An antenna shoots up.)*

WHEELS: *(Into walkie-talkie.)* Miss LaRue? *(Taps machine.)* Ein, zwei. Roger. Over.

LARUE'S VOICE: Arrow?

> *(The Actress plays both Wheel's and LaRue's voices.)*

WHEELS: Eet's for you.

ARROW: *(Taking walkie-talkie.)* For me?

LARUE'S VOICE: Oh, Arrow—

ARROW: Watch what you say in front of Wheels here—

LARUE'S VOICE: He can be trusted.

ARROW: Can you be trusted?

WHEELS: *(Offended.)* I can be trusted.

ARROW: He can be trusted.

LARUE'S VOICE: Arrow, I hate to bother you on the street, but get in that play.

ARROW: I'm on my way to the play.

WHEELS: She means *get in the play.*

ARROW: Get in Gib's play??????

LARUE'S VOICE: Arrow, if you don't, Gib will never leave that theater alive.

ARROW: Is this a trap?

WHEELS: Save Meester Geeb. Save heem.

LARUE'S VOICE: Believe me.

WHEELS: Beleeb her.

LARUE'S VOICE: You see, Arrow, I know who killed Stockton.

ARROW: Who, LaRue?

WHEELS: Who, Mees LaRue?

LARUE'S VOICE: It's—It's—It's—Oh no. No. No.

ARROW: Yes?

WHEELS: *(Takes walkie-talkie.)* …The machine is dead…

ARROW: If Miss LaRue is the same, you won't have a leg to stand on. Get me to that theater. Quick.

WHEELS: Quick????

ARROW: Pronto, Spicko.

WHEELS: Ohhh, kweeek.

ARROW: Brett Arrow's got some acting to do.

WHEELS: Thees way!!!!

(Thrilling Chase Music plays. Arrow hops on the back of Wheels's dolly. Darkness. Voices: "You can't come in here. The play is on." Sounds of slugs and hits and people falling. Then patriotic music plays. Tootling fifes and drums. A little stage wheels on, big enough for the two actors. Curtains part. Marilyn Monroe and George Washington are in bed.)

MARILYN MONROE: I don't want you doing that anymore to me, George. You hear?

GEORGE WASHINGTON: *(His head under the covers.)* Yum yum yum yum yum yum yum yum.

MARILYN MONROE: You've got wooden false teeth, George. And I've got splinters everywhere. Either you take those wooden false teeth out and give them to the termites or you leave me alone. I'm just a young girl, a very young girl, and don't take, Mr. W., you shouldn't take advantage of my youth. Oooo. Ouch. George!

GEORGE WASHINGTON: *(His head pops out of the covers.)* Look, I found you at Valley Forge and I can drop you back at Valley Forge—

(Arrow plays all the Presidents like Groucho Marx.)

MARILYN MONROE: *(Looking strangely at this new performer. Beat. Then:)* Oh, George, Mr. W., I know I should be really grateful that you're going to make me the symbol of the country—

GEORGE WASHINGTON: *(Pouting.)* Some girls would love to be symbol of a new country. I wrote you a song today!

MARILYN MONROE: A song? For me?

GEORGE WASHINGTON: *(Sings vaudeville-style.)*

DaDaDaDa Dot Dot
Your cunt
Tree, 'tis of me
Sweet land o'

MARILYN MONROE: Where did you learn all these things?

GEORGE WASHINGTON: Martha was married before. *(Ducks under the covers.)*

(A clock begins ticking throughout the rest of the scene.)

MARILYN MONROE: What did Millard Fillmore always say? Time goes by so quickly. Here it is: fourscore and seven years ago already.

(Arrow appears from under the covers as Abraham Lincoln.)

MARILYN MONROE: Couldn't you at least take off your shawl?

ABRAHAM LINCOLN: *(Again as Groucho.)* I need it to keep warm, Marilyn.

MARILYN MONROE: It makes me feel old. And those warts. I have to put up with your warts. You leave indentations in my skin. I don't want indentations in my fresh white skin.

ABRAHAM LINCOLN: Think of them as dimples, Norma Jean. Dimples that fell out. Babies have dimples. Dimples are young. I leave dimples in you. *(Vanishes under the covers.)* I need you. *(Sings.)*

My country, 'tis of you
Sweet land of libertoo
Yum yum yum yum yum yum yum yum yum yum yum yum yum.

MARILYN MONROE: You're so wise. Oh yes. I like that. Yum yum.

(Arrow leaps up as Teddy Roosevelt.)

THEODORE ROOSEVELT: Speak softly and carry a big shtick! *(He's back under the covers.)*

MARILYN MONROE: Oh, Teddy, shoot me a bear and keep me warm!

ARROW: *(Under the covers, keeps repeating over and over:)*

My dear little pussy,
My dear little pussy,
Dearest darling little pussy,
Puss puss puss puss.

MARILYN MONROE: *(Gradually mounts in ecstasy.)* Oh, Woodrow, I feel so old. Oh, Calvin, say something. Harder Harder Harder Harding. To think one day Herbert Hoover would be mine. Oh, FDR, your braces are cold against my legs. You don't tell me, Harry, you learned that from Bess. Oh, yes, Ike, you put me to sleep. Hold me, Daddy Ike. Oh, Jack. We're young. You and I are young. *(Becoming an Old Lady.)* Bobby, answer the phone? *(Gasps for breath. Desperate. Then bright and Marilyn again.)* Hey, hey, LBJ, where'd you learn to kiss that way? *(Then as Old Lady.)* Bobby? Answer the phone… *(Then Marilyn.)* OooooooooOO, Mr. Nixon. Just 'cos I'm dead doesn't mean you can treat me like that. OooooOO. *(Old Lady.)* Bobby? Answer the phone! Say… we're both… young… both still… the dream… Bobby… *(She dies, then brightly appears as Marilyn.)* My last wish was to have my ashes scattered among you, among my fans. *(To Arrow, below her.)* Hurry. Hurry.

(Arrow appears with an Uncle Sam hat on. He carries an ashtray full of ashes and a little battery-operated fan. He blows the ashes into the audience.)

MARILYN MONROE: I'm now a part. A part of you all. Breathe. Breathe so very deep. *(The curtain falls on the Little Theatre. Boos and applause. Arrow and Marilyn appear through the curtain for bows. She blows kisses.)*

ARROW: Porno Smutto… If one mind has got bended out of shape by this… *(They finish bowing. Move back behind the curtain. The theater rolls away. They are now backstage.)*

MARILYN MONROE: Who are you? You're Mondo Perfecto.

ARROW: I'll kill him. Out of my way, lady. I'm here to save Gib.

MARILYN MONROE: *(Blocking his way.)* And who, Mondo Studdo, do you think you're talking to?

ARROW: *(Pulls back; looks at script.)* The Role Of America Growing Old will be played by—

MARILYN MONROE: Hi ho, Mondo Mondo.

ARROW: *Gib!!!!!!!!*

(And a shot rings out. Gib leaps into Arrow's arms. Arrow draws his gun. Footsteps echo through the theater.)

MARILYN/GIB: *(Terrified.)* Save us?

ARROW: Get in this trunk.

(Which Gib steps into—an old theatrical trunk.)

ARROW: Gib, your cousin LaRue asked me to save you. Which I have done. *(Stirring music plays underneath.)* But I can't guarantee what will happen when you and this Porno Smutto arrive in Washington, DC and J. Edgar and his boys get a hold of you.

GIB: *(À la Judy Garland.)*
  "Anyone can be born in a trunk
  But how many get to die there?"

(He slams the trunk down on Gib. The footsteps resume. He sneezes.)

ARROW: This American Beauty is giving me the—Wait—this isn't an American Beauty—this is a bloodstained—Oh, no. Because the only other blood is the blood on the— *(He takes out the list.)* Then that would mean that this was a blood-stained—

(And Gardenia Gertie appears with a gun drawn.)

ARROW: Gardenia Gertie.

GARDENIA GERTIE: I pay you to be a flower sniffer?

ARROW: Gertie, we're on the honor system here. Go down to the precinct and turn yourself in.

(Advances toward her. She cocks the gun.)

GARDENIA GERTIE: Dance, Arrow.

ARROW: *(Dancing.)* Why'd you do it, Gertie? Why?

GARDENIA GERTIE: You think I liked being old so the only thing could love me is a cat? I fed it and it scratched me. I petted it and it bit me. I treated it good. It should love me. But when you're no longer young, power is your only weapon. So I killed him. I done it and I'd do it again.

ARROW: But, Gertie, power is a wonderful thing.

GARDENIA GERTIE: That's right, Arrow, and the power makes me feel young and I'm going to travel the whole woild—Europe, Asia, everyplace—showing I'm powerful and beautiful and still the dream. Say I'm young. *(She waves the gun.)*

ARROW: You're young. You're young!

GARDENIA GERTIE: *(Laughs insanely.)* You'll never catch me. Never.

(Backs out the door. There is a deafening scream of hundreds of meowing cats. Arrow dashes out. Then returns, clutching his stomach.)

ARROW: *(To us.)* Stockton's revenge. Devoured by an alleyful of insane felines. All that's left are her crutches and the cats are using those for toothpicks.

(LaRue crawls on, dying.)

ARROW: A goddam messy case.

LARUE: I'm dying, Arrow. I've been working for a foreign power. Don't ask me any more. Not yet. But they had seen you coming to One Million Park. They heard me warning you. They got me. Right here. I did some surgery and got the bullet out—but it went through the heart—Oo oo oo—

ARROW: Steady, girl. Steady.

LARUE: I'm all right now. And I crawled out of my apartment, down those eighty-nine flights, wanting to get to you, needing to get to you, crawling all the way here.

ARROW: Crawled?

LARUE: Oh, Arrow, rats on Park Avenue. Mice on Madison. A Fifth Avenue bus ran over me, but I'm here.

ARROW: You got the messy end of this case.

LARUE: *(Snuggling painfully in his arms.)* Yes. But I met you. *(Sings.)* Whodunit, my love? You done it, my love.

ARROW: *(Holding her.)* Don't die, LaRue!

LARUE: Keep America young for me. You have to keep us young. At any cost. Keep it young for La—oo oo oo—Rue. *(She dies.)*

ARROW: Who are you? CIA? FBI?

LARUE: *(Eyes opening. Sings.)* If you beat me to death with your gun… Oh, Arrow. DOA. *(Dies in his arms.)*

ARROW: *(Clutching her.)* No! *(Tries not to cry.)* I'll get you— *(And his eyes search the theater.)* for trying to kill off America. I know you're out there, Mr. Big. I'll get you, all you Commie Jewo Niggo Dago Woppo Mafio Faggo Russki—I'll get you I'll Get You I'll Get You I'll Get YOU I'LL GET YOU I'LL GET—

(And the Strobe light begins flashing on the screen behind. Arrow keeps yelling his threat over and over again. The sound of vroom vroom vroom of cars starting and stopping fills the theater. The Lights are Up and the stage is bare. The Policeman is taking tolls in a tunnel. In a deep anger:)

THE POLICEMAN: Five exits down. Dim your lights. Ten exits down. Read the signs. *(The Girl waits her turn behind a car. She comes to him. He reaches his hand out to take the toll, then see it's she.)*

THE GIRL: I walked through the tunnel.

THE POLICEMAN: *(Angry; not looking at her.)* Only cars are allowed here. No pedestrians in the Lincoln Tunnel. *(To a car:)* Three exits down. Turn off after the bridge, dope. *(To her:)* Get out of here! You deaf? *(To a car:)* Where'd you learn to drive? *(He pushes her behind him.)*

THE GIRL: You had the operation, didn't you?

THE POLICEMAN: *(Pause. Then, to a car:)* You don't got nothing smaller? Four exits down.

THE GIRL: Is that why you don't want to see me?

THE POLICEMAN: *(Looks at her; fumbles. Then, to a car:)* Look at your map… *(Pause. To her:)* And before the Novocain had wore off, they shipped me here as additional punishment for consorting with a known demonstrator.

THE GIRL: I—I would've come visit you…

THE POLICEMAN: You stay away. I got to earn my way back into the Force. Boy, did you dupe me. You Commie, carrying signs. You with your thinking. If you people would only stop to think where your thinking leads you—Boy, I had a chance in that hospital to do a lot of thinking and, boy, did you knit sweaters over these eyes. Well, now my eyes are clear and, boy, do I see.

THE GIRL: *(Not comprehending.)* But—you and—we were going *steady.*

THE POLICEMAN: *(Tough. To a car:)* Six exits down. Turn off by the fork. *(To her:)* It all comes back to me now. You trying to put thoughts in my head. You'da been happy if I wasn't *even* a cop. Well, I am a cop and I inhale every car that goes by, so the fumes will make me madder and tougher and, every tenth car, I steal fifty cents and put it in the PAL Fund. *(To a car:)* Fifty miles ahead, asshole. *(To her:)* So we'll have more cops. Younger cops. Teach kids to be cops right at birth and give them vasectomies and drill them—five-year-old, six-year-old police—that's what we need—And every kid in this country will wear navy blue and at high noon the universe will be blinded by the sun fingering the gold on our brass buttons. "LeasePo LeasePo" the world will sing because the screws are turning, baby. You got the blackies all riled up and you'll probably start working on the Chinko riots and get the Indians all on warpaths again. Well, your days are numbered. Because there is going to be a White the Whitest of White on White Revolutions you ever saw and all the people who want this country to to be what it can be, well, we are going to win. It's war, you Commie Dope Dupe. I had a lot of time to think in that hospital… Oh boy, my eyes are clear.

THE GIRL: Here's fifty cents. Treat me like any other car. *(Starts to go.)*

THE POLICEMAN: Right into the PAL kitty. This is gonna be the fattest kitty on the block. Oh, I love my operation. I feel I finally belong. I am finally something. *(Becomes aware that she is looking at him. He fumbles.)* I—I—I—

(She picks up a sign and begins picketing defiantly in a circle around him.)

THE POLICEMAN: I have my cophood. I have my promotion.

(She stops by him. He fumbles.)

THE POLICEMAN: I have my stick. I have my uniform.

(She stops by him. He fumbles, but stops looking at her and begins beating his club against his palm—think thonk thonk thonk—trying to pull himself together. She moves faster and faster. He becomes tougher and tougher.)

THE POLICEMAN: I have my *teeth.* I have my *fists.* I have my *spine.*

(She stops by him. He is no longer self-conscious. He is beaming ferociously.)

THE POLICEMAN: I have my *cock.* I have my *gun. Lease-Po. Lease-Po. Leasepo. Leasepo.* You stop picketing. You stop running. You stop it. You stop.

(She is running in a full circle, desperately.)

THE POLICEMAN: I'm warning you. You stop.

(She throws down her sign and leaps off stage. She runs up the aisle. He shoots her. A deafening Blast. Blackout.)

(Thonk thonk thonk thonk. One spot overhead down on him, his cap pulled down to the bridge of his nose. He beats his stick as at the very beginning. Ten counts. Blackout. He exits. Then House Lights Up. The Actress lies in the middle aisle till the audience goes home. Then she gets up and leaves.)

END OF PLAY

Home Fires

CHARACTERS:

Peter Smith: Patrolman for the Police Department of Lynn Massachusetts

Nell Schmidt: his 17-year-old daughter

Rudy Smythe: his 25-year-old son

Margaret Ross-Hughes: Rudy's fiancée and an elegant heiress

Mr. Catchpole: an undertaker

The Sullivan Family, an ideal American family who can sing and dance

TIME:

November 12, 1918. The night of the day after the signing of the Armistice ending World War One.

PLACE:

Catchpole's Funeral Parlor. A very posh establishment on Ocean Boulevard in Swampscott, Massachusetts.

HOME FIRES

Before the Curtain: The sound of foghorns and people cheering.
At Curtain: The curtain rises on a dark room. Offstage the sound of general
consternation.

MR. CATCHPOLE: *(Offstage.)* And don't come back.

PETER: *(Offstage.)* You can't kick them out! Please—come back—Wait— *(A door slams.)*

MR. CATCHPOLE: *(Offstage.)* Oh, can't I? We shall see, my good Officer Smith. Smith, is it? More likely Schmidt, shall we say? Or Schmitter or Schmarter or Schmatter. The door is closed on them. They are all gone.
(The door opens to this room. Light from the hall spills in from the hall. Mr. Catchpole is dragging an enormous spray of red roses in through the door. Officer Peter Smith is on the other side of the flowers, pleading with Mr. Catchpole.)

PETER: But they are my—my—my—

MR. CATCHPOLE: *(Triumphant.)* My my my. Relatives, is that what you're stuttering out? Or friends. I look in your guest book, your libra memoria, and I see in spidery foreign handwritings the names Dunkel. Dunkelmeyer. Webernbach. Hasseldunk. Wuderlich.

PETER: You do not understand—

MR. CATCHPOLE: I understand, Officer *Smith,* that a war is over, that an Armistice has been signed by the same spidery foreign hand, that the Doughboy's hobnailed boot has squashed forever the scourge of the Spiked Helmet. And do I see any joy? No, only the tears of a loser. Tears of defeat.

PETER: My wife is dead!

MR. CATCHPOLE: Hah! *(And he sweeps into the room, giving the roses a tug through the door. He switches on the room light. Lights from chandeliers flood the room. Little gold chairs for mourners to sit on are scattered and tossed on the floor. Everybody evidently left in a hurry. If there is a coffin in the room it must be there in that enormous garden of flowers filling almost half the room. Sprays in the shapes of stars and horseshoes and circles all have banners reading "Sympathy" and "Good-bye" and "Regrets" and "Oh No" draped on them. Mr. Catchpole adds this latest spray of roses to the array.)* It's très très misterioso,

Officer Smith, that I should receive money, enormous quantities of lucre via telegraph with anonymous orders to report to Twenty-nine Lyman Street. Vingt-neuf Lyman Street in *Lynn* of all places. Lynn, Lynn, City of Sin. My stomach is still disgusted from my trip to Lynn.

PETER: But from whom was the telegraph?

MR. CATCHPOLE: *Anonymous!* Anonymous orders to bring the earthly remains of Mrs. Peter Smith to these premises, Catchpole's Funeral Parlor. Right by the sea. And then all these Germans appear. On the very night that we have put the kibosh on the Kaiser. A war has ended and you appear. Strange. Very very strange. *N'est-ce pas? (Sings to tune: "Battle Hymn of the Republic:")*

> We have made the Kaiser wiser,
> We have made the Kaiser wiser,
> We have made the Kaiser wiser,
> And all you men appear...

PETER: *(Who has a very heavy German accent.)* Ohh-hhh, is that what you're thinking? I see what the trouble is—Ohhhhh, you think I'm... No, I'm not German.

MR. CATCHPOLE: And then all these flowers arrive.

PETER: Maybe we won a prize. My wife was always very lucky.

MR. CATCHPOLE: Thousands of dollars worth of flowers and not one card. One reads. One hears rumors that despite last night's truce the Hun in typical crafty fashion is preparing one last desperate attempt to capture the United States and hold us in her Satanic power. *(The Lights in the room Flicker. Foghorns hoot on the sea outside.)* What more ideal place of entry than Swampscott. The gateway to New England! We're right on the ocean. The foghorns are hooting. This strange woman wearing a very shabby dress is brought here under the guise of death. One reads. One hears rumors that the Kaiser is a lady.

PETER: *(Hushed.)* The Kaiser is a lady?????

MR. CATCHPOLE: The New York *Tattle* cannot afford to go around printing lies. How do I know this woman is not the Kaiser?

PETER: *(Peering into the coffin.)* That's my missus...

MR. CATCHPOLE: I'm going to make a few calls of inquiry on Mr. Bell's invention. A few pertinent *sub rosa* inquiries. If I discover, Officer Smith so-called, that that woman is indeed guilty of Germanity, out she goes.

PETER: No! No! You can't!

MR. CATCHPOLE: Into the street. La Rue. Die *Strasse*. Does that make you understand? I know you Germans. I didn't fight in the Spanish-American War for nothing. I have purple hearts. I have medals of honor. You don't fool with ex-Lieutenant Tom Catchpole. Not on Armistice Night. Not in Catchpole's Funeral Parlor. What's your badge number?

(Peter holds his hand over his chest. Catchpole pulls his hands away and pulls at Peter's badge.)

MR. CATCHPOLE: Hmmm. Two. All right, Officer Smith, the investigation has begun. Smile. This is a wonderful night. *(Opens the door behind all the flowers to proceed into an adjoining room. He beams as much as he can.)* Ahhhhh, Widow Sullivan. Don't you look lovely! Red, white and black. *(Glares at Peter and exits.)*

(Peter starts after him but the front door opens and Nell runs in. She is a pretty and chubby little schoolgirl of seventeen. She wears a cape over her school uniform and her hair is an extraordinary network of braids woven up around her ears and in coronets on her head. She has been running and can barely breathe.)

NELL: Oh, Papa. Are we safe? Papa, they were so hurt. Papa, I ran after them as far as the trolley. Uncle Otto. Uncle Wilhelm.

(Peter shushes her. She runs into his arms, gasping. He strokes her braids.)

NELL: Oh, Papa, I didn't know what to say. Why are we here? Then why did that man want to throw us out? So many unanswered questions. Why, Papa? Why? Oh, where is Rudy? Why isn't he here?

PETER: He'll be here.

NELL: How can we be sure? We have not seen him in three long years. How do we even know the telegraph wire we sent to his hotel in New York, the Hotel Brevoort, his last known address, ever reached my dear brother? Why are we here? Has Rudy deserted us as well as all reason?

PETER: Rudy will be here. *(Sings.)*
When there are blue skies,
If I want new skies,
I ask my boy.

If I am troubled
And burdened
With grief
My boy will bubble
And life turns over
A brand-new leaf.

If life comes a-cropper
Will he save his papa?
You ask my boy.

(Turns to Nell.) Now what I want you to do is—

NELL: Yes? Yes?

PETER: Run home.

NELL: It's three miles to home, Papa. The last trolley has left. We're trapped here, Papa. Trapped. *(Weeps.)*

PETER: But I need your birth certificate.

NELL: *(Stops weeping instantly.)* My birth certificate is always on my person.

PETER: Give it to me. I'll show that pig foot what country *you* were born in. *(Nell turns her back to the audience and plunges her hands into the depths of her clothing. She turns to her father with the birth certificate in hand.)*

NELL: Papa, you'll see the information that I, your daughter Nell, was indeed born in the United States of America in the city of Lynn.

PETER: I'll show him who's born a German.

NELL: Read on, Papa. The document identifies me as Nell Schmidt, born to Peter Schmidt and Gertrude Kappel Schmidt of Hamburg, Germany. *Schmidt,* Papa. It reveals our true identity.

PETER: You got any friends you could borrow their birth certificates? You got any friends named Smith? What do I send you to school for you don't make friends named Smith?

NELL: *(Appeals to the bank of flowers.)* Oh, Mama. Help us. Look down from your new home in heaven and speak.

PETER: Leave her alone.

NELL: Papa, remember when the City Hall burnt down with all the records? Mama said she'd love to be born in Lynn. You could lie about your age and always stay young.

PETER: *(Bitter.)* But she didn't say it in English, did she? Even her laughing. Ha ha ha. She'd go ha ha ha and you'd look in the dictionary to see what she was saying.

NELL: She just couldn't learn it, Papa.

PETER: *I* learned it. Rudy and your mama and I stepped on that boat in Hamburg eighteen years ago without one word of English in our mouths. And the minute I touched my tootsies onto the Boston pier, the electricity of America jiggled every word in my head into English.

NELL: You had the gift of tongues, Papa. Like the prophets in the Bible. Which I also keep on my person.

PETER: Every pebble was a Plymouth Rock. You happened in America, Nell, our first night here.

NELL: *(Embarrassed.)* Papa!

PETER: The words you got made in was English. You wasn't conceived in no

German. I made love to your mama in English. "Hey, Baby." And Mama talking German eighteen years. I couldn't even understand her last words. And that Catchpole is kicking us out! I'm all wound up. It's from your braids. Make your hair down loose. You're so pretty with your hair down loose like the lady on the silver dollar.

NELL: *(Clutching her head.)* Never, Father. The tying of these braids was Mama's last act on this earth. She tied the braids and off she went.

(The door opens and Mr. Catchpole enters carrying party hats and red, white and blue bunting and patriotic Kewpie dolls hanging on striped canes.)

MR. CATCHPOLE: The investigation has begun, Officer Smith. Badge Number Two. Numero deux. Nomber *zwei.*

(Hands them two party hats. Nell and Peter are petrified and put them on. Mr. Catchpole begins draping the bunting over the room.)

You'd be wise, Smith, and that goes for your little Empress of Austria here, to take a lesson from the Sullivans who have the rooms next door. They are not letting selfish grief get in the way of joy at the Armistice.

(Music strikes up. The room lights up. The Sullivans dance in. They are a healthy, wealthy bunch of four or five bright Men, Women and Children, or as many as the stage will hold, all dressed in black clothes with red, white and blue mourning bands on their arms.)

THE SULLIVANS: *(Out to the audience.)*

> We have made the Kaiser wiser,
> We have made the Kaiser wiser,
> We have made the Kaiser wiser,
> And we won't eat sauerkraut.
>
> For many years the Germans fought,
> Their slogan greed and gain.
> The world is wrong and I am right
> Imprinted on his brain.
> The U.S.A. has won today and Yankee Doodle we will play
> You bet your life we made the Kaiser wiser.

(They repeat the chorus out to the audience and try to get the audience to sing along with them with the aid of a bouncing white ball and then they dance out, throwing flowers from the bier out to the audience. Mr. Catchpole follows them out. He turns to Peter.)

MR. CATCHPOLE: The investigation has begun. *(Exits. We hear the murmuring and laughter from next door.)*

PETER: *(At the door.)* Listen to them, Nell. All speaking English.

NELL: *(Looking at the birth certificate.)* Schmidt... what a lovely name that is, Papa.

PETER: It's very exciting, Nell, to hear a woman speak English. It's very French. Very oo la la.

NELL: *(The beginning of self-discovery.)* Schmidt. Gertrude Kappel Schmidt.

PETER: Listen to that English.

NELL: Beautiful.

(Starts to hum softly. The tune is not identifiable at first, but is quite lyrical and nostalgic. Peter begins humming along with her. He crosses to her and tenderly holds her hands. Then they break into the words of the song.)

NELL AND PETER:

> Deutschland, Deutschland
> Uber alles!!!!!!

PETER: *(Realizes what he is singing and claps his hand over Nell's mouth.)* You don't sing that song!

(The door swings open. Mr. Catchpole glares in. Peter sings to the same tune.)

PETER:

> Swampscott Swampscott MassaChooosetts
> Fa la la la la ladeeda!

(Laughs merrily. Mr. Catchpole exits. Peter swings Nell around.)

PETER: Is your noodle crazy? This is no time to go singing the German National Anthem.

NELL: *(Crying.)* Oh, Papa, where's Mama?

PETER: *(Distracted.)* Over there in the corner...

NELL: Why did she have to go? Why? Why? What are all these flowers? Why are we here? Papa, help me. You're mother and father to me now.

(Peter holds her in his arms. He is frightened and sad and lost.)

(The door opens—the main doors—and Peter and Nell gasp. There at the top of the stairs appear a marvelous Man and Woman. All the lights in the room come up a point and you'd swear the couple caused it. He wears a polo coat with a fur collar and a striped suit underneath and a carnation in his lapel and she is in baby blue and ermine and feathers. They glow.)

PETER: *(Overwhelmed.)* You must want the Sullivans. The... Sullivan wake is next door.

THE MAN: You are the people we want.

NELL: *(Frightened.)* But, good sir, I think you know not who we are.

THE MAN: *(Sings.)*

> When there are blue skies,
> If I want new skies,

I ask my dad!

(He takes off his hat.)

PETER: *Rudy!!!!!!!!!!*

NELL: *Rudy!!!!!!!!!!*

RUDY: *(Swaggers with style and élan into the room, leading the Lady by the hand.)* When your telegram arrived, I tried to hire a biplane to fly to your side with the greatest alacrity, but President Wilson has instituted a blackout of the entire Eastern seacoast, should the German Armistice prove a ruse. *(Suddenly fumbles just a bit. Peter and Nell are terrified of him. He is suddenly very self-conscious.)* So we took a train. Two of them. *(Nervously holds up two fingers.)* We... we had to change at New Haven.

(The Lady coughs delicately. Rudy is all style and swagger again.)

RUDY: Forgiveness, kind folk. Joy at this reunion mixed with the grief of the occasion should not cancel etiquette. Let me present Margaret. Margaret Ross-Hughes.

MARGARET: *(Extending her hand.)* Rudy has spoken of nothing else since the unfortunate telegram arrived at his hotel.

NELL: It arrived! It arrived! The miracle of modern communication!!!!

MARGARET: He could not place you at first, but once he did, the tears *flowed.*

(Peter and Nell react.)

RUDY: Margaret, this is Nell who has been like a sister to me, and this sprightly gentleman is dear Officer Smith whose only lack is the equally dear lady now buried somewhere in those flowers.

(Margaret extends her hand graciously. Nell curtsies and Peter follows suit. Then Margaret sneezes quite loudly.)

MARGARET: Excuse me! I fear I've a touch of the flu that is sweeping the country.

NELL: That's what carried Mama off.

MARGARET: Pray, let me not give it to you.

(During the above exchange, Rudy, under the guise of paying his respects, has palmed a number of cards into each of the bouquets of flowers. He crosses himself and stands up.)

RUDY: Lovely flowers! Margaret, breathe deep.

PETER: Rudy, it's a mystery from where they are from—

RUDY: *(Reaches into the flowers and takes out the cards one by one. Reading.)* Oh, J. P. Morgan. Ah, Jay Gould. Ah, Mrs. Astor. Boss Tweed. How nice. Flo Ziegfeld. How sweet. *(Starts.)* Johnny Rockefeller! *(Throws the card down in anger.)* That phoney baloney!

(Margaret gasps.)

RUDY: Oh, dear Margaret, I hate to use such language in your presence, but he's a fraud and a cad and I do hate him.

PETER: *(Picks up the card.)* Rudy, you *know* Johnny Rockefeller?????

RUDY: Of course, Papa…

PETER: I'm glad to see you're making friends in New York.

MARGARET: Papa?????

RUDY: *(Brightly.)* They'd all stop up here on day trips from Newport. Gert, here, would cook for them. They don't forget. Not the big ones.

MARGARET: She must have been a marvelous cook. She died yesterday? Would there by any leftovers perchance? The trip has made me suddenly ravenous.

PETER: *(Puzzled.)* But she was a rotten cook—You should speak good of the dead, but, boy—

MR. CATCHPOLE: *(Enters. To Rudy.)* Sir, may I have words with you? I saw you step out of the taxi-meter cab and have prepared your way at the Sullivans'. You obviously want the grief next door.

RUDY: The grief here is sufficient, thank you.

MR. CATCHPOLE: You want these grubbies?????

RUDY: Enough, sir!

MR. CATCHPOLE: Wait!!! I suddenly understand! *(Takes Rudy aside.)* You're from the newly formed Federal Bureau of Investigation!

RUDY: I beg your pardon!

MARGARET: How amusing!

MR. CATCHPOLE: *(Squeezing Rudy's arm.)* I have reason to believe this woman in the flowers is none other than the Emperor of the defeated German peoples.

MARGARET: How doubly amusing!

RUDY: Sir, this woman at best was the Empress of the hearts you see here tonight. She who had been like a mother to me had little enough while alive. The least she deserves is a posey or two.

MR. CATCHPOLE: You are the author of the anonymous telegram!

RUDY: I know not of what you speak. All I know is I cannot have my friends show me up.

(Rudy takes out a roll of money. Everyone's eyes, except Margaret's, pop.)

RUDY: More flowers. Even if you have to send to Marblehead or the moon. I want mountains of the rarest of blooms.

MR. CATCHPOLE: *(Looking at the cards.)* These were not here before. *(Takes the money proffered by Rudy.)* These cards were not here before. *(Exits with suspicious glances.)*

RUDY: *(Brightly.)* Well!

PETER: All that money!!!!

NELL: Rudy, are you really from the newly formed FBI?????

MARGARET: Rudy, may I have a word with you?

RUDY: Certainly, darling. *(Gives the roll of money to Peter and Nell.)* Take this. You might find it amusing. *(Moves to Margaret.)* Yes, my sweet?

MARGARET: *(Pointing into the bier.)* Rudy, the ring the lady is wearing looks *very* much like the ring you described as belonging to your mother.

RUDY: *(Looks; fumbles.)* It couldn't be the same ruby ring. Mother and Dad are in Honduras for the vapors. Surely they would have informed me had the ruby disappeared.

MARGARET: *(Sotto voce.)* You're so trusting, Rudy Who Makes My Heart a Cathedral of Love. Servants steal. No matter how long you've had them, or how much you trust them, they steal. Look at them. Counting that money.

RUDY: You're so wise, Angel of My Cardiovascular System.

MARGARET: *(Indicating Peter.)* And what is that vulture dressed as? Some kind of night watchman? And that girl. Her hair puts knots in my stomach.

RUDY: What an eye you have.

MARGARET: For the real thing.

(He moves to kiss her. She pulls away.)

MARGARET: Not too close. Remember. My influenza.

(He pulls a surgical mask out of his pocket and puts it on his face. They kiss, deeply. He holds her in his embrace. They turn out front. Music plays.)

RUDY AND MARGARET:

> Don't let the Love Bug bite,
> Don't let the Love Bug bite,
> Don't let the Love Bug bite.
> He'll get you hot
> And you'll catch your death of—
> He'll get you hot
> And you'll catch your death of—
> He'll get you hot
> And you'll catch your death of
> Cold.

(They embrace. Music stops.)

MARGARET: Oh, I'm quite out of breath.

RUDY: *(Takes off his mask.)* Darling Nell, do you think you could take Miss Ross-Hughes to a room where she might freshen her person?

MARGARET: I'm so covered with soot and cinders and epidemic flu germs that a drop of Belladonna might do us all a world of good. Lead on, little Nell. I'm so sorry to meet you when the hands of Time's clock are draped in black but perhaps the next time we meet the color of Time will be garlanded with bridal bouquet and the tears will be tears of joy.

RUDY: *(Thrilled.)* Do you mean that!!!!!!

MARGARET: *(Tapping her finger.)* The ring, Rudy. Don't forget the ring.

PETER: The ring?

RUDY: Miss Ross-Hughes is one of New York's most noted opera buffs. She remarked to me a moment ago that now that hostilities have ceased, Wagner's Ring Cycle might finally be sung again.

MARGARET: *(Sings the cry of the Valkyries.)*

Toy O Toy Ho!!!!

(She and Nell exit. Peter and Rudy look at each other. There is a long pause. It's as if all the color and style had drained out of the play.)

PETER: Maybe Rumpelstiltskin switched you in the cradle.

RUDY: Papa, do you think me an awful rat?

PETER: You really call Johnny Rockefeller Johnny Rockefeller?

RUDY: Papa, it's for her. It's all for her. Margaret. For Margaret Ross-Hughes. Papa, I think she's going to be Mrs. Smythe.

PETER: She's gonna marry another fella?

RUDY: No, Papa. Me!

PETER: Smythe?

RUDY: Do you like it?

PETER: Do I like what?

RUDY: S.M.Y.T.H.E.

PETER: Ohhhhh, Smythe. With a Y. That's you?

RUDY: Classy, huh? But not pompous, you know?

PETER: Noooo. Not at all. Smythe. Where'd you find that name? The hero of some Mary Pickford movie? You phoney baloney. You're another Johnny Rockefeller.

RUDY: Don't give me that. Four years ago you wake up Mama and Nell and me in the middle of the night and tell us from now on to start calling ourselves Smith.

PETER: *(Nervous.)* A little quiet about the names. The walls keep check around here.

RUDY: *(Whispering fiercely.)* All my life I'm Rudolf Schmidt and because of some rum-dum war a million miles away, you settle for Smith. *(Loud.)* Smith! *(Soft.)* Smith.

PETER: *(Quiet.)* Nobody trusted a German copper since the war. They said either change your name or get off the Force.

RUDY: Then, Papa, I change my name because of the peace. I'm going to be

King Somebody. Rudyard Smythe. Oh boy, people listen to a Rudyard Smythe. Where do you think I got all the money to pay for this place? To pay for the flowers? To pay for my suite at the New Ocean House?

PETER: *(Truly impressed.)* You're staying at the New Ocean House??? Wooo...

RUDY: Look at these duds! Look at these threads! Where do you think I get the money for polo coats and flowers?

PETER: Is this a confession? Come home with me while I get the handcuffs. Even my own son, I don't care, justice must be done.

RUDY: Papa—

PETER: *(Turns his back.)* So you better escape now while I'm not looking.

RUDY: I'm no bank robber! Papa, that's an insult.

PETER: You're not? What am I supposed to think? You leave home three years ago to play baseball for the Buffalo Buffaloes.

RUDY: A wonderful team!

PETER: Then I get a postcard you're a desk clerk in a hotel in San Francisco. Then you write you're panning gold in the Ohio River. I'm afraid to open the mailbox.

RUDY: Papa, I'm in show business.

PETER: *(Turns away in disgust.)* The traveling carnival? Oh, you make me so proud.

RUDY: Papa. New York. Broadway. The Big Time.

(Peter looks at him.)

RUDY: I'm an agent!

PETER: An agent?

RUDY: I personally represent the Ben Hur Animal Stables. Till I took it over, it was the biggest dog account in the whole William Morris Agency. They gave me the account as a baptism of fire to see what I could do and, boy, christen me Big Shot because the Ben Hur Stables is now the fourth biggest account we handle right after Will Rogers, Miss Fanny Brice and the Creole Fashion Plate. All thanks to me. I got the Met doing twelve Aïdas. That's six camels right off and they don't come cheap. The Hippodrome's got two elephants and a diving palomino that leaps right into the pool for Annette Kellerman's finale and Mr. Ziegfeld's got six, count 'em six, white horses in his climax alone. It's been the best theater season in years! Mr. William Morris *himself* patted me right on the head—this head—and he said, "What's your name? You're going far." The breath all went out of me, Papa, and that night I got all dressed up in my white tie and tails and stood outside the Follies waiting to see my acts. I also got three afghans in the

First Act finish when who comes along but—Do you remember Pepper Giambarino and Felix Wunderlich?

PETER: Your best boyhood friends. They were here tonight. You had some wonderful times together—

RUDY: Picking up dog dirt to sell to the tannery? You call that wonderful times? Going around with a bucket and shovel to pick up dog dirt to sell for a few rotten cents from the tannery?

PETER: You were twelve years old—

RUDY: And thirteen years later, two months ago, I'm standing in front of the Nieuw Amsterdam Theatre—me, Rudy Smith, in my white tie, top hat, cape with a silk lining, feeling my head like it was a crystal ball and Mr. William Morris had read the future in it—and I look up and I see there's Pepper and Felix down from Lynn on the prowl and they get a look at me in my glad rags and the crowd is hurrying in to see the show and you can hear the overture out there on Forty-second Street and my boyhood chums pick up dog dirt and start throwing it at me and barking, and the carriage trade is watching and traffic is stopped and even Mr. Ziegfeld's top assistant, Goldie, comes out to see what the noise is. "Let's go sell it," Pepper keeps yelling, and Felix is in the background laughing and barking. Woof. Woof. I turned my back on them and walked into the theater just as fifty of Mr. Ziegfeld's finest twinkled and beamed and turned into naked rays of sunshine for Irving Berlin's "Fountain of Youth" number. As the audience gasped and applauded, I changed my name on that spot to Rudyard Smythe and if the applause wasn't for me, it was good enough and I said I'm never going back to Lynn till I'm something, Papa, till I'm better than dog dirt. That was two months ago and look at me, Papa! Since I changed my name, I got this wonderful girl who I'm hoping will accept my hand and my arm and all of me in the state of wedded bliss. She's so classy, Papa. Take her to Lyman Street? Oh, boy. Even Swampscott isn't good enough for her. You should see her apartment, Papa. Her bathroom alone is all red velvet. All of it. The seat. The chain.

PETER: She must be very neat.

RUDY: And she sleeps with her hands in dishes of cream scented with mint and rubs honey under her eyes so she won't ever get a wrinkle, and for perfume she rubs, really soft-like, Grand Marnier Brandy all over her body and the smell of it lingers so soft...

PETER: She doesn't take a bath?

RUDY: Papa! Three times a day! In a tub that looks like a golden swan. And the water spouts are the breasts of a China lady and the water sprays out and you turn it off by moving these gold and silver feathers. Silver for hot. Gold for cold.

PETER: She must have a very nice job.

RUDY: *(Transported.)* Papa, she's Anna Held's roommate! *(Sings to illustrate:)*
> Every little movement has a meaning all its own,
> Every little meaning has a movement all its own,
> Every little movement,
> Every little meaning,
> Every little movement has a meaning all its own.

Anna Held, Papa! The famous Ziegfeld star and ex-wife of same and the roommate of *my* Margaret Ross-Hughes.

PETER: You know Anna Held????????

RUDY: Not personally. When Margaret's home, Anna's out and when Anna's got company, Margaret and I take our palette and paint the town red. But, Papa… I… I did a silly thing.

PETER: *This* I want to hear.

RUDY: I promised her Mama's ruby ring.

PETER: *(Pause.)* That's why you're here? I haven't heard from you five months now and you show up for ruby rings?

RUDY: No! *(Pause.)* Not just for that.

PETER: Leave, you vampire. I'll tell the owner you're a German.

RUDY: *(Indicating the bier.)* Papa, there's a ring in there. You're going to bury it with her?

PETER: It's her ring. She can do with it what she wants.

RUDY: Papa, she's at peace. You're an officer of the peace. The world is at peace. Is it too much to ask for me to be at peace? As soon as we're married, I'll explain everything to Margaret and I'll invest her money and make a fortune and bring you to New York and even introduce you to Anna Held. But, Papa, I can charge clothes. I can charge night clubs. But I'm having a little trouble with a big hunk of jewelry and look at that. Just sitting there!

PETER: *(Sitting down.)* I want you to go…

RUDY: *(Kneeling by him.)* Papa, on the train trip up, when it got dark, they started shooting up these fireworks so it looked like something had happened to the sun and Fourth of July came in the winter. Please, Papa, let me have the ring?

PETER: *(Stands up.)* Where's Nell? I want Nell.

RUDY: *(Follows him.)* And at Saybrook, Papa, they stopped the train and had a band on the platform and made everybody get off because it was a small town and they had nobody to celebrate the Armistice with. Everything is at peace and I want you to be proud. Please, Papa. It's just a ring.

(The main doors open and party noises bubble in and Margaret sweeps into the room with a champagne glass and a turkey leg that she takes little elegant nibbles from. She is followed by Nell, who still wears her party hat.)

MARGARET: Rudy!!! Next door is such fun!!!!

NELL: *(To Peter.)* Papa, she put liquor on her.

PETER: Grand Marnier. I know. I know.

MARGARET: Rudy, the Sullivans—charming people—have plugged in this enormous electrical crystal set right under the coffin and you can hear Elsie Janis singing "Over There" right in the middle of Times Square, only it sounds as if it's coming out of poor Grandfather Sullivan. Rudy, it's so amusing and the food is so good!

RUDY: Even in death, dear democratic Margaret, I snub the Sullivans. Lace curtain Irish in a tar paper shack. That's who they were. There are some respects a Smythe will not pay.

MARGARET: But, Rudy, it's so gloomy here in the servants' mortuary when Times Square explodes with excitement right next door.

NELL: Papa, we heard New York so clearly. And a naked lady rode right out on Forty-second Street bareback on a white horse. But I closed my eyes. I didn't listen.

RUDY: Right out on Forty-second Street??? That's not in that horse's contract. I better get on the telephone—

MR. CATCHPOLE: *(Enters, triumphantly waving a piece of paper.)* This has just been found!!!!

NELL: *(Feels the bodice of her clothes.)* My birth certificate!!!!!!!

MR. CATCHPOLE: Nell Schmidt born to Peter Schmidt and Gertrude Kappel Schmidt.

RUDY: I'm sure it's no one here.

MR. CATCHPOLE: Foreigners!!!!! Look at those foreheads. Look at those noses. You people are all Germanoids. *(Pulls a gun on them.)* You'll never take Swampscott while I'm alive!

RUDY: Let me explain—

MR. CATCHPOLE: Back!!!!

(All cluster in a bunch and raise their hands. They are terrified.)

MR. CATCHPOLE: First on the agenda, out she goes. *(With the gun drawn on them, he maneuvers to the flowers which he starts knocking over purposefully.)* The tide is high. You can all jump in the box with her and paddle your way back to Berlin.

(The radio from next door gets louder and louder with its static-filled singing and celebration.)

NELL: *(Loud.)* Please, sir! I fling myself on your mercy!

MARGARET: I'm going to faint! Not swoon, but faint!

MR. CATCHPOLE: *(Loud.)* Foolish Fraulein, I should show mercy to the enemy? *(Suddenly the lights in the room flash and Black Out. The radio is silent. The wind blows. Doors slam. General terror. Mass confusion. Total darkness.)* Is this the invasion!!!! Has it come? Are you landing? *(Sings.)*
> Deutschland, Deutschland
> Uber Alles.

NELL: My song!

MR. CATCHPOLE: I surrender.
(The Sullivan Family enters from next door illuminated by matches and sparklers that they carry.)

MR. SULLIVAN: *(A thick brogue.)* Tom Catchpole? Are you in there???

MR. CATCHPOLE: Is that the Kaiser? There's sugar hoarded in the basement. Take it! Welcome to Swampscott.

MR. SULLIVAN: *(Flashing a light around.)* Tom? It's Harry Sullivan. *(The light catches Mr. Catchpole standing terrified on the window ledge.)* Tom? Our electrically power crystal set I fear has blown a fuse. I thought your house had modernically sufficient wiring. Where would the fuse box be, I pray you?

MR. CATCHPOLE: In the—in the Embalming Room.

MR. SULLIVAN: Can I help you down?

MR. CATCHPOLE: I'm all right, thank you. *(Hops down and trips and falls. To Peter and Rudy and Nell.)* I'm not afraid of any of you. You hear??? You hear????? *(Runs out and trips repeatedly as he goes. The Sullivans follow him out. Mrs. Sullivan lights a light in front of Peter.)*

MRS. SULLIVAN: I hope the darkness hasn't intruded on your grief. Would you be liking some beer till the lights come back?

PETER: *(Flustered.)* Are you the Widow Sull—I—Danke. But no. Nell. I—I—

MRS. SULLIVAN: *(Blows a kiss to him and she leaves.)* If you'd like any, I'll be next door. *(The room is pitch black.)*

RUDY: *(Lighting a match.)* Margaret?

MARGARET: *(Her face lit by the match. She is eating.)* The ring? The ring? Did you get the ring? *(The match goes out.)*

RUDY: Papa? Papa?
(Trips against something. Strikes a match. His father is sitting by the overturned flowers, his head in his hands.)

PETER: *(Lit by the match.)* Goddam you and goddam your mother and goddam me and goddam us all. *(Blows out Rudy's match.)*

MARGARET: Your mother? Rudy, just who is who here?

RUDY: *(Lighting a match.)* Who's Who! Look us up. We're all right there! Page eighty-two!

PETER: *(Kicks Rudy from behind.)* You're not getting that ring.

(Match out. In darkness, we hear slapping sounds.)

RUDY: Ow! Ow! Ow!

MARGARET: *(In dark.)* Help! Help!

PETER: I'm going to hock that ring and buy me a wife that speaks English and I'll invite all the policemen to my house and she'll cook and I'll change my name to Smithereens! To hell with you, Rudy. Your papa's going to be somebody first. Police Chief!!!!

(The Lights Flicker, then come on bright. The radio in the next room whirrs up to full blast. Voices all cry "Hooooray." We see Peter has struck a Napoleonic pose in the dark. Rudy rubs his rear end. Margaret is caught by the light with a mouthful of turkey. She pats her mouth.)

MARGARET: *(Looks in the bier; then screams, her mouth full.)* The ring!!! The ring is gone!!!!

RUDY: The ring!

PETER: *(Pulls out his police whistle.)* Police!!!!!! Police!!!!! *(Pause.)* Oh. *(Feels for his holster.)* My gun!!! Where's my gun???????

MARGARET: *(Screams.)* Aaaaaaaa!!!!!!!!! The girl!!!!!!!!

(Faints and Rudy catches her. Nell is in the far corner of the room. She stands up threateningly, from behind a potted palm. She points the gun at them. Peter, Nell, and Margaret leap again into a cluster.)

NELL: *(Triumphant.)* I have the ring and I'm going to hock it and sail back to Germany and find my name and find my relatives and apologize to them for losing the war and become Nell Schmidt again.

PETER: *(Approaching her.)* Nell...

NELL: *(Waving the gun wildly. Peter leaps back.)* Do you know what Mama said? Close enough to the end to be her last words. She said Ich Blein Nicht Blicht Vaterland. I shall translate. The trouble with this country, Nell, it's not a Fatherland. It's not even a Motherland. It's an Uncleland. And we all say, *(Sings:)*

"We're dear old nephews of our Uncle Sam."

And all nieces and nephews can ever be to each other is cousins. I want to go to a country where we're sons and daughters. I want to go home. And Mama's ring will get me there.

(Suddenly a Voice comes from the bier. Margaret and Rudy leap away from it in fright.)

THE VOICE: *(A high eerie lady's voice.)* Nellllieeeee. ...Puuuuutt downnnnnnnnn the gunnnnnnnnnn...

(Nell screams.)

PETER: Quick, Rudy, get the gun!

(Rudy wrests the gun from Nell. She collapses, crying.)

MARGARET: *(To Peter, pointing wildly to the bier.)* It talked! It talked!

PETER: *(Without moving his lips.)* Ventriloquism is only one of the arts an officer of the law Ust Aster.

MARGARET: Ust Aster?

RUDY: *(Proudly giving the gun to his father.)* Must master!

PETER: *(Proudly.)* Son!

NELL: Oh, Papa, I'm so unhappy.

PETER: *(Comforts her. Sings:)*
> When life is unhappy
> Trust in
> Your pappy.

(Takes the ring from her and goes to the bier. He stops and turns and gives the ring to Rudy.)

RUDY: Dad! *(Rudy puts the ring on Margaret's finger.)*

MARGARET: May I consider us, dear Rudyard, engagée?

RUDY: *(Pointing to the coffin.)* Till that do us part!

RUDY AND MARGARET: *(Sing.)*
> He'll get you hot and you'll catch your death of,
> He'll get you hot and you'll catch your death of,
> He'll get you hot and you'll catch your death of
> Cold.

(He kisses her.)

RUDY: Your germs are mine.

PETER: *(Wagging his finger.)* Oooops, nothing German!

(General merriment.)

MARGARET: Now, dear Rudy, may I employ the telephone to make a call of great distance? There is someone to whom I must tell our joyous news.

(Rudy hands her the telephone. She lifts the receiver off the hook and speaks into it:)

MARGARET: Great distance, please. Operator? In New York City, I wish to speak to Miss Anna Held. Rhinelander three four five.

PETER: *(Straightening his tie.)* Anna Held???????

(Margaret sits. Rudy pulls Nell furiously to the other side of the room, out of Margaret's earshot.)

RUDY: What do you think you're doing? Embarrassing me in front of the lady.

NELL: *(Weeping.)* I hate you and think you're terrible and fake and rotten. No wonder Mama wouldn't speak English. It's a language for lies and I'll get to Germany somehow and never speak English again. Let me go! Let me go! *(Peter and Rudy restrain her.)*

PETER: Listen, miss, you cannot back to Germany go. Germany for us is Verboten.

NELL AND RUDY: Verboten???

PETER: Why do you think we left, your mama and I? I stole that ring.

NELL AND RUDY: Stole!!!!!

PETER: I stole that ring to give to your mother. When we were found out, we escaped and came here.

NELL: But you're a policeman!

PETER: Repentance. Everybody on the Force has a record in another country.

RUDY: Extraordinary!

PETER: But true. In America, everything is wiped clean.

RUDY: That's the operative word. *Clean!!!!!*

NELL AND PETER: Clean????

RUDY: Nell, it's a whole new beginning. I remember, though but a child, sailing here to this land.

PETER: Thirty days it took us in those days. Thirty days and thirty nights.

RUDY: Thirty days of clutching my stomach in pain, for I knew full well the entire Apache army led by Sitting Bull himself waited for our scalps at Boston Harbor.

NELL: *(Clutching her hair.)* No!!!!

RUDY: But we stepped off the boat and the Indians in my head vanished to be replaced by ordinary people like you and me who bowed to us and smiled.

PETER: And instead of teepees and buffaloes, we had Lyman Street and our faithful German shepherd, Rex, who it's a shame we had to shoot when the war broke out.

RUDY: Nell, you are the only one of the family to be born in this country, in this century. America reads the golden globes of our magical heads and cries out: "What do you want of life?"

PETER: I said "Life, I want to be a policeman for there must be law."

RUDY: And I chose the arts for there must be order. The future is wide open and this country is so very young. Nell, what do *you* ask of Dame Life????

NELL: *(A pause.)* To keep my braids.

(Stirring music begins to play. Rudy undoes Nell's hair so it falls to her shoulders.)

VOICES OFFSTAGE: *(Sing to the tune of: "Battle Hymn of the Republic.")*

> The war to end all wars is over,
>
> The war to end all wars is over,
>
> The war to end all wars is over,
>
> And we'll never fight again!!!!!!!

RUDY: *(Over the music.)* Nell, put on Margaret's ermine wrap.

> *(She does so.)*

RUDY: Nell, put on Margaret's hat.

> *(She does so.)*

RUDY: We saw socially acceptable young men next door. Go meet them. Go marry them. Get that Sullivan money. The two of us together can form a dynasty. Oh, Nell, we're tomorrow's royalty!!!!

PETER: *(Smoothing his mustache.)* I think I'll pay my respects to that nice Widow Sullivan.

NELL: Papa, am—am—am I beautiful?????

PETER: *(Tenderly.)* You're good enough for all practical purposes.

NELL: *(Hugging him.)* Oh, Papa, thank you!

PETER: And you speak English like a native.

NELL: But, Papa, I've just learned a great, great lesson. A lesson as vast as this victorious land. I *am* a native. Ohhh, thank you, Rudy. Thank you.

> *(The Three join hands and come downstage and sing triumphantly.)*

PETER, RUDY AND NELL: *(Sing.)*

> The war to end all wars is over,
>
> The war to end all wars is over,
>
> The war to end all wars is—

(Mr. Catchpole and All the Sullivans burst through the door. Mr. Catchpole carries a telephone.)

MR. CATCHPOLE: Quick! Pick up your phone!!! Someone is calling Anna Held!!!!!!!

(Peter and Rudy and Nell in unison point to Margaret, who stands up and glares at them. The Sullivans and Mr. Catchpole retreat.)

MR. CATCHPOLE: Forgive me. It's just that it's such an honor. Anna Held! On *my* phone! Why didn't you tell me—

PETER: Please leave us. Aus. Aus. Aus.

MR. CATCHPOLE: Mademoiselle Anna Held. Why didn't you tell me you were French! *(Sings "La Marseilles.")*

PETER: *(Ferociously.)* Did you not hear me????? Aus!

> *(They all leave.)*

PETER: Widow Sullivan???

(The lady freezes at his command.)

PETER: You stay here...

MR. CATCHPOLE: *(Closing the door behind him.)* Please forgive us. Yes, Officer Smith. Oui.

(Mr. Catchpole and the Sullivans are gone except for the pretty widow. Peter moves toward her.)

MARGARET: *(Into phone.)* Yes... Operator... That's Miss Held... Yes, please get off... Miss Held??? This is Margaret. No, your bath is not drawn. ...No, Miss Held, I shall not be in ever again... I am in Swampscott, Massachusetts, with the man I am going to marry and we have used your bath and used your bed and I have learned from you to hold out for only the best... I'm sorry if your milk bath has curdled, but, at this moment, I am probably wealthier than you... Go to hell, Miss Held. *(Hangs up the phone. She turns to Rudy.)* Rudy? Can you forgive me? I love you so much I wanted you to know the truth. The ruby gave me courage. Say you're not angry. Rudy?????

(The Curtain comes down as Rudy faints in his father's arms and the foghorn gives a good healthy raspberry. Marching bands in the street play joyfully. The Curtain keeps rising and falling, revealing frozen tableaux of general confusion.)

END OF PLAY

Marco Polo Sings A Solo

MARCO POLO SINGS A SOLO

ACT ONE

A galaxy of stars. A man in a silver space suit appears floating in space. He takes off his helmet: Stony McBride. He is absolutely amazed. He talks to us.

STONY: I feel myself changing. I twist the gauge. I lift up. Is change this easy? Through stratospheres. Dodging quasars. I will get to you, Frank Schaeffer. You are the best part of me! This is the me I always wanted to be! To think! I woke up this morning a vegetable and here I am by nightfall a new sign of the zodiac! Stony McBride! Children born under this sign can change their lives at will. I've done it. How did I do it? Was change all this easy? Remembry. Dismember. Membrotic. Membrosis. A new word for the neurotic and panic-stricken act of obsessive memory. I, membrotic. How did I get here? How did I make the change? Did it begin only this morning? Membrosis. Membrotic. A man. A woman. A Norwegian breakfast. Napkins strewn between them like rumpled bedsheets. Membrosis. Membrotic. Remembry. Dismembry. Dismember. Remembry. Changing. I heard. I did not speak. I saw. I did not act. I watched. I did not move. Only this morning… only today…

(Stony fades into dark as the lights reveal an iceberg. Some genius has carved a flat plane out of this great, Titanic-killer of an iceberg floating in the Norwegian sea. It's the time of year when the Arctic sun never rises, but high-tech heat lamps provide the necessary light and warmth to make this space more than livable. The dining table is set quite elegantly, a baby carriage is off to one side, and, of all things, a Baroque grand piano is tied with an enormous pink bow on its leg and an extravagant bouquet of lush flowers set on its closed lid. Outside the area of light, the ice makes chaotic shapes. At the moment, in the light, two extraordinarily attractive people are at the table finishing a breakfast.

Diane McBride is a lush, indolent beauty in her thirties. This is the year

1999 and the clothes that year you'll remember were reminiscent of 1940s erotic glamour with a good old-fashioned self-aware salute to Buck Rogers and Flash Gordon. A century is ending. People were very cheery.

Across from her, as crazy about her as she is about him, sits Tom Wintermouth, late thirties. Yes, the one the evening news is about. The one on the front page of the morning papers. He's handsome. He's beautifully tailored. The 1990s were a lucky time to contain such a confident leader.

They are served by Freydis, a spunky Norwegian country girl who looks like an escapee from a Brueghel painting. She's very clean, pours wine for them both and steps back to a respectful distance. Tom and Diane clink their glasses...)

DIANE: You said the Sandstones? That's fine, Freydis.

TOM: The Shootselfs. I said about the Shootselfs.

DIANE: Keep it coming, Tom. Oink is right into the trough. I am starved for every syllable that's happening down there in the real world.

TOM: Bob and Stephanie Shootself—

DIANE: We're up here in Reality Heights.

TOM: —flew to Idaho, right to a mountaintop, and repeated their marriage vows.

DIANE: But Tom, they had to. In their ten years together, between them, they've suffered so many nose jobs, chin jobs, eye lifts, ass lifts, breast lifts, name changes, I don't think there's any of the original bride and groom left.

TOM: I'm all for change.

DIANE: But they take it too far. Last year, didn't Stephanie have her entire body relifted? Flying from Palm Springs to Palm Beach, the altitude unraveled the stitches. The silicone zinged out. The whole new ass falls off. Broke the stewardess's foot. They had to turn the plane back. Put her ass in intensive care. I've heard of having your ass in a sling, but in this year of 1999, Stephanie carried it a little too far.

TOM: That space between your eyes and your ears. Blind people can see there. Facial vision they call it.

DIANE: Freydis, that's enough. Eeenooof. *Prego. Prosit. Skol! Exit. (Freydis leaves. Diane's manner changes. She leans forward urgently, passionately.)* Why didn't you write? I thought you had died. I thought you were dead. I thought you'd forgotten me. I heard a commotion. A delivery being made. A piano being lowered down out of a helicopter.

TOM: Not just a piano. Edvard Grieg's piano.

DIANE: As if the piano had flown here under its own steam. Pursuing me. Had Pegasus been transformed into a piano? It's my wedding anniversary. My fifth wedding anniversary. I go back to my room. Why is there a piano here? I look in mirror getting ready for a party.

TOM: Your thighs. Your skin. The way your hair grows out of your skull.

DIANE: A party in the Arctic Circle. I see my life with such a sudden clarity, the precision of it kicked the air out of my lungs. I said: "No, it's not oxygen there's a shortage of in Norway. It's light. Remember light? Six months of no oxygen?" Wanting to call you. Not knowing where you are. Paris? Washington? Have you died? Have you forgotten me? Is there somebody new? *(They kiss. The baby cries. Diane goes to comfort the baby. The baby is quiet. Diane is in emotional turmoil.)* I sit in the mirror getting ready for a party and look at this portrait of myself trying to guess what those eyes are thinking. What holiday that face is a mask for.

TOM: I flew to Bergen.

DIANE: A hand appears on my breast.

TOM: I rented a boat.

DIANE: I cannot see beyond the horizon of the frame—

TOM: A hydrofoil.

DIANE: —to see who the hand belongs to.

TOM: I sailed up.

DIANE: The hand on my breast speaks.

TOM: The first time we made love.

DIANE: The face moves into the frame.

TOM: You had just had a child.

DIANE: The face speaks.

TOM: *His* child.

DIANE: Have I gone crazy?

TOM: Your breasts were filled with milk.

DIANE: Tom?

TOM: I pressed you to me.

DIANE: Tom Wintermouth?

TOM: The milk spilled over us. I was in Washington. That's all I could think of. The purity of that first fabulous time. We made love. Your legs. Your ass. I love the way your lips join the line under your nose.

(They embrace.)

STONY: *(Offstage.)* Diane?

(Tom and Diane break apart. Stony comes into the light from out of the darkness. We see him now as he generally is: a man who appears to have at least five radios going on in his head at once, who valiantly tries to give the impression

of control and serenity. His clothes suggest speed, a combination of jogging-racing-cycling-skating. You feel in his happy calm he might just explode.)

STONY: I did it. On the spur of the moment I just shot the last scene of the film. Was it the light? The look on my father's face? Inspiration.

TOM: You finished the picture? You shot the last scene?

DIANE: They don't shoot films in order.

STONY: Marco Polo has been sidestepping death. Wandering through all these new worlds. He's seen so much. He's witnessed so much. But he has nothing of his own. He wants to change his life. Twenty-four years have gone by. Marco Polo comes home to Venice. To be recognized. And this is the scene. No one in Venice believes his life. His family thinks he's a beggar. He slashes open his ragged cloak and this proof of rubies and diamonds and pearls and emeralds spill out of him. This weary traveler with this waterfall of hidden treasures pouring out of him. Giving his life credence. He stands there emptied. Home. Changed. Ready to begin again. Hello.

DIANE: Brilliant. Absolutely brilliant.

TOM: Marco Polo in Norway?

STONY: It's fantastic for filming. The light's always the same. The control it allows you. The security it gives you. The dependability of the dark. Plus you can save a lot of money. You want the Great Wall of China? Carve it out of ice. Venice in the thirteenth century? We just carve the icebergs into any shape you want. *(To Diane.)* Oh, I bet you thought I'd forgotten. *(Hands her a script.)* Happy anniversary, darling.

DIANE: *(Looking at the script.)* You've dedicated the film to me?

STONY: History may have supplied the facts, but this woman supplied the spirit. My wife is my life.

(Lusty McBride enters in a rage. Lusty is a great Hollywood star in his sixties—the last time anyone looked like this in a movie. Try to find a still of John Wayne in Barbarian and the Geisha.*)*

LUSTY: False pretenses!!!! *(Lusty rages off into the dark. He is gone.)*

STONY: No false pretenses, Dad. *(Stony follows Lusty off.)*

TOM: *(To Diane.)* Your wrists. Your teeth.

(Lusty rages back on, followed by Stony and Mrs. McBride—late fifties, she's dressed as a Renaissance Italian princess.)

LUSTY: I left California for this? The house is damp. I'm freezing. Standing there in the water up to my ass in Mongolian hordes. Wearing this costume.

STONY: Tom, Diane, I'll be right with you.

TOM: *(To Diane.)* Your skull. Your skin.

LUSTY: He says Dad, change your ways of working. Dad, treat it as a musical experience. Dad, open yourself up. I've learned one thing in my life, son, it's easier to open yourself when you're sitting around a pool in Palm Springs.

STONY: Dad, it's 1999. I want to help the audience recuperate from the entire twentieth century. Marco Polo sailing out for new worlds. Always enriching. Never destroying. He always took what he needed and gave what he had.

LUSTY: Spaghetti and gunpowder. I'll give you one hour to give me heroic stature and three good laughs. Or you'll find me back at that pool in Palm Springs. Don't think because we adopted you, don't think I'd hurl you back into the abyss. I wouldn't do that, boy! You're my son. But there are priorities. *(Lusty leaves.)*

MRS. MCBRIDE: Stony, I have a wonderful present for you that will make you feel so much better.

STONY: Mom...

MRS. MCBRIDE: Stony, don't let him make you crazy.

STONY: To be a father figure to my own father.

TOM: *(To Diane.)* The way your shadow moves after you.

(Mrs. McBride tries to embrace Stony.)

STONY: Mom, please. We have guests.

MRS. MCBRIDE: Don't I see—

STONY: Mother, have you met... *(Starts to introduce Tom.)*

MRS. MCBRIDE: No names, please. I know how it is with you great men. Being married to one myself, I know how you treasure your anonymity.

TOM: I know who you are.

MRS. MCBRIDE: Who am I? I won't look. Should I guess?

TOM: When I was a kid, I had that picture of you over my bed, you burning the American flag, singing "The Ending of the Age of Pisces." I nearly wore that record out. You were the first naked woman I ever saw.

MRS. MCBRIDE: Well, I hope you've seen more since.

STONY: Mom, go rehearse your scene.

MRS. MCBRIDE: You try to give somebody a present. A pleasure. *(Sings.)* "It's the ending of the Age of Pisces/Some call it Piskus/My blood boils and freezes/At people who say Pieces/It's Pisces! Pisces! Pisces!" *(Mrs. McBride stumbles out.)*

STONY: Mom's been taking tranquilizers.

DIANE: Not nearly enough, I'm afraid.

STONY: It seems you've come in the middle of a little artistic crisis. What were you saying?

TOM: Let me bathe in this atmosphere. The wild Arctic raging right out there. The house so cold and damp. Yet under these heat lamps, it's so serene. How absolutely brilliant to force the Arctic to accommodate you, Diane. Feel this heat. My body feels so alive. You've heard the grape about Skippy Schaeffer?

STONY: I'm afraid we don't get much grape in Norway. Working around the clock—

(Tom whispers in Diane's ear and begins fondling her blatantly.)

DIANE: What? Skippy Schaeffer kidnapped from the White House? Frank Schaeffer in outer space?

STONY: What are you saying?

TOM: Excellent authority. Privileged source.

STONY: What about Frank Schaeffer? I am consumed by Frank Schaeffer. I think about him. I dream about him. This hero out there in space. Giving us legends. What are you telling her?

DIANE: Go on. Go on. Don't get him started on Frank Schaeffer. Yes. Go on. What!? Thrown down on a bed in the Lincoln Room??? Frank Schaeffer's wife, Skippy, has been kidnapped and taken to the White House??? They've inserted a metal disc into a transformer that will transform as transformers do transform that semen into nuclear bolts that will travel through space to find their destination, the metal disc with Skippy?

STONY: Let me get this right. Nuclear bolts traveling through space to find a metal disc within Skippy?!

TOM: Yes, from an impeccable source.

DIANE: Well! That's a brilliant public relations job, correct?

TOM: Perfect! Frank Schaeffer will impregnate Skippy through space. The theory that all the knowledge of the world, the truth, all that's best, rises and actually lives in outer space.

DIANE: Not another investigation on Hegel. Why can't they leave poor Hegel alone?

STONY: Hegel?

DIANE: George Wilhelm. The spirit constantly maturing. Constantly evolving. Thesis. Synthesis. Antithesis.

TOM: Of course. Hegel.

DIANE: But not in that order. Hegel puts it so hauntingly. Desire transforms being.

STONY: Man as an individual trapped by his structure.

DIANE: Freydis?

FREYDIS: *(Appears.)* Ya?

DIANE: Is there a diet fudge? A diet soda? Anything so long as it has diet in the title.

FREYDIS: Ya? *(She curtsies and goes.)*

TOM: They won't even bother with an election. The world will drag Frank Schaeffer out of that spacecraft when he returns and crown him king of the world.

DIANE: Brilliant. Absolutely brilliant.

TOM: With what's left of the world. Poor Italy. Shaped like a boot.

STONY: Tom!

TOM: The heel fell off.

DIANE: What are you saying?

STONY: Don't tell her.

TOM: This morning.

DIANE: No!

TOM: Twenty million dead.

STONY: I wasn't going to tell her. An earthquake. Italy's gone.

DIANE: *(Desperate.)* Gian-Carlo? I have to get through to Gian-Carlo?

STONY: You can't get through.

DIANE: Yes, I will. Adriadne? I need to talk to Adriadne. Freydis?

FREYDIS: *(Appearing.)* Ya?

DIANE: Get my address book.

STONY: Calm, calm!

FREYDIS: Add-Dress-Buk?

DIANE: Do you understand me? Call. Quick. Pronto. Dial. Telephone. Somehow get through to Italy.

FREYDIS: Eee-Tall-Lee. *(She curtsies and goes.)*

DIANE: *(Calls after.)* Keep calling every name in the Italian section until you find a friend who answers. A friend who's survived.

STONY: I tried. We won't know who survived for days.

(Stony goes to Diane, trying to comfort her. She backs off.)

DIANE: Italy gone. *All* of Italy? Not some of Italy?

STONY: Gone.

TOM: I'm sorry. I didn't mean to be the one to tell you.

DIANE: No. I do not want to be touched. I'm just going off from under these heat lamps and lie down in the snow for a bit. *(She goes into the dark and lies in the snow.)*

STONY: *(Calls after her.)* Diane? It will be the same as when Hawaii went. The good thing about earthquakes is it gets rid of the people you wanted to get rid of anyway. It cleans out your address book. Everything will be all right.

TOM: Diane, are you safe out there?

STONY: *(Takes Tom by the arm.)* She'll be fine. When I came downstairs before and saw this man talking to my wife, I thought it was a holograph. An astral projection. Tom Wintermouth here? I knew my wife had a chum named Tom but I never knew that her Tom was that Tom. *The* Tom. Why don't *you* run for President, Tom? With Adalbert in Washington and Frank Schaeffer up there in big Frank Schaeffer country, you could just walk in and pick up the marbles. I mean, you'd split the votes in this house. I have to go with Frank. Is that what you're planning?

TOM: No, I'm only the power behind. Adalbert or Schaeffer. It makes no difference to me. I work behind whoever can give me what I want. The power to wage peace. Anonymous. Never up front. Not like you. The artist. Your name, plastered everywhere.

(Larry Rockwell, thirties, comes into the light. Even though his legs have been mangled sometime in the past, he moves with incredible speed thanks to his silver canes. He is in a constant state of rage. Freydis follows carrying a birthday cake.)

LARRY: "Happy anniversary to you/Happy anniversary to you/Happy anniversary dear Stony and Diane/Happy anniversary to you."

FREYDIS: "Hippy. Hippy. Anna-vish-new."

LARRY: *(Finishes singing. Freydis continues.)* Thank you, Freydis.

FREYDIS: Yer velcome. *(Freydis curtsies and leaves.)*

LARRY: If the two of you don't recognize the fact, I do. You've been married five years today. Do I have to remember everything? Diane, will you get out of that snowbank. I brought you a present. Not one of the new books. I mean, Caroline Kennedy's *Memoirs* are a toilet. This is a very old book, long out of print. I went to a great deal of pain and trouble and difficulty in locating it, but it's all for you, Diane and Stony. Diane!

(Diane comes into the light. Larry blows out the candles.)

STONY: *(Opens the gift and reads the title.)* Living Well Is the Best Revenge.

LARRY: By Calvin Tomkins.

DIANE: The one about Gerald and Sara Murphy?

TOM: Gerald Murphy, wasn't he…

LARRY: They were only Scott Fitzgerald's models for Dick and Nicole Diver in *Tender Is The Night.* She had an affair with Hemingway… he with Cole Porter. Together they dug out the legendary beach at La Garoupe with their own hands and invited the twenties.

STONY: Larry, have you met our friend, Diane's friend really. This is—

LARRY: I am perfectly aware of who this person is. Jung says the only sin is to be unconscious. I have committed no Jungian crimes. I am perfectly aware of *who* this person is. But *why* this person is.

STONY: Tom, have you met our friend Larry Rockwell? He's head of the five thousand Chinese extras.

TOM: What an extraordinary job description.

STONY: Tom's a friend of Diane's too.

LARRY: Don't you think every golden age has an inseparable couple that sums up that age? Gerald and Sara Murphy the twenties. Fred and Ginger the thirties. Jack and Jackie the sixties. John and Yoko the seventies. Bob and Stephanie Shootself the eighties. Stony and Diane the nineties. "Hippie Anna VishNew." To quote the domestics.

STONY: Think of it, darling. We're the nineties.

DIANE: Well, if we stay together into the next decade, will we be the nothings? the zeros? I don't know, what do they call the first ten years of the new century?

LARRY: I don't want you lending this book. This book is intended only for the two of you to read. In your bed. In your room. The two of you. I mean you're really cleaning up today. A rare book from me. A piano from whoosi—

TOM: This is not just a piano. This is the piano Grieg composed the concerto and "Peer Gynt" on.

STONY: Two pieces she always said made her seasick.

DIANE: That is so hardly the point.

TOM: Thank you, darling.

STONY: Do people confiscate pianos as presents if they don't expect something in return?

TOM: No, they don't. Quid pro quid.

(Freydis enters with a tray and a glass of cola.)

FREYDIS: Diet.

TOM: Du lingner Skippy Schaeffer.

FREYDIS: I want to learn your English.

TOM: Ah, yes. You look very much like Skippy Schaeffer.

FREYDIS: Skee Pee? I not Skee Pee. I Freydis. I clean. I am gut. I am gut.

TOM: Yes, yes, you're very gut. In this strange, artificial light, she almost looks like a version of Skippy Schaeffer. You don't suppose Skippy Schaeffer came up here to change her life?

DIANE: Freydis? Could you bring out some of those diet hors d'oeuvres? Those little Norwegian meatballs you make with the Kleenex and the snow?

FREYDIS: Ya. *(Freydis goes out.)*

DIANE: What would I have done if any of you had been in Italy? It would have been so easy for any of you to be in Italy. I don't know what I would have done. I feel so whole now. All the parts of my life together. *(Diane kisses Larry, then Stony. She approaches Tom, who shakes her hand tenderly.)*

TOM: All that I told you about Frank Schaeffer. Skippy Schaeffer. All that was classified information.

DIANE: Who are we going to tell? Donder? Blitzen?

LARRY: Diane, don't forget we have theater tickets tonight. We're flying to Oslo to see that production of *A Doll House*. Don't you dare forget. Do you hear me? You do not forget. *(Larry goes into the dark.)*

DIANE: Anyway, I say good for Frank Schaeffer, in any case. It takes all that for him to get it up, for him to father a child, then I say go to it. Poor grotesque sad Frank.

TOM: Not like us.

STONY: Five years ago today, Frank Schaeffer stepped into his spacecraft vowing to bring back to earth that new planet strapped over the fender of his spacecraft like a deer at the height of hunting season. I had become separated from my father in the rush of people there at Cape Kissinger. And there in the cool, in the shade, sitting at a piano, waiting for a concert to begin, sat Diane. We met. We talked. She gave me peace. She gave me comfort. And the sudden harmony of Frank Schaeffer in space, Diane in the cool, Dad looking for me, pulled us together in this chemical equation. The four of us in this perfect emulsion. This divine parallelogram. All the parts of *my* life together. My wife is my life. Tom, why are you here? Are we the new chic? Christ, I am so vain. Thinking you've come to see us. Scandinavia. Sweden. The Nobel Prize. How many Nobels is that you've won now? And the Peace work. I mean, Saudi-Israel. What a brilliant solution to a previously tragic impasse.

TOM: Actually, I've come to see your wife. The first time we made love, she had just had a child. Your child.

DIANE: Could we at least start considering dinner?

TOM: Her breasts were filled with milk. I pressed her to me. The milk ran out of her breasts down my chest down our sides. We drank it.

DIANE: Or is it time for breakfast?

TOM: During certain hearings at the UN last summer...

STONY: The Wintermouth hearings! Do you hear that? He calls his own hearings "certain hearings." She always had fabulous friends. All her men friends.

DIANE: *(Calls off.)* Freydis?

TOM: A message was sent to my table. It said: "If you look up, you will see a woman in a flagrant red dress standing by the exit door."

DIANE: Is there any of that reindeer bacon left?

TOM: Was it an assassin? Was it my savior?

DIANE: Let's just call it six P.M. Okay? That's a good sturdy time.

TOM: I stood up. There she was. "Exit" over her head.

DIANE: We'll send for take-out. That's what we'll do.

TOM: I took this woman in her fragrant, flagrant red dress.

STONY: Peking has the best take-out. They can jet it here in two hours. Would you like that?

TOM: I took her from under that exit sign into a cloakroom deep within the United Nations.

DIANE: What do you think about paella? We could call Madrid. Order it *al presto.*

TOM: Our clothes vanished like anger at the end of a war.

DIANE: Or there's that wonderful trattoria in Rome.

STONY: No, no, no, the mozzarella always came cold.

TOM: Sex is sex only with you.

DIANE: *(In despair.)* I forgot Rome, I forgot Italy. Oh God.

TOM: With anyone else, you say let's make love. Have an affair. Tender raindrop walks on a beach.

DIANE: Twenty million dead?

TOM: With you it's all hot and scorching and fierce and hungry.

STONY: Twenty million dead. At least.

DIANE: I don't see how we can ever eat pasta again.

TOM: —And our mutual orgasms hurl us out of time and space—

DIANE: Hawaii lost into the sea… And now Italy… Oh God…

TOM: —And when we finish and check that we're still alive we crawl up out of the ocean of ourselves gasping for air onto the beach of reality.

DIANE: *(Anguished.) Roma! Firenze! Milano! Siena!* The entire *Renaissance* gone. No!

TOM: Sex with you is lurid and gaudy and hot and brazen…

DIANE: Sometimes we just have to say no to Mother Nature.

TOM: My lungs can't get enough air.

DIANE: I will not eat again until Mother Nature straightens herself out.

TOM: Your eyes. your skull. The roof of your mouth.

DIANE: Dinner. Dinner. We'll eat one last dinner tonight and that's it.

TOM: I won't say your wife brought peace to the world.

DIANE: One feels so powerless in this vast universe.

TOM: But after our fabulous commission of love in the UN dashiki-filled cloak-room, I saw a way out after many years of not seeing a way out.

DIANE: Man stumbling into the new century.

TOM: Without dressing, I drew up a document. I created Saudi-Israel. I took her naked hand.

DIANE: Changing. Yearning.

TOM: I guided it with mine over the newborn treaty. My signature. Our signature. Brought peace, at least to one part of the world.

DIANE: It's our only salvation.

TOM: We dressed and stepped out into a world, that your wife, as simple as this, had made a little bit better. *(Tom takes Diane into his arms and kisses her deeply.)*

STONY: Well, I hope you let her keep the pen. *(Singing.)* "I'd like to see that midnight sun come up..." This has got to be our best anniversary yet. We weren't in Italy. We have a visitor. Frank Schaeffer is in that sky. I think we need a little celebration. *(Calls off.)* Freydis? Could you bring some of that veal wine out here?

TOM: Veal wine?

STONY: Do you think I'd crush a grape to make a sip of wine for my own personal pleasure? But take one live juicy living veal. Ground it into a fluid. Ferment it. Two or three days. Perfect. Grape wine takes years. Why? The grape is fighting off death. The grape wants to live. But animals want to die. If we don't kill them, they think we're bored with them. Not being killed is the same as not being noticed. They die from boredom.

TOM: An interesting theory.

STONY: Theory? You call scientific fact theory? It's mankind's problem in a nutshell. We never go far enough. We have to keep pushing ourselves further and further to recognizing the needs of others. I recognize the needs of the grape. The grape wants to live. The veal wants to die. Why should I stand in the way of the veal? Deny the grape. So locked off from life with your peace work. Don't you know anything? Next life around, I'm coming back as a vegetable researcher. I'm committed to being an artist in this life. But one feels so inadequate when I compare the work I'm doing to the work they're doing on vegetables. Have you ever heard the cries of the asparagus? *(Stony takes out a pocket cassette and presses a button. Agonizing screams are heard.)* Granted, zucchinis are dumb. *(Moans are heard.)* But radishes are brilliant. *(More squeals.)* If we could just break the code... All the money wasted trying to break the language of the dolphin. They finally do. What are the dolphins saying to us? These high, reedy, squeaky voices singing: "Sun goes down, tide goes out, darkies gather round and dey all begin to shout." I have no sympathy for mammals. Meat can run away. Meat has wings. Meat has gills. Meat has hooves. Meat can escape. Meat can change. Meat can die. Meat wants to die. But plants have roots. Plants are trapped. Plants are dependent. Plants know about survival. Plants have to stay there. One of the great fallacies of science is aligning man with the mammals. Man is a plant. We may look like meat, but we're not meat. We can never escape. Nor change. We are planted firmly in the ground. We are what we grow out of. My plant nature. I celebrate that.

(Freydis enters with wine.)

STONY: Ahhhh, veal wine. Thank you, Freydis. You certainly have fabulous friends, darling. Tom Wintermouth himself flying up from Washington? The world of politics! Tom, why *is* New Zealand bombing the hell out of Toronto? Explain New Zealand's anger? I mean, what happened to negotiations?

TOM: *(Fierce.)* Let me explain negotiations. *I. Want. Your. Wife.*

(Stony suddenly breaks away from Tom. A spotlight comes down on Stony.)

STONY: Frank. Schaeffer. Has. Found. The. New. Planet. He flies beyond the third moon of Venus. A green shadow blurs that part of the galaxy. This planet is on no map. A green planet so fertile it looks like a ball of manure popped out of a black hole in space. Frank Schaeffer lands on the new planet. The earth will never go hungry again. He is elated. Immortality guaranteed. He toasts the plants that live on this planet with powdered champagne. One special plant dances by. Frank Schaeffer is aroused. Frank Schaeffer is lonely. Frank Schaeffer has been without contact for five years. This plant may not be human but it beckons to him, waving its leaves. Frank Schaeffer risks death. He takes off his space suit. He stands naked. He stands erect. The green plant wraps its tendrils around him. Frank Schaeffer forces the green plant down. The green plant tilts Frank over. The plant overpowers Frank. Pistils. Stamens enter Frank. Green sap spills. Bursts. I've lost contact. My head is dead.

(The lights come back up. Diane comforts Stony.)

STONY: I can't go into the new century this frightened.

DIANE: You're not frightened. You're brave.

STONY: Insignificant. No air. No breath. All my life I've lived in my father's shadow. The great Lusty McBride.

DIANE: You're not the son of Lusty McBride. You're adopted. You have to say that over and over, and know it.

STONY: I'm adopted. I'm adopted.

DIANE: You have no share in his genes. He didn't pass on any worn-out genes to you. You are not his son.

STONY: I am not his son.

DIANE: No blood to live up to.

STONY: No past. No heredity.

DIANE: You can invent yourself.

STONY: I can invent myself. I am Frank Schaeffer.

DIANE: No, you are not. Frank Schaeffer is up there in space finding a new planet that will feed the world. You're here in Norway making a film about the life Marco Polo that will—I don't know what it will do.

TOM: You're in touch with Frank Schaeffer?

DIANE: No, he's not in touch with Frank Schaeffer. Stony projects his life onto the life of Frank Schaeffer the way you would project a film onto a screen to give himself size. To give himself shape.

STONY: I used to get us all mixed up. I got Diane mixed up with me. I've got that straightened out now. She's Diane. I'm Stony. That's Frank Schaeffer up there. *(To Tom.)* I'm not too sure about you.

DIANE: I hate this year. 1999. All those nines. So negative. *Nein. Nein. Nein.*

TOM: Diane. Diane. I went into a record store in Rio and there in a discontinued bin were all the recordings you had made. All your smiling faces beaming up at me with a promise of what your future could be. Before you married this man. Before he got you pregnant. Before he brought you to the Arctic. Before. Before. *(Tom gets album covers from his briefcase.)* Look at yourself. Look at what you could have been. Look at your past! Before you married this man and he scooped your insides out. *(Tom holds several album covers with Diane's face on them.)*

STONY: She doesn't play anymore.

TOM: This is you, Diane.

STONY: She let her fingernails grow.

TOM: This is the best part of you.

DIANE: If I played now, it'd all sound like Carmen. My fingernails castanetting against the keys. Click. Click. Click.

TOM: I've just come from South America.

DIANE: Is there someone else? Who is she? Don't betray me.

TOM: *(Extracts a small piece of paper from a cylinder that is handcuffed to his wrist under his jacket.)* A lone doctor in a jungle outpost hospital in South America has discovered the cure for cancer.

DIANE: My God! Let me see that!

TOM: This lone doctor contacted me. I flew down there with a battery of physicians from Columbia-Presbyterian. They were overwhelmed by the beauty and ease, by the architectonics of the cure. On their way back to New York, the plane crashed. They were all killed. This is the only copy extant of the cure for cancer. I'm on my way to the UN to deliver it. I want you to be at my side when I deliver it. Already hospitals are closing entire wings. Patients who were considering suicide are signing up for dancing lessons. Pain is about to be stopped. The world will be at peace. *(Music begins playing in the distance: shepherd's pipes and drums. The sun is rising. Colors play against the sky.)* Diane! See that! That yellow! That blue! That gold! That red! The winter's over. The summer can begin. And change is coming into our lives as surely as the light gathering strength to appear. Day and night. Light and dark Indian wrestling on the edge of the universe. Diane, are you with me? You have no choice. Hear the bells ringing? Diane, are you with me? The fish have leapt out of the sea. The snakes sprout feathers. The birds test the air. Diane, a fuse lights beneath the present. Now becomes a Hiroshima. Diane, pack your bags! Cancer is cured and we're in love!

(Tom and Diane embrace. The sound of an air taxi is heard. Larry enters dressed for evening.)

LARRY: It's the air taxi, Diane. I called the air taxi.

STONY: What are you talking about? We have work to do on that other island.

LARRY: Diane and I have a date in Oslo.

TOM: Oslo! You're leaving with me!

DIANE: Tom, we have theater tickets.

TOM: Theater tickets?!?!?!

LARRY: Diane, you promised. I'm in pain. I hurt. I have an extra ticket.

(Diane, Tom, and Larry go off. We hear the air taxi taking off as Lusty comes on.)

LUSTY: Stony! Do I have to wear this goddam hat? Did you get me three laughs? Don't forget I'm photographed from the left side only.

STONY: I've got it all right here, Dad. We've got the light. We're going to be all right. It's day. It's finally day!

(Stony and Lusty go off. Freydis comes on to clean. Mrs. McBride comes on.)

MRS. MCBRIDE: Stony? Does any women go off to see forty-one different productions of *A Doll's House* if she's not trying to tell her husband something? Stony?

(Mrs. McBride goes off. The air taxi is gone. Silence. Then a beeping noise begins. Freydis looks up from her scrubbing to locate this mysterious piercing noise. She stands up. She realizes that the beeps seem to be coming from her. She hears a great Whooosh from above. A man in a silver space suit descends to earth. He takes off his helmet. He is Frank Schaeffer, in his thirties.)

FRANK: Hello, Skippy. Guess who's back?

FREYDIS: *(Drops her accent.)* What are these beeps? What have you done?

FRANK: I have come the distance of forty moons to tell you the good news. We're going to have a baby.

FREYDIS: What are these beeps?

FRANK: Come back to Washington and we'll talk.

FREYDIS: No babies. No Washington. I have a life here. I'm very happy.

FRANK: This is no job. Honey, you've been elected the Fourth Most Admired Woman in the World, thanks to me. Looking up in the heavens waiting for me these past five years.

FREYDIS: I have a stiff neck and a broken heart and I want to be left alone. Don't even talk to me. Two months ago I went into the White House to accept that award and instead was dragged into a dark passage, thrown down on a bed in the Lincoln Room…

FRANK: How do you think this job makes me look?

FREYDIS: Rude hands spread my legs and inserted into me, Skippy Schaeffer, a disc. A metal disc that is burning in me right this moment.

FRANK: If you'd stop being hysterical and let me explain—

FREYDIS: I was held prisoner in the White House. I'm not talking about Tijuana, Mexico. I'm talking about the White House.

FRANK: Our new address if you don't go humiliating me.

FREYDIS: A marine guard played the cello while they tied me down on Lincoln's bed.

FRANK: So you wouldn't be frightened when the bolts came.

FREYDIS: I waited till she dozed.

FRANK: The cello was to wile away the terror.

FREYDIS: I picked up that bow and plunged it through her heart. I ran out of the White House. I got to a heliport where I commandeered a helicopter. Get me out of light. Get me to darkness. This burning within me. My helicopter exploded. I Icarus through the sky. Land in the North Sea. Eliza across ice floes. Dolphins take me on their backs to Oslo. I go to the Oslo Employment Agency. I want to be pure. I want to be clean. They say Ahhh, you want to *clean*. They give me job. I sail forty miles out to sea. To this iceberg. *(She resumes her Norwegian accent.)* I Freydis. I cook. I clean.

FRANK: The child was supposed to be born in the White House. You're so goddam selfish. I'd splash down New Year's Eve as 1999 becomes 2000. You'd present me with the perfect child. Give the world a new legend.

FREYDIS: *(Begins scrubbing the ice with a vengeance. The beeps grow louder. Freydis is terrified.*) I have burned my house. I am cleaning the world. I am trying to be a Saint, in the church of life. I am trying to purify myself.

FRANK: (*Unzips his space suit and steps out of it, now in his NASA long johns.*) Okay, Skippy. Deny the world dreams. Deny the world legends. I'm sorry, but my kid is going to be born in the White House or not at all. Skippy, put on the suit. It's the only thing that can block those bolts that are coming down on you.

FREYDIS: I not Skippy. I Freydis. You leave me alone. The woman you married no longer exists. I have changed myself. I am a brand-new person. Oh God, reinvent fire and burn Frank Schaeffer in his spacecraft. I am no longer married to you. I have changed myself. I am happy! So happy!

FRANK: Honey, I found the new planet and I took the liberty of naming it after you. There's Saturn, Uranus, Pluto, Neptune, Earth, Venus, Mars, Jupiter, Mercury, and now Skippy!

(*Mrs. McBride, Lusty, and Stony come on. Mrs. McBride is soaking wet and wrapped in a polar bear blanket. Frank hears them coming and hides behind an iceberg in the darkness.*)

LUSTY: Give my boy a break. It worked once for Walter Huston being directed by his son John in *Treasure of the Sierra Madre*. But they were real father and son. That must be the ticket.

STONY: Dad, *Treasure of the Sierra Madre* was an adaptation. *Marco Polo* is an original.

LUSTY: Well, I'm going to be an original postage stamp. The United States Post Office has picked me to be a commemorative stamp for the end of the twentieth century. I got the six-cent slot. Beat out Paul Newman. Beat our Gary Cooper. How come the United States government can see the ache in my eyes that the prairie is dead and my son can't.

STONY: You'll love being a postage stamp. You've always wanted people licking your backside.

LUSTY: Did I hear right?

STONY: I'm sorry. It just popped out!

LUSTY: You be careful the way you address an actual commemorative stamp.

MRS. MCBRIDE: Stony? Did you like the way I played my scene? That was my idea to jump into the Arctic with my clothes on. I jumped into the Arctic all for the sake of art and my son's film.

LUSTY: You're disgusting. You never were any good with your clothes on anyway. Here! (*Hands her papers.*)

MRS. MCBRIDE: What are these?

LUSTY: Divorce papers. I want my girlfriend Bonnie by my side. I need my Bonnie. You get me Bonnie. *(Lusty goes off.)*

MRS. MCBRIDE: Why didn't Dad talk to me? Tell me he was unhappy with me? You're not unhappy with me?

STONY: Mom, you have a little problem that makes it difficult sometimes to talk to you.

MRS. MCBRIDE: You call a little grass, you call a few vitamins, a problem?

STONY: Let's not have any pretenses. They're not vitamins. Just leave me alone. I look at you and I don't know who I am.

MRS. MCBRIDE: But, Stony, you're the most wonderful extraordinary person in the whole wide world.

STONY: Sure, Mom. The best. Mom, I'm nothing.

MRS. MCBRIDE: I have a little anniversary present for you, my darling. Along with the pianos and the books, I have a wonderful anniversary present for you. *(She hands Stony a paper.)* You're hardly nothing.

STONY: It's a birth certificate.

MRS. MCBRIDE: Of course it's a birth certificate.

STONY: But it says here Stony McBride, born January 1, 1965, New York Hospital. It says here Mother: Debbie-Lisa Dempsey. That's you. It says here Father: Philip McBride. That's Dad. This is not my birth certificate. On the birth certificate I used all my life, it said Parents Unknown.

MRS. MCBRIDE: That was a forgery.

STONY: Then this is real? You're my real parents?

MRS. MCBRIDE: Are you embarrassed?

STONY: Why did you tell me I was adopted?

MRS. MCBRIDE: Your father's name was Elliot.

STONY: Wait a minute. My father's name was Philip. Changed to Lusty.

MRS. MCBRIDE: As I was saying, your dad, your pop, your father's name was Elliot. And Elliot fell in love with a man named Philip McBride, whose stage name was Lusty, and Lusty was the word for Elliot's feelings, for the feelings that lived in his heart. He followed Lusty across country. He followed him every minute. He captured his garbage that Lusty would throw away and the edges of the half-eaten lamb chops, pork chops that Lusty would eat for breakfast. And all the time, Elliot was blocked from Lusty by the rows, lines, hordes, of girls that continually surround the great, the growing greater, the soon-to-be-a-star, soon-to-be-a-legend, the great Lusty McBride. And Elliot would hear the groupies talking, how great Lusty was, how each of them balled him, how beautiful Lusty's body was inside them. Elliot looked at his body in the mirror and was consumed with hatred for the appendages that dangled off it and blocked him by a simple biological, physiological fact from knowing the warmth of Lusty McBride. So Elliot, being the ultimate fan, the ultimate worshiper, removed himself from the sight of Lusty and went on a little trip to Johns Hopkins Hospital in Baltimore, Maryland, and stayed there a year, like a virgin preparing for her marriage, a nun in a convent of silence preparing for Jesus to come to her. And Elliot left Maryland for New York where Lusty was starting auditions for his new musical, *Skin,* and the new Elliot auditioned and Lusty McBride in the dark audience out there said, "Nudity is required for this role." Ahh, yes. "Would you take off your clothes so we may see your body, ahh yes." Drums fanfared in Elliot's head. Elliot removed his clothes and like Venus on the half shell wept as Botticelli must have the first time he realized what his painting "The Birth of Venus" was turning into. Elliot stood naked and everyone came near respectfully, hushed, a sound I've only heard at the feet of the Winged Victory in the Louvre Museum since. They came to me. Touched me with their eyes. Asked me my name. I said, "I am Debbie Lisa." They said the part was mine but Lusty's eyes said I want you. As they say, the rest was show biz history. On opening night in front of fifteen hundred people we made love and sang "It's the Ending of the Age of Pisces" and had simultaneous orgasms and the critics ran out of their seats and the reviews were all on the front page. We married at the opening night party. We flew to Woodstock where we would have a cottage. I changed into a nightgown. Lusty's naked body came through the door. He throws me violently on the bed. Ahh, life. Ahh, love. Those were my words. I opened my eyes. Lusty held out the telephone. He threw the phone on the bed. "Dial him," he commanded. "Dial who," I said. "Dial your brother." I said, "I don't have a brother." He said, "Don't give me that. Why do you think I hired you? Why do you think I married you? You are the spitting image of your brother. The only man I ever loved that I could never have. Your brother followed me for two years, always on the outskirts of the crowds of worshipers. I would play for him. I would leave half-eaten chops in the trash and watch behind curtains as he would go through my trash and munch on them and I could feel my lips receive his bits and munches through the glass. He never spoke to me. I tried to catch his eye. Nothing. I've been able to ball everyone I wanted in my life. Except him. He knew the groupie girls. I'd ball them so they might tell him that I was available. That I wanted him. That part of me that wanted him would stick onto those young groupies' voices and he would hear me through them like some celestial ventriloquist act. Then he vanished for a year. I went crazy.

Where was he? I couldn't play Madison Square Garden. I could play nowhere. Where was his face? I learned his name. I sent detectives. Find me Elliot. No Elliot. Vanished. I would perform no more. I would become an actor and lose my identity. I invented the role of Ulysses. Searching. Searching. Then you appeared. Elliot's face. But the body of the enemy. I checked into you. You and Elliot had the same last name. You and Elliot lived at the same address. You and Elliot had the same birthday. Elliot's twin sister. I loved you. You and Elliot have been conceived at the same moment. Floated in the same womb. The same face. Even though I hate women, you were different. You were a link. Call him. Call your brother. Bring Elliot over here." Well, I didn't want to tell him I was the brother, I mean it was his wedding night too. So I dialed a number and then said, "Hi, Elliot!" All the while the weather report is going in my ear. Sunny in the afternoon. Winds at twelve degrees from the North. Barometer's falling. "Hi, Elliot, it's your sister, Debbie. Debbie Lisa. Can you come over? You'll never guess who I married. Lusty McBride. Come on over and help us celebrate." So here I am. Spending my wedding night with the man I love. Locked in passion? Oh no. Talking to my former self. Lusty's eyes were filled with tears. "What is he saying? What is Elliot saying?" I can't tell him Elliot is saying ten percent chance of showers in the afternoon. I said, "Lusty, Elliot doesn't want to come." Lusty says, "Let me talk to him. I love him. I love him. I'll give him money. I'll kill myself. I'll kill you." I held the phone away from my ear. I said, "Elliot has hung up." Lusty wept in floods in spite of the ten percent chance of showers. I comforted Lusty. Held him. Touched him. I was finally where I wanted to be. "Elliot will come for Christmas." Lusty looked up like a baby. "You promise?" I kissed him all over. "Mommy promises." That was our married life. Elliot held us together. And Lusty would say, "When is Elliot coming?" And I'd be in the tub washing the body I had built for Lusty and I'd say "Godot will show up before Elliot." And Lusty would say, "What did you say?" I'd call out, "I talked to Elliot today." Lusty opened the bathroom door. "He said he didn't want to see you, Lusty. He didn't even watch your TV show. He threw his TV out the window so he wouldn't have to watch you." And Lusty wept these great Garden of Gethsemane tears and would run out of the house, our mansion, our estate, and I would leap out of the tub, let the wind dry me off, hide in the back seat of his Maserati while he drove to the more unsavory sections of whatever city we were in, and the car would stop, but the motor kept running and Lusty would mention money and a young man would get in the front seat and they would drive off to

Mulholland Drive or some enchanted vista and I would lay there in the back seat in a puddle of bath water, listening to my husband and a stranger make love and my husband cry out the name Elliot. "Elliot." I grew to love Elliot so much that I became insanely jealous of him, passionate about him, thought every moment of Elliot. I traveled back to Baltimore, Maryland. I went to Johns Hopkins. Before my change, I had made a deposit in the sperm bank. The doctors were only too happy to transplant the first womb into my body. They inserted my deposit. Elliot entered me on the operating table. I became pregnant. You were born. Named Stony after Dr. Stevens and Dr. Antonacci who had created my life. They found the truth of me. I wanted you to have that truth. Your real name is Stoneyacci. You were a love child, Stony, with all the love in the world because I loved myself when you were born. And you're famous. I gave you that much. You're in all the medical books. I tried to shield you from the truth. I didn't do wrong. You're making a wonderful movie. You've got a wonderful wife. Have good friends. Given me grandchildren. And you're all me. Everything about you is me. I filled your head with great men because you are like the first person born out of twenty-first century technology. I filled your head with heroes because I think I was a hero. Or a heroine. And if you ever read in any of those books written about the sixties that someone else claims to be the First Flower Child, you tell me and I'll sue because your Mom, right here, little Debbie Lisa, right here, can produce interviews on old yellow pieces of paper that prove she was the first flower child of the whole wonderful sixties.

STONY: *(Looks at her and begins screaming. He runs in an ever-widening circle until he's lost in the dark. He screams and screams. He returns and sits by her side. He is very still. A spotlight appears on Stony.)* Constellations of stars have fallen out of another galaxy. They hurtle towards earth. Frank Schaeffer steers his spacecraft into the eye of the lost constellation. He destroys it. Star shards sprinkle down on us. Order is restored. Frank Schaeffer is victorious again. *(The lights return to their normal state.)* I am not you. My parents were teen sweethearts in Idaho. Iowa. Wisconsin. No, no, no, no, I am not you. I am so happy. I am Frank Schaeffer. I am in space. I am anybody in the world but you.

MRS. MCBRIDE: Don't try to escape emotional family traditions. This is a beginning. My friend. My son. My self. Man to man. I'll pass on the only bit of wisdom I ever picked up in my entire life. We were born for chaos. That's our natural state. Chaos comes natural. Give in to it. Serenity you got to bust your ass for. Go through hell for. I look back on those days of my torment and yearning and anguish and I say That was the happy time. That was life.

STONY: I am anybody in the world but you.

(His scream is drowned out by the sound of the air taxi descending. Enter Larry, Tom, and Diane.)

LARRY: Ibsen knew everything. Even though you know the plot of this play, you lean forward, Ibsen makes you lean forward. Perhaps tonight will be different. Tonight the play that insures Ibsen's place in world drama will change and Nora might not leave.

TOM: Yes, for a play that was written a hundred years ago...

LARRY: 1879. 1879. *A Doll House* was written one hundred twenty years ago. Didn't you read your playbill?

TOM: Freydis? *(Calls off.)* Would you begin packing Mrs. McBride's clothes? She'll need the barest minimum down there at the Equator. Freydis? Where is she?

LARRY: And it's not *A Doll's House*. The accurate translation is *A Doll House*. Not the house of the doll, but the house itself.

DIANE: Stony, I brought you a little present. God, the production was incredible. They sold video cassettes of the production in the lobby right next to the orange drink. I brought it home to show you. Larry, flash it against that iceberg over there, please.

(Larry takes a video projector from under the dining table and inserts the cassette into it.)

TOM: I think Ibsen would be very happy to know his play had caused a woman to walk out on her life.

DIANE: Her alleged life.

TOM: And in leaving that life, find a better life. A truer life.

DIANE: The actors played *Doll House* entirely on trampolines. Nora doesn't just walk out the door, she leaps this incredible bounce into freedom. Into infinity. Stony, it was done by Ingmar Bergman's son and I thought of all these great men surpassing their fathers.

TOM: I'll set up the video, Diane.

LARRY: *I've* set up the video, Diane.

(Larry projects the image against an iceberg. A video shows a man and woman in dour nineteenth-century dress bouncing up and down wildly on trampolines, flipping over as they recite Ibsen's closing lines:)

HELMER: Men jeg vil tro pa det
Nevn det! Forvandee oss salede at—?

(Helmer does a back flip.)

NORA: If Samliv mellow oss to Kunne
    Ble et ektestap. Farvel.
    (She flips and tumbles out of sight.)
HELMER: Nora! Nora! Tomt. Hun en her
    ikke mer. Det vid underligste.
    (He laughs and bounces high. A door slams.
    Freeze frame on his bouncing.)
STONY: Isn't it incredible. Here it is 1999 and people still miss the point of that play.
TOM: And what is the point of the play?
STONY: Nora never left.
TOM: Pardon me while I laugh, but the entire point of the play is...
STONY: Nora never left. Ibsen's entire point is Nora's husband knew she was leaving and, quick as a shooting star, he constructed a new living room that enclosed the outside of the front door. So when Nora left, she found herself not in the outside world, but in another, a newer, a stranger room. And since there was no door in that room, she drew a window and quickly climbed out of it. But her brilliant, heroic husband built a new room off that window. And she beat down the walls of that new room and the walls crumbled and her hands bled and the dust cleared and she found herself in a newer room still damp from construction. And she crawled through the ceiling, gnawing, and her husband dropped a new room on top of that escape hatch. So the wife invented fire and burned down all the rooms and her skin blistered but she smiled, for she knew she would soon be free. And the smoke cleared and an enormous igloo domed the sky and she ripped out her heart and intestines and forged them into an ice pick and chopped her way out through the sky and she opened the ice door that would lead her into the nebula, the Milky Way, heaven, freedom, but no, she chopped back the door to heaven and was warmed by the glow of a cozy room, her Christmas card list, a lifetime subscription to a glossy magazine called *Me,* her children, her closet crammed with clothes, her possessions, her life sat waiting for her in a rocking chair.
MRS. MCBRIDE: Stony, can't you see anything? Your wife is pulling the big ankle like little Nora in the *Valley of the Dolls* playing against that iceberg over there. Your little wife is leaving you.
STONY: She's right here, Mom.
DIANE: Debbie Lisa, could you please not butt in—
MRS. MCBRIDE: My life is here screaming in front of you. Can't you hear me? Can't you acknowledge what I've just told you? *(Mrs. McBride goes off.)*

DIANE: Listen to that bell on the mainland. It rings all night. I hate that damn church bell ringing all night.

STONY: Why didn't you say so, Diane? I have a horde of five thousand Mongolians at my command. You just have to tell me what you want. You want that bell stopped? I'll stop it. I take my directions from you. You are my life. My wife is my life.

(Stony runs off. Tom rewinds the video and plays it again.)

TOM: Watch Nora bounce. Watch Nora leap.

DIANE: Oh, God, to be that free.

TOM: *(Snaps the video off.)* But you've been that free. That's what keeps us in common. You're no stranger either to the icy blasts of greatness. Tchaikovsky competition. Gold Medal. Moscow 1992. Monte Carlo Music Festival 1993. Juilliard Great Alumnae Performers, 1994. Carnegie Hall, 1993. Requiem for poor dead King Charles, Westminster Abbey, 1994. I bought the records. I play them. You know what's amazing?

DIANE: Everything.

TOM: Your unerring sense of the inner...

DIANE: ...structure.

TOM: Structure. Exactly.

DIANE: You're not the first to say that.

TOM: Your way of leaning on the inner structure so as to reveal the composer's secret intention.

DIANE: It's all in the structure.

TOM: *(Spreads the tapes and record jackets in front of her.)* This is you, Diane. This is the best part of you. This is the you I want to give back to you. Diane de la Nova. Metropolitan Opera House: Great Solo Performers Series, 1994. Your last concert. Your last program. Bach. Beethoven. Schoenberg. Schumann. Satie. Ravel. What a program. *(Tom picks up a tape at random and inserts it into a cassette that he carries in his pocket. Piano music flows out, Satie's "Gymnopedie.")*

DIANE: I recorded this three times. Once when I was twenty-eight. Then again when I was eighteen. Then again when I was eight.

TOM: Which is this?

DIANE: *(Listens.)* Eight.

TOM: Eight! Eight years old! Do you realize how small an eight year old's hands are?

DIANE: I really started cookin' when I was eight. I sat down at the piano as I had every day since I could walk, threw back the lid of the Knabe-Bechstein-Steinway and there on the keys was Mozart. I was never lonely playing the piano. Brahms was always there. Bach. Chopin. And here was Mozart. Hi, Mozart! Only this time he had a raincoat on. A little raincoat. Now I had been told to beware of men in raincoats, but after all, it was Mozart. Mozart's no degenerate. Mozart's no creep. You can trust Mozart. The cool water of Mozart. He says, "Hello, little girl. You gonna bring me back to La Vie?" I said, "Golly, I'll try." And I began playing that Köchel listing I had been practicing for a year with that magical imitative brilliance that children can have. The technical mastery and total noncomprehension that children can have. I lifted my hands, dug them into the eighty-eights and Mozart says: "Yeah. Give it to me." I look down. Mozart. The raincoat. Opened. The keys became erect. Black. White. I became terrified. Mozart! This isn't a school yard. This is a hall named after Mr. Andrew Carnegie and I'm only eight years old and what the hell are you doing??? "More. More. More," says Mozart and he throws back his head. "Dig those digits into these eighty-eights. Bring me back to life. Bring me back to life." Mother??? Dad?? They're in the wings blowing kisses at me. Holding up signs. "You've never played better." Mozart moans. It's a short piece. It ends. Mozart spurts all over me. I'm wet. Mozart wet. Frightened. The audience roars. This child prodigy. Can't they see what's happened? I look down and hear a chorus of "yeahs" coming from all those little dead men in raincoats. There's a scuffle and Brahms leaps on the keys. "Me next! Me next! Bring me back to life." My fingers dig into Brahms. Well, I started to like it. Mozart lives. Brahms lives. For the next twenty years that was my life. Diane de la Nova and her Circus of Music. Diane de la Nova and her Massage Parlor of Melody.

TOM: You were brilliant.

DIANE: It's so easy to get brilliant reviews. You simply sit at the piano every day for twenty years with the moss growing up your legs, sparrows nesting in your hair, bringing dead men in raincoats back to life.

TOM: *(Reads a jacket.)* "Diane de la Nova has reached a pinnacle of perfection."

DIANE: That was the day I called Uncle. Closed the lid on all those dead men who had shot their wad all over me for twenty years. Used me. I dried myself off… Went to a tattooist. Had a life line inserted on my palm. Said: "Where does life begin?" Stony comes into view. The day of my last concert. The day Frank Schaeffer shot into space. I closed one door. Opened another. Now I close that door and open yet another.

TOM: Nora slammed the door behind her and Modern Drama was born.

LARRY: Don't you love people who manage to squeeze, to actually use, the phrase "the birth of Modern Drama" in everyday conversation?

TOM: Where did you say you met this man?

LARRY: She ran over me in a car crash, Wintermouth, and you know what? It's still the luckiest thing that ever happened to me.

DIANE: Let's not play this record over again please.

(Larry turns on the video for its last moments.)

TOM: That's the end of the film. Nora leaves.

DIANE: Run it again.

LARRY: *(Stands in front of the projector blocking the image.)* But this is a warning. If she does leave him, you cannot lock me out.

DIANE: Nor will we. No one's locking you out. Move out of the way—

TOM: Exactly. Open door policy. Christ, a key. You can have a key. Dinner anytime you want. Dinner or lunch or breakfast. A plate. A permanent plate nailed on the table.

LARRY: I'm not sucking around for dinner invites. I have credit cards. I have dozens of credit cards. I have a very high credit rating. I have all the major credit cards. I can eat at any restaurant in the world and take anyone I want with me. I am included in the structure of their lives. Her life. She can leave him. I don't mind. She can go anywhere she wants, but she can't lock me out of the structure of her life. When her kid was born, I went to the hospital secretly and picked up the still damp child, still damp from birth, and screamed at the child: "Don't think you can lock me out!!!" I come in the package. I am in the bloodstream. I am in the bones. I am in the marrow.

DIANE: Freydis? Would you bring down Mr. Rockwell's suitcase? Larry, you've carried your new legs with you long enough. You must be used to them now. Get those useless pins sawed off. The new legs... the doctors just screw them on.

(Freydis comes on dragging Larry's suitcase. She tries to pay no attention to the beeps.)

FREYDIS: Ting a ling a.

LARRY: I am not a prejudiced person but I think I hate the Norwegian language more than...

FREYDIS: Ting a ling a

LARRY: Hoona Hoona Hoona.

FREYDIS: Ting a ling a Him. *(Points to Tom. She goes off.)*

LARRY: I think there's a phone call for you, Tom. That's all it sounds like to me. Hoona, Hoona, Hoona.

TOM: No one knows I'm here. *(Tom leaves.)*

LARRY: Is that all you want from me, Diane? Why didn't you say that's all you wanted? *(Opens the suitcase to reveal a pair of new plastic pink legs.)*

DIANE: Put those away! I want to see them under your trousers, not in a box.

LARRY: Between the plastic legs and the new medical shoes, I'll be much taller.

DIANE: Larry, I am not going in the house until you apologize to me for this unapologizable outburst. Put those legs away! I thought you were—

LARRY: Were? Were?

DIANE: Are my friend, my ally.

LARRY: You I thought told me I had to be more curious about life. You ran over me and pulled me out of that wreckage. You gave me mouth-to-mouth. You gave me ear to ear. Hummed me love themes from operas. Told me what it was like for a man and a woman to be in love. What they did. The secrets that happened between men and women. And then the ambulance came and you got in with me. I could be the world's richest cripple from the way you ran over me, but instead I kiss these limbs because you brought me home with you. You told me I could have life any way I wanted. You told me... you told me... *(He cries.)*

DIANE: Now, Larry.

LARRY: Yes?

DIANE: Could you have electricity put in the legs so you could receive phone calls and I could always call you?

LARRY: I could have hot plates on the knee caps. Whip up a soufflé. Plug in for a cup of coffee. Hot and cold running water.

DIANE: A little drawer here for your valuables.

LARRY: So there won't be any unsightly bulge in my trousers.

DIANE: So you can stand up straight and tall and be presentable and attractive and meet people and lead your own life?

LARRY: I'm doing a good job on the movie.

DIANE: Larry, training five thousand Chinese not to look in the camera as they run by screaming is not a life's work.

LARRY: When you two leave, I'll leave with you. You can drop me off at Helsinki. That's where they do the operation. That's the least you can do.

DIANE: The least. Hurry.

LARRY: Is this all you wanted from me? Why didn't you say? Freydis? Freydis? Help me with this.

(Larry goes off with his suitcase. Tom comes out of the house, highly upset.)

TOM: Mxmmmmamfmatmaffsssfmmm.

DIANE: Tom? What happened?

TOM: Adalbert. Stroke.

(Freydis runs past. Her beeps louder, more insistent.)

DIANE: Freydis, please. Tom, look at me. Stop shaking.

(Larry rushes on with a radio. He listens to it.)

LARRY: Listen, everybody! President Adalbert has had a stroke. The Vice President has committed suicide. The government is in chaos. Military rule in Washington.

TOM: They want me to go back. President.

DIANE: President!

TOM: This cure for cancer makes me a very powerful man.

LARRY: *(Quoting radio.)* "Thomas Wintermouth is mentioned to be interim President. Plans made to find Frank Schaeffer in space and bring him back from wherever he is in space."

TOM: I'm afraid! I said it. Oh God.

DIANE: This is not the Thomas Wintermouth I know. Larry would you go in the house and find Tom? This isn't Tom. This must be an astral projection.

(Larry goes back into the house.)

TOM: I... afraid... I say I don't know...

DIANE: It's your time in history, Tom. It's our time.

TOM: What an incredible turn of events. Did you think this morning when you woke up you'd be the wife of the President of the United States? Before night fell?

DIANE: I take strength from the words Bob Dylan wrote so many years ago: "Take what you have gathered from coincidence."

TOM: And I strength from you.

DIANE: Call Washington.

TOM: Washington.

DIANE: Tell them you accept.

TOM: I don't have to call. I left them on hold.

DIANE: I love you.

TOM: And I you. Oh, I you.

DIANE: I want you.

TOM: And I you.

DIANE: Strong.

TOM: Your mouth.

DIANE: Powerful.

TOM: Your breasts.

DIANE: Loving.

TOM: Your eyes.

DIANE: Tasteful.

TOM: Let me kiss your breast. Just for a moment.

(Tom buries his head in Diane's breast. Stony comes on carrying a large bell.)

STONY: I took the motorboat over to the mainland. I found the bell. I bought it.

DIANE: I don't care. It's too late.

STONY: Too late?

DIANE: Too late too late too late.

TOM: Too late?

DIANE: Not you. Strong. Powerful. Loving. The best.

TOM: Just for a moment there I had a lapse. Never again. I apologize. I don't know what came over me. President. Lean on me. Depend on me. *(Tom goes into the house.)*

STONY: So.

DIANE: So.

STONY: I have my film.

DIANE: I have my life.

STONY: My life is starting.

DIANE: Ditto.

STONY: My father and I finish this picture. My life begins.

DIANE: Ditto the dittoes.

STONY: Frank Schaeffer's in that sky. Soon you'll be in that sky. The sky's the place to be.

DIANE: Tom has a friend who's lending us his ranch in South America. He raises leopards. Lobotomizes them. Takes out their vocal cords. Grafts on the vocal cords of hummingbirds. Amputates their tails. Grafts on coral snakes. Quite striking.

STONY: Why?

DIANE: When evolution takes a turn, beauty must be included.

STONY: I'm not asking why some South American asshole is grafting snakes onto leopards. I'm asking the larger Why. The cosmic Why. The reason why Why was invented. Why didn't you leave me before. Why when I was a wreck. Why when I was falling apart. That kind of Why.

DIANE: I don't leave wreckage behind. I don't desert sinking ships. When five thousand extras arrived last week to be citizens of Venice and Mongolian hordes, you had them line up on the decks of this flotilla of Venetian gondolas carved out of ice. High noon. Pitch black. You sailed between them, a spotlight on your face. The only lighted thing around. You introduced yourself. Welcomed them. Told them how much this film meant to you. Five years of work beginning to culminate. Your father playing the lead. How much that meant to you. And I looked at you and said Yes. Here is a man I can leave. You see, I only leave the best for the best. Tom is the best. Now you're the best. I can leave.

STONY: Did you tell him you were pregnant?

DIANE: I shall.

STONY: Is it mine?

DIANE: Of course it's mine. It's yours. None of your business. It's mine. It's yours. Yes.

STONY: Why did you get pregnant if you were leaving me?

DIANE: I wasn't leaving. I hadn't heard from Tom. I thought he'd forgotten me. You're up here filming over on that other iceberg all the time. No sunshine. I don't even cast a shadow. Who needs me? I wanted something in me so I wouldn't float away.

STONY: I'm glad I could be of service. The worst of a kid. Joined at the hip whether you like it or not. Never really separate.

DIANE: I really hate the weight of this child already beginning to claw its way out of me…

STONY: The child will be born. You'll have to tell me. I'll have to see it. Visitation rights.

DIANE: Second month. Fingernails starting. Like I'm trying to claw my way out of you.

STONY: Custody battles. Sicknesses. Christmases. Graduations. Weddings.

DIANE: Let its eyes develop so it can see you for the fool you are. Let its sex develop into a man so you can see the man you should be. Let its ears develop so it can hear the shit I have to contend with. Let his feet form so he can run away from you. Let his spine develop so he can stand up straight. He'll be born in the year 2000. He's due to be born in the last week of December 1999, but I'm holding him in. I don't want this kid born in any century that contained you.

STONY: What am I supposed to do? Nail your shoes to the floor? Tie your hair to the trees? Drop you in a block of ice and freeze you here?

DIANE: I want more.

STONY: I want more.

DIANE: You have your film. Your film will be great.

STONY: I've already started on my next project.

DIANE: That's wonderful. What's it about?

STONY: You.

DIANE: Really? What is it called?

STONY: Whore. Slut. Pig. Death. Die. Go.

DIANE: I must look for it. *(Diane starts to leave.)*

STONY: Diane? Don't leave me.

> *(Stony runs after Diane as Lusty comes on with his luggage.)*

LUSTY: Son, Bonnie's waiting for me. I'm going to go see her.

STONY: What are you talking about? We still have to film the key scene. Diane, wait—

(She's gone.)

LUSTY: You've got enough footage. End the picture now.

STONY: Marco Polo has to sail out for new worlds. Diane!

LUSTY: What new world? Looks like the same old world to me. Mother shooting up. You ranting and raving.

STONY: Dad, I have a new project. There's a lot of money in it—for you. *(Pause.)*

LUSTY: What kind of project?

STONY: *(Improvising wildly.)* I've—I've—I've negotiated for the rights to the new Marcel Proust western. *Kill My Palomino.*

LUSTY: Marcel Proust western? Are we talking about the same Marcel Proust?

STONY: People think he spent all his time in his room writing *Remembrance of Things Past.* He wrote that on a bet to show anything could sell. What he thought he'd be remembered for were these four hundred really first-rate Western novels he wrote under his real name: Pancho Diehard. You know all that faggola stuff??? Asthmatic? That was all publicity. He was Jewish. That much is true.

(Mrs. McBride wanders on.)

MRS. MCBRIDE: Stony? Lusty? Did you see my little yellow case? It has some needles, in it, some white powder, a rubber hose and a spoon. Have you seen it? I need my little yellow case. *(Mrs. McBride wanders off.)*

LUSTY: I want Bonnie. I want all this insanity out of my life.

STONY: *(Tries to block Lusty's way.)* Dad, I'm remembering a time. I've never told you this. You took me for a walk. And then there was the time. Well, I don't have to tell you. And then I'm remembering the time. The emotional shorthand. An eyebrow tilt. A shoulder shrug. More weight that the entire works of Balzac. And what about the time! And don't forget the time! Are you remembering the same time too? This is ESP. Wasn't that a time!

LUSTY: Let me go!!!!!

(Lusty throws Stony aside into a snowbank and is gone. Diane comes on with her suitcase. We hear the sound of very loud beeps. Freydis crawls on in pain.)

DIANE: Freydis, where are my traveling shoes? I can't travel in these shoes. I can't travel in this dress.

FREYDIS: Madam, I am in pain.

DIANE: What? Shall we put handkerchiefs over everyone's pain and clap for our favorite? I am on my way to the White House. I'm going to send for you and the baby in about a month. You like that? Big trip across ocean? I'd like the baby to lose about five pounds. Never too early to start slimming. Willpower. Freydis? You hear me? Willpower. Those beeps? What are those beeps?

(Diane goes off into the house. Stony crawls out of the snow into the light.)

STONY: Frank Schaeffer, who art in heaven, keep my family here. You have your structure. You have your life-support suit that controls you and feeds you and keeps you alive. Keep me alive. Keep my wife here and my father here and my son here. Help me, Frank. Bring something down. Give me a sign. What do you want in exchange? Take anything of mine you want. I sent my dreams up to you like incense. Help me.

FREYDIS: *(Crawls after Stony.)* Master, I am in pain.

(Stony looks up as he hears Frank's voice boom out of Freydis's body.)

FRANK'S VOICE: Skippy? Tonight's the night. I hope you're all cozy there in the White House.

STONY: Did I do it? Did I contact Frank Schaeffer? There is a Frank Schaeffer who hears my prayers? The powers in my mind. The untapped powers. Diane? Diane?

(Stony goes off. Frank runs into Freydis. He carries his space suit in his hand. He places his space suit beside her. Overhead, the sky begins to change with strange swirling streaks of violent color.)

FRANK: Okay. Now, Skippy. Listen to me because in a few moments, very colorful bolts containing my semen will zap down on you. I know you're going to say Why. Well, blame it on the media. They wanted your impregnation to be this physical Fourth of July. Right now, these bolts containing my semen are gathering force to zap down on you, change you into a pregnant woman with the twenty-first century man. You'll be hearing my voice. Oh, it's the big production. You'll be a technological madonna. Me, Frank Schaeffer, I'll be a technological messiah. Don't be afraid when the bolts come down. You'll put on my suit. Nothing can hurt you. If we can't do something right, we won't do it at all. You'll put on the suit and we'll sit back and laugh.

FRANK'S VOICE: I hope you're feeling as romantic as I am, little missy.

(Lights start flashing under Freydis's skirt.)

FRANK: That's my voice, darling. Broadcasting out of that little disc. Now put on the silver suit. It's the only thing that can stop the bolts.

(Diane comes into the light.)

DIANE: What is that little voice? Why are we having ventriloquism at this point in my life? And why is your lap doing imitations of Times Square at New Year's Eve—

FRANK: Will somebody help me put the suit on her?

(Freydis knocks Frank down and runs off. He dashes after her.)

FRANK: Wait a minute. Skippy!! Please???

(Larry comes on.)

LARRY: What's going on? The sky is swirling with light like some terrible Van Gogh—

DIANE: Stop it with the artistic analogies!!

(Frank and Freydis dash past Larry and Diane and run off.)

LARRY: *(As Frank runs by.)* You're Frank Schaeffer!! It's Frank Schaeffer!

FRANK: Write NASA. They'll send you an autographed picture.

(Frank runs off after Freydis. Mrs. McBride wanders on, happily.)

MRS. MCBRIDE: Fillmore East. That's what the sky looks like. Fillmore East. Does that mean anything to anybody? Back in the sixties when psychedelic was a brand-new word.

(Stony comes back on and sees Frank's space suit lying on the ground. Stony picks it up.)

STONY: Is that a sign? Frank Schaeffer wants me. Frank Schaeffer is sending me transportation. Frank Schaeffer wants me!

(Stony rushes off with the space suit in his hands. Freydis and Frank run on and off.)

FRANK'S VOICE: Do you have your little government-issue negligee on? Are you all hot and sexy?

MRS. MCBRIDE: Hey Hey LBJ How Many Kids Did You Kill Today!!

(Tom comes on.)

TOM: *(To Diane. Very formal.)* Darling, how to put this. I have to fly to Washington immediately. I said I'd be bringing my new bride. They said she's still married. Give her up. They said this is no time for a new President to be breaking up homes. It's really outrageous, but what I will do is send for you in about three months.

(Diane faints.)

TOM: Just let me get the world in order. Get the President and the Vice-President swept under the couch with all the other dustballs of history. Diane. Get up. Please. Diane.

MRS. MCBRIDE: *Ho* Ho Ho Chi Minh. NLF Is Gonna Win!!!!

(Frank comes back with Freydis in his arms.)

TOM: Hello, Frank.

FRANK: Hello, Tom.

TOM: Frank Schaeffer!?! *(The bolts begin.)*

(Zap!)

FRANK: Where's the suit? Who has the suit? Skippy, dodge those bolts!!!

(Zap!)

(A bolt hits Larry's suitcase. Flames!)

LARRY: My legs!!!

(Zap! A bolt hits the piano. It begins playing a Grieg concerto. Zap! A bolt hits the carriage. Zap! A bolt hits the cure for cancer in Tom's hand. Zap! A bolt hits Freydis. Everyone is in a daze. Freydis is lying against a wall of snow, knocked out, smoke steams around her.)

FRANK: Skippy, tell me you like it. Oh, God, Skippy, I'm sorry. It was all supposed to be in Washington. Skippy? I meant well.

MRS. MCBRIDE: *(Begins ringing the bell that Stony brought from the mainland.)* Relax. The chaos won. Give into it. The chaos won. We're home!

(Stony comes on, wearing Frank's space suit.)

STONY: This is the me I always wanted to be! I'm on my way, Frank!

(Stony begins to ascend into space, into the light. Frank's Voice comes out of Freydis.)

FRANK'S VOICE: Hail Skippy full of grace. Now you're filled with the twenty-first-century man.

MRS. MCBRIDE: LBJ pull down your pants! All we are saying is give peace a chance. *(Mrs. McBride sees smoke coming out of the baby carriage. She hears the baby crying. The carriage begins shaking. She looks into the burned carriage.)* Kid, make it a learning experience. *(She rocks the burned carriage and sings.)*

> "It's the ending of the Age of Pisces/
> Some call it Piskus/
> My blood boils and freezes/
> At people who say Pieces/
> It's Pisces! Pisces! Pisces!"

(Stony ascends and is gone.)

CURTAIN

ACT II

A few moments later. The baby carriage, burned, glows. All the furniture is burned and scattered. Grieg's piano lies on its side. Larry's legs gape out of his scorched and battered suitcase. Everyone lies in a daze. Freydis is already at least nine months pregnant. We hear one final rumble in the sky. The sky is clear. Everyone slowly revives.

MRS. MCBRIDE: Stony? Wasn't there another iceberg over there? Wasn't there a big white cube with the Great Wall of China carved out of ice on it? Wasn't there a film a man put five years of his life into? Wasn't Dad having a comeback in it? Wasn't I an Italian princess? Wasn't life over there?
(Mrs. McBride wanders off. Tom shakes the container holding the cure for cancer. Ashes fall out of it.)

TOM: The cure for cancer? Where is it? It was right here. *(Tom begins searching frantically for the cure.)*

DIANE: The carriage containing our child has been hit. Why am I afraid to look in the carriage? Stony?

LARRY: Look at my luggage! What was in those bolts?

FRANK: I am truly, truly sorry.

LARRY: Forty-five alligators did not give up their lives so you could say I'm truly sorry. Stony? *(Larry stuffs his new legs into the ruined suitcase and goes off looking for Stony.)* Stony? Stony?
(Diane crawls with great trepidation to the glowing baby carriage. She looks in it. She screams.)

DIANE: The baby's been burned! It's been hit. Get a doctor! Stony? Help!

FRANK: *(Looks in the carriage.)* The baby's fine. I think. Yes, he's fine. What a fine little boy. He's just a little dusty.
(Diane takes the child out of the carriage and begins bathing him. The baby cries. Diane sings a lullaby. Mrs. McBride comes on. She holds a piece of fruit in her hand. Frank goes to her.)

MRS. MCBRIDE: Have I gone bonkers? On my way up from the beach, I slip. Reach out in the dark to regain my balance. Squish. Have I squeezed a pair of polar bear's nuts?

FRANK: It's a mango.

MRS. MCBRIDE: A mango, he says. And what are those flashes of pink in the sky?

FRANK: Those are flamingoes.

MRS. MCBRIDE: Flamingoes?

FRANK: Hawaii fell into the sea. The entire pineapple industry lost. I negotiated for Norway to buy the rights to the Gulf Stream before I left for space.

The Gulf Stream is on its way up here now. Nuclear re-routing. I guess the bolts made it all happen sooner. Oh God.

MRS. MCBRIDE: Norway. The pineapple capital of the world. *(Mrs. McBride goes off.)*

TOM: *(To Frank.)* Pardon me. You haven't seen a piece of white paper in your travels? Have you? Rectangular? White. Official looking. Lots of C's I remember. Lots of CH's. Square roots growing off into hexagonal shapes? It was in my hand for a second. Then it wasn't there. It was in a lead container. A lead asbestos flame-proof container. It's not important. It's just the cure for cancer and the UN general assembly is waiting for me and I'm supposed to be President of the—

(Frank buries his head in his hands.)

TOM: Oh well. Nothing really out of the ord. Nothing really spesh. Take over the shards of government. Cure the world. It was right here. The piece of paper. In this hand. It was right here. *(Tom continues searching.)*

FRANK: *(To Freydis.)* Darling, I didn't mean it to be this way. There's a perfect child in you right this moment, but it's not in Washington. It wasn't filmed. This will be our Bethlehem. Come back to DC. At least. The child will be born there.

FREYDIS: The child will be born of Freydis. In the woods. On the cliff. Overlooking the sea. Private. Quiet. I do not know the father. This sometimes happens to country girls. Men from other farms attack us on spring evenings and fill us full of baby.

FRANK: You're my wife.

FREYDIS: Naughty Freydis. No ring on any finger.

FRANK: Skippy. Give me a hold. I'm so lonely. It's not like there's any USO in outer space.

FREYDIS: Skippy was your wife. When Skippy was your wife, Skippy would hold you. I no Skippy. *(She contracts with labor pains.)* Mrs. McBride, please forgive. Dinner be slightly late this evening.

(Freydis and Frank go off. Diane puts the quiet child back into his carriage and rocks it gently. Tom crawls by on his search. He looks up at her.)

TOM: It might have seemed back there as if I didn't.

DIANE: Didn't? Didn't what?

TOM: You know.

DIANE: Yes?

TOM: Love you.

DIANE: Oh, no.

TOM: Us leaving together. It was just inopportune.

DIANE: Of course.

TOM: With the new developments.

DIANE: History in the making.

TOM: The President's stroke.

DIANE: Vice-President's suicide.

TOM: Moral tone. Me. Provide.

DIANE: Moral leadership.

TOM: Exactly. I couldn't break up a home at this moment.

DIANE: Wouldn't look right.

TOM: Hold the world together.

DIANE: You must.

TOM: You understand.

DIANE: Always.

TOM: I'll send for you.

DIANE: Never.

TOM: But if I can't find the paper and lost the Presidency and Frank Schaeffer goes to Washington instead of me plus I can't find the cure for cancer plus all the peace work goes to hell, we can start up again? I can't lose everything plus you. You have to stay with me.

DIANE: I loved you.

TOM: And I you.

DIANE: Can't you even squeeze out the verb? You come all the way up to Norway and you can't even squeeze out the verb?

TOM: Your breasts. Your eyes.

(Diane looks at Tom and goes off. Tom continues to search for the cure. Frank comes back on.)

FRANK: The baby's dead. The baby ran out of her. A boy. Skippy was only pregnant hardly any time, but the nuclear transformers sped the gestation. Our child would be the Twenty-First Century man. That's what I was promised. Conceived from space. I felt like God the father. Skippy ran to a cave. Opened her legs. Did you hear her scream? Tropical birds looked down from the sky. Our child was not delivered. He strode out of her womb. Enormous. Tall. Golden. Wet. I went up to him. "I am your father. Hi!" He looked in my eyes and said "You are not pure. You are corrupt." At that very moment a group of unsuccessful lemmings crawled up out of the sea and ran up the cliff to make the leap again. My son looked around at the world and looked at me. He joined the lemmings. He leaped over the cliff. They were all successful this time.

(Mrs. McBride comes on carrying a frozen flamingo.)

MRS. MCBRIDE: I don't know much about symbols, but I'd say when frozen flamingoes fall out of the sky, good times are not in store.

(Diane comes back into the light carrying her suitcase and wearing a traveling cloak.)

DIANE: *(To Mrs. McBride.)* Could you look after your grandchild just for a bit? I have to go over to the mainland.

TOM: *(Leaps up in exaltation, waving a piece of paper.)* I found it! I found the cure! "Dimethylene carbonitrate square acetycyclic bionic methyldratic acid benzoid!"

DIANE: *(Reads it.)* This is the label for my Diet Pepsi.

(Diane goes. There is sudden darkness. The darkness of outer space. Comets, asteroids, novas swirl by. Stony appears in space.)

STONY: Bolts came. I was on earth. Now I am here. I dodge quasars. I am not hallucinating. Hallucinations never bring peace. This is real. Glass-of-milk real. I ascend through space twisting, turning, to show gravity does not apply. I am being carried home. Frank Schaeffer waits for me on the new planet. We shall re-enact some primitive conception. Become true father and son. The answer to some prophecy at last. I count the one moon we know. Two moons. Three moons. Four. Forty moons! The silver suit knows the way to its rightful owner. We pass a third moon of Venus. There it is. The new planet. I see Frank Schaeffer's space craft on it. Sending out beeps. I land on the planet. So green. *(The light around Stony becomes lush and green. He takes off his helmet.)* Hellooo?? Frank Schaeffer??? Anybody home? Am I alone on the planet? A light rain falls. I hear a music like two crystal glasses rubbing together. I feel around. A green plant dances by, its tendrils reaching out to me. It must recognize my plant nature. I want union with this green plant. I want to set roots down here. I risk death. I take off my suit. I stand naked. I stand erect. I take the plant and hold it to me. We breathe. The plant shudders with delight. In an instant, I see little images of me run up the stem, fill up the stamen. These perfect representations of me pop out of the petals. I take another plant. That plant becomes pregnant, wrapping its leaves around me. More mes pop out of the petals. This is the world I want! A world populated by only me. I hear a scream. One me hits another me. Is that rape? One of the mes rapes another me? More mes now march out of more petals. Mes fill the horizon. Downtown India is a ghost town compared to all the mes screaming in fear. Me! Me! Notice me! Each me screaming to be heard. Me! Me! Each one moaning, whining Me! This is not the me I had planned to be. I came up here to find Frank Schaeffer. My true self. My true father. My true son.

All I see are these mes. I take an axe. I slash the plants. I stomp the roots. I take a gun. I shoot all the mes. I take flame. I burn the planet. Flames in space. I burn the new planet. I don't care. I want these mes out of me. I have killed a planet. *(The planet turns bright red and then disappears. The blackness of outer space. Stars. Comets. Earth comes into view.)* I put my suit on. I twist a gauge. I plunge down toward earth. Is the fear out of me? I am so quiet. I have killed me. I want no more solos. I crave duets. The joy of a trio. The harmony of a quartet. The totality of an orchestra. Home. I head for home! Duets! Trios! A quartet! Yes, even an orchestra. Make some music out of my life. I descend on my garden. I am home.

(The clear light returns to our iceberg. Everything is as it was before. Frank is alone picking out a simple melody on Grieg's tilted piano. Stony descends, enters.)

STONY: Hello? Hello? Where is the other iceberg? Where is the Great Wall of China? Where is my film?

FRANK: Gone.

STONY: The crew?

FRANK: Gone.

STONY: There were five thousand Chinese extras.

FRANK: Gone.

STONY: Diane?

FRANK: *(Stops playing the piano.)* Gone.

STONY: Larry?

FRANK: Gone.

STONY: All dead?

FRANK: Not dead. Just gone.

STONY: I can't tell if you look familiar or not.

FRANK: I'm nobody. Who are you. Are you nobody, too?

STONY: Are you Emily Dickinson?

FRANK: I have other news for you. Your father.

STONY: Gone?

FRANK: He wouldn't wait for anyone. He took off in the air taxi. Bolts hit the helicopter. It exploded. Your father's dead.

STONY: What a rotten comeback he's having. Oh boy. Oh God. All those years trying to connect with him. I'm remembering a time. No, I'm not. Nothing ever happened between us. My father's dead. My film is gone. My wife is gone. I've killed a planet. On top of everything, I killed a planet that was supposed to feed the world.

FRANK: Oh, you found that planet too? You saw yourself? All the versions of yourself screaming Me Me? I found that planet. I killed it. It grows back. Don't worry. You didn't kill it. You only saw yourself.

STONY: Why is it that all the things that should hold us together, help us change—love, creativity, sex, talent, dreams—those are the very elements that drive us apart and the things that you think would separate us—hate, fear, meanness—those are the very things that bind us together and keep us from growing. Keep us from changing.

FRANK: By the way... your son.

STONY: My son. Nothing's happened to my son.

FRANK: *He's* not dead. The bolts hit your son's carriage.

STONY: What are you saying?

FRANK: The bolts that so speeded up my own wife's gestation so that the greatest creation known to man was accomplished in a matter of a few moments... Those bolts hit your son.

STONY: Why am I afraid to look in the carriage?

FRANK: After your wife left, we thought everything was all right. But as you can see, I guess it's not.

STONY: *(Looks in the carriage. The carriage begins to glow. He's shocked.)* I've seen my life. I don't want... *(Stony runs into the darkness and scales an iceberg.)*

FRANK: *(Yells after him.)* You can't run away from it. You can't hide from it. Open your eyes to it. You can't close your eyes to it. *(Frank is left alone.)* Now let me see, what are my choices? Should I go back into space and become a hero or stay here and try to win Skippy back? The world on one hand. Me on the other. *(Frank takes a burned flower from the bouquet and begins plucking the singed petals to make his choice.)* The world. Me. The world. Me. *(Frank wanders off.)*

(In the distance Tom calls to Stony. The carriage glows and begins to shake violently. A large hand appears over the edge of the baby carriage. Then a large leg follows. The baby emerges. He looks exactly like Stony. He is wearing "Doctor Denton" pajamas and is sucking a juice bottle. The baby walks unsteadily over to the table and pulls at the tablecloth until it comes off, spilling the dishes onto the floor. The baby sticks his head through one of the holes burnt in the tablecloth and crawls around the ice dragging it behind him. Tom runs into the light.)

TOM: *(To the baby.)* Stony! God, where have you been? Everybody's vanished off this island. I felt like Robinson Crusoe all of a sudden. My man Friday! *(Tom slaps the baby in an attempt at good humor. The baby cries.)* Oh, Christ. I'm sorry. Did you get a vaccination? I hate it when people do that. Hit you in the arm right after you've been shot up with... Stony, you've got to help me. I have to come right out and say it. Hide me out just for a while? Let me work on the film. Stop crying, Stony. Let me work on the film. I've been impressive. Been referred to as impressive and even felt impressive. But now maybe it's time for a change. A change of direction. Time for, say, Art. I've been in the library in your house dipping into, God, like Chekhov while I was waiting for your wife to leave you. And by the way, I hope that silly misunderstanding is over. Please say something to me? Please? This is no time for vindictiveness. What I'm asking for is a job. Anything where my face won't be seen. Where I can work with the creative sides of my personality. I'm not going to trod on your toes. On your territory. I've got— it seems I've got the entire UN waiting for me. It seems I had announced the cure for cancer all ready, that I held it in my possession. Thousands of people have swarmed out of hospitals and are waiting at airports for me to return. I have to—vanish seems too melodramatic a word, using a word like vanish at a time when ironically I feel so present, when I feel so there. You see, I feel my soul has moved finally into my body and I could be such a good helper on your film. Carry the film to the drugstore or wherever you go to have it developed. I could get coffee. I could work on the costumes. Stony, wait till you see what I found. *(He takes a rusty tin box out of his jacket breast pocket.)* I was down at Flamingo Beach and saw a flamingo pawing the sand. The sun glinted. What was buried there? I pushed the flamingo away and dug this up with my bare hands. *(Tom opens the box. He takes out a pile of letters.)* Wait till you see what this is. *(Tom reads the letter.)* "Mein Liebstram Eva… Die Lieblich, Adolf." Yes! Can you believe it? Hitler's love letters! This place was built as a summer house for Hitler when the war would be over and he and Eva could come up here and relax. Isn't it extraordinary? You decide to make a film about heroes and about men who wanted to change history and, my God, you move inadvertently into Hitler's hideaway. The world of Art! My God! Does it always create this chain on which every event fits in some crazy exact magical pattern? The World of Art? Let me move into it. I'll hide anywhere. Hear the exclamation points I'm talking in. My mind makes spears out of exclamation points and nails me right onto the world of Art. Right onto your life. Let me stay. I can't go back. I am a laughingstock, Stony. I heard on the radio that my name has passed in the vocabulary. Not since Wrong Way Corrigan. As sure as Benedict Arnold is a synonym for traitor so will Tom Wintermouth pass into everyday speech as a byword for asshole. For one who promises and cannot deliver. For one who has a smugness and a self-pleasure. For one who… Stony, say something. Help me? Let me stay?

BABY: Ga ga splee do. Juice. Up! Up! *(The baby holds up his arms. Tom picks him up and carries the baby to the couch.)*

TOM: Stony, you want juice. Anything you want, you can have. I wish you'd get that tablecloth off your back. I'm not much into fashion, but I don't think tablecloths are in anybody's fashion forecast. You're impressive. You're the director. Stony, while we're having this heart-to-heart, let me tell you an idea I had. After I found Hitler's love letters which I just leave with you as a bread and butter gift, look what else I found. *(Tom unfurls a giant painted map of the world. It covers the entire garden floor.)* Isn't that something??? A map of the world circa 1935. Hitler's map! Showing what he hoped the world would look like after the war was over. Forget that. I use the map as a prop to tell you my idea. Why start with Marco Polo? The world needs heroes or at least people who dare dream beyond themselves. It'll soon be the new century. Take a hero—representative—from each of the last ten centuries. Leif Ericson here in Norway—man going out to search for New Worlds. Then the Twelfth century. Abelard, down here in France! Abelard! Man moving into his mind. New World's within. Man thinking for himself! Then we leap to Italy and look all the way to China. Marco Polo is a wonderful idea!! Thirteenth-century man going into New Worlds and taking from them what he needs and giving what he has. Mutual enrichment. Stony, don't turn away. Hear me out? Please? Next century: Francis Bacon, I thought. Science is born. Man learning to use this world. Next century— I don't know—Rembrandt! Man trying to capture this world on canvas. Eighteenth century we leap from Holland to America because you have to do George Washington. I could even play George Washington. I mean, I've had experience in front of the TV cameras. The Wintermouth Hearings. I've had my own hearings. And your wife who is the smartest person in the whole wide world said I have dreams where other people have pupils. My eyes alone. Destroy my face. I don't care. Look, Stony, your wife sleeps with me and that gives me some rights around here. For the Nineteenth century I haven't decided fully on Marx or Freud. Then for the Twentieth Century Man, we could— *(Tom leaps across the "ocean" again and plunges through the map. Vanishes. The baby looks up at the sounds of an air taxi landing. Diane comes on carrying her suitcase. The baby toddles to her. She sits beside the baby.)*

DIANE: I called my old piano teacher in Paris. Could I see her? I flew there. Such a lovely day in Paris. April. I went into her studio and lifted the lid of the old Knabe-Bechstein-Steinway and Mozart and Brahms were there in their little raincoats and if they didn't exactly break out into "Hello Dolly it's so nice to have you back…" I got through the Mozart—Köchel listing 453A. Started in on the Brahms. She stopped me. My old—my very old—piano teacher said if I practiced two years, three years, eight hours a day, then perhaps she could begin with me again. But really I was too old to think of starting a career again. I was a child prodigy and I'll always stay alive in the history books, but I had stayed away too long to resume an adult career. She said, "You have a nice husband. A child." I said, "I hate my husband. I'm having an affair." She said, "Stages. Compromises. Phases. Settle." I said, "But I want to keep my lover and have my marriage and resume my career." And she said, "Yes, and I wish it were 1938 again and World War Two hadn't happened and I still lived in Vienna." Stony, I sleep with Tom.

BABY: Go da splee do.

DIANE: I know you know. I want to continue. Darling, what did you spill that you're all wet? Poor Stony. Trying to find life-size. Is that why we're all so afraid? It used to worry me that I gave you nothing. That you got nothing from me. It used to hurt me that I wanted nothing from you. That you had nothing to give me. I see now, darling, that's our secret weapon. We can be together and always leave each other alone. Darling, I got frightened after I left. I got rid of the baby. I wanted to start all over again. I'm not pregnant. It was easy. I feel fine. I feel great.

(The baby tries to nurse.)

DIANE: No, darling, don't think you have to compete with Tom. No! Don't kiss me with so much passion. I don't want that. I want you to go out and do what you have to do and I'll go out and do what I have to do and then we'll come home and beg forgiveness and we'll both swear we'll be different and both swear we'll change but our secret that holds us together is that we secretly love and adore the way we are. I don't want you to change. But we'll keep the promise of change. Let's just hold each other and heal our wounds and call that growing.

(The baby cries.)

DIANE: What? You don't believe me? You think I'm going to leave you? What do you want? Silence? You want silence? You never lied to me. I certainly don't want to lie to you. *(She turns on a cassette tape of a piano recording.)* One of my best pieces. "The reason the piano was invented." I was the best. I thought if I were the best in music… *(She goes to the piano and slams the lid on her hand.)* I was then the best in it all. *(Slam.)* I see. *(Slam.)* I see. *(Slam. She cries in pain. She holds up her hands. They are bleeding.)* See what I've done for you, darling? Music with anyone, but silences with you.

Where is Tom? I want Tom. Freydis? Somebody? Could I have a valium and some gauze? Are you in there?

(Frank appears dressed as a Norwegian peasant. He carries a glass of water and some bandages.)

FRANK: I am Einar.

DIANE: Anything you want to be.

(He bandages her hand. Mrs. McBride comes out.)

DIANE: Debbie Lisa? Were you ever happy?

MRS. MCBRIDE: Only once really. On my way to Johns Hopkins. It was my last day as a man. I took a walk before the operation. I had made a choice. There was a beautiful little girl playing in a field. I would soon be like her. But I also felt a strong feeling for her I suppose was sexual. Pre-sexual, if there's such a thing. And I did something I never did before or since. I opened my raincoat to her. I exposed myself to her. She was so beautiful. I wanted myself with her. I probably frightened her. I don't care. I don't think it was sick. I wanted somebody to see me as a man. I was proud at that moment to be a man. I was proud I would be a woman. I was proud I had made a choice. She was such a beautiful girl.

(Freydis appears in tatters.)

FREYDIS: Was that in Baltimore? Baltimore, Maryland? 1965? I don't think I ever saw a happier human being. I followed you to the door of the hospital. I waited for you to come out. You never did. All my life I have dreamed of those eyes. I married Frank because I thought the joy I saw in his eyes was the joy of a man who has made a choice and revels in it. Let me look in your eyes. Yes. Those are the eyes.

MRS. MCBRIDE: Is it you?

FREYDIS: Let me sit on your lap.

MRS. MCBRIDE: Of course. You come sit in my lap.

FREYDIS: *(Sits in Mrs. McBride's lap.)* I need a comfort zone.

MRS. MCBRIDE: Of course you do.

FREYDIS: There's a little cottage at the far end of this island that's filled with food and chintz curtains. Come live with me and I'll take care of you. I'll grow you poppies. I'll make you drugs. I'll grow you hash. It'll be a wonderful new century. I want to get back to what I am.

MRS. MCBRIDE: I'll walk you there, but it's too late for me to get back to anywhere near where I was.

(The sound of the air taxi descending. Mrs. McBride and Freydis go off together. Frank/Einar picks up the baby and carries him out. Larry enters very happy.)

LARRY: So. I go to Helsinki, say: I lost my legs. Got a spare pair? They say "sure."

I see my new legs waiting for me. Beautiful. Shining my legs. And I thought, I can go anywhere I want to. I am free. And I thought, "But the only place I want to go is here." Isn't that a hoot and a howl???? The doctors… they were surprised. I mean, I left a lot of dislocated jaws in that hospital. "But your new legs," they said. "You're in a great deal of pain," they said. I tipped my hat, picked up my old kit bag, turned to the doctors and said, "Doctors, why go anywhere when you're where you want to be. After all, pain isn't the worst thing in the world." Isn't that a brilliant choice? Absolutely brilliant? I'm home. I came home. Diane, did you see there's another production of *Doll House* in Oslo? This time on roller skates and surfboards! Why not?

(Tom pushes himself up through a hole in the ice, supporting himself on his elbows.)

LARRY: Tom, if I were you, I'd get out of that water as quickly and as quietly as I could. On my way back here, with all the tropical waters coming up here, for the first time in Norway, there's a piranha scare. *"Peerannnaskeeren,"* I believe, is the latest addition to the Norwegian dictionary.

DIANE: Piranhas? Tom? Get out of the water!

TOM: I *am* out of the water. This is all there is. They already, it would appear, have got to me. I have read how your body produces morphine to deaden pain at times of great shock and loss. It's really not so bad… I want to cry. But it's really not so bad…

DIANE: *(Kneels beside Tom.)* I've made bargains with Stony, Tom. We can make love anytime we want to. It's all arranged. We have no illusions about what we need from each other. It's all worked out, Tom. You can fill me. *(Pause.)* What do you mean this is all there is of you? Tom, get out of the water. Tom, come into me. Tom, I need you. Just for a moment. Tom, it is very undignified to beg for comfort.

TOM: I've been reading Chekhov. *Three Sisters.* Those poor girls, all the time trying to get to Moscow. I looked at this map before I went through it. The town they lived in was only forty-eight miles from Moscow. In 1999 that town is probably part of Greater Downtown Moscow. They were in Moscow all the time. Those three dumb broads. There all the time. We spend all this time talking about the future. We're here. Baby, we are the future.

(The sky begins to darken.)

DIANE: No. This is not my life. The clock has not yet started ticking on my life. I'll let life know when I'm ready for it to begin. My parents told me I could have life anyway I wanted it. When I have a life, it's going to be a wonderful thing. A treasure you can put on a shelf. Warmth. Passion. Golden. Light. Freedom.

(Frank/Einar comes on carrying a door.)

FRANK/EINAR: *(In a bad Norwegian accent.)* I am not ready to go through any doors, but what I will do is fix this door so when I am ready to go through a door, I will have the door with me. *(He leans the door against an iceberg and begins fixing it. Mrs. McBride and Freydis come on. Freydis carries a tray of champagne and glasses. She hands glasses to everyone. Mrs. McBride takes out a cassette and puts it in the player: Guy Lombardo's recording of* Auld Lang Syne.*)*

MRS. MCBRIDE: Now, it's not too late to start planning for a New Century Party. Oh, I know you're going to say the new century doesn't start till 2001, but as far as this little girl's concerned, when that taxi meter of time goes click click click and tumbles into Two Oh Oh Oh, that's the new century and *2001* is just a darling sweet old movie I saw in a museum just before I came here. Stanley Kubrick hobbled out. So charming. We must have him. And Guy Lombardo if they can unfreeze him in time. And we'll have the powdered champagne—I'm sorry, but I love it—and midnight will come and we'll all toast so quietly so we won't frighten the new century away and we'll all whisper: Happy New Year.

(They all freeze in the midst of their toast with their champagne glasses. Stony comes on holding his space suit in his hands. The lights slowly dim until only Stony is illuminated by a single spotlight. He talks to audience.)

STONY: I looked at all these people waiting for a future that would never come and when it did come, when the new century finally did arrive, they would wait another hundred for yet another century and then a hundred years for another, waiting, waiting, always for rebirth. Should I reveal myself to them and explain and cry and he saids and she saids and forgives and forgets and going backs and resumes? Or should I simply twist the gauge again, lift up there in space, spend years ruminating about the events of these days, holding them to me until they finally cripple me.

Remembry.

Dismember.

Membrotic.

Membrosis.

A new word for the panic-stricken act of obsessive memory? And I realized what I would have to do. Draw the curtain. Say good-bye forever. Take my son. Go out into the now. Out there where you live. Into the present. Out there where you are. Grow. Change. My plant nature. Our plant nature. To celebrate that. *(Stony holds up his hands. Two green plants appear in them. Curtain.)*

END OF PLAY

Moon Under Miami

MOON UNDER MIAMI

A Man—is it an Eskimo?—appears in a parka, mukluks. Snow falls on him. Wind. He lowers his binoculars.

OTIS: *(To us.)* I love the way Alaska feels. You have all the dark at once. And then you have all the daylight at the same time. It's neater. The hard part of it is it is harder to shadow people. First of all, there are no shadows. Fashion wise, it's harder to trail people because everyone looks the same. But that's all democratic and good. In the Inuit—the Eskimo language—Alaska is the word for Great Land. And it is a great land. Look! A caribou leaping! I sit on an ice floe here at Point Hope and watch Russia on the horizon across the Bering Strait. To see your enemy that close. Oh, I know, I know. The evil empire is gone, but the Russians are still over there, nabbing our whale blubber, and the Federal Bureau of Investigation of which I'm an agent—Hello—Special Agent Otis Presby here—accept no substitutes—the bureau is nothing if not vigilant. The lesson of the caribou, mountain goats, fur seals. They are peaceful because they're vigilant. They know who their enemies are. I like an enemy. Some people say the lonely quiet must drive you crazy, but No! I have all these icebergs for company. I look at my icebergs sailing by, all grand lumbering innocence like great thoughts as yet unthought. Yes. All great ideas started out as icebergs. The wheel. Language. Love. Democracy. The Federal Bureau of Investigation. America. Each great idea began as an iceberg floating down to us, tilting, calving, melting until those ideas become part of our souls. *(Ominous music.)* And then one day an Eskimo floated by on an ice floe. Dead. And another. And another. And another. Their faces blue. Bloated. I know the Eskimos put their dead on ice floes and send them out to become part of the great—the Great Idea—but this one. I rake it in. This Eskimo is clutching in his dead fist two things. A hypodermic needle and a campaign button. "Time for a change. Vote for Reggie Kayak." He's the congressman from Eek. Is there any connection? I hold up the empty bag that had contained the Chinese cut heroin. *(Otis looks at the label.)* I can't read the label in this light. Only the chlorine blue light of the iceberg. Wait. The death dealing snow has a label. A street name. It says "Moon Under Miami."

(A trio of Mermaid Voices sing:)

MERMAIDS: *(Offstage.)* "A new kind of moon…"

OTIS: *(To us.)* It's Friday afternoon. I follow the congressman from Eek. He's in a panic. I call his office, pretending to be the telephone repairman. "Is the congressman from Eek there? He's making an emergency trip out of town? Thank you." Hmmm. Won't let him out of my sight. I have frequent flyer miles. Be back at my post on Monday. Nobody will know I'm gone. What can go wrong?

(A Voice booms out:)

VOICE: "The important thing in life is to have a great aim and to possess the aptitude and perseverance to follow it."

OTIS: Yes! Thank you, sir. Mr. Hoover said that. *(He begins—well, it's not a striptease, but he starts to take off his clothes. He gives new meaning to the layered look.)* I had planned to stay in Alaska forever but sometimes you have to leave town. The trail leads me south. I mean, up here, anything's south. No. I mean, *south.*

(He pulls off his mukluks. Otis is stripped down to a Hawaiian shirt and Bermuda shorts. He puts on sunglasses. The iceberg recedes into darkness as a trio of Mermaids appear behind Otis and take him into the darkness.)

MERMAIDS: *(Sing.)*
Follow me down
Down to Miami
It's Paradise
To dream on the sand.
The Bay of Biscayne
Will simply drive you insane
Its breezes calm you
And then embalm you.

(All sound is drowned out by bongos. The Mermaids lead Otis into a nightclub, all South Sea grandeur, and seat him at a table. Otis looks in wonder at the giant Easter Island statues, bamboo thatching, zebra skin banquettes, ancient signed photos of ancient celebrities on the red walls. Some of the guests enjoying their evening are simply painted behind those banquettes. The Mermaids make sure Otis sees The Man seated at the other table. The Man is the congressman from Alaska, waiting nervously. The Mermaids join the painted guests. The bongos play wildly. Suddenly a spotlight swings around the room.)

VOICE: The Boom Boom Room of the Fountaine Moon Hotel proudly presents the one, the only, Fran Farkus.

(The spotlight comes up on Fran Farkus, an aged, ageless platinum blond.)

FRAN: *(Sings.)*

> "I go to Hawaii
> When I want a good lei
> Now we're in Miami
> Going down at the Moon!
> I keep a big heart on
> My sleeve so I can say
> I'm loving Miami
> Going down at the Moon!
> Miami's romance
> Knocks you off of your feet
> I'll show you my pants
> Can you stand the heat?
> So stay in Hawaii
> If you all wants a lei
> Or else come to Miami
> And park your carcass
> On top of Fran Farkus
> And let's all go down to the Moon!!!"

Good evening, ladies and gentlemen. Welcome to Miami's own Boom Boom Room, where the elite meet to eat—anything. Anyone. The food here is shit. Let me see that menu. Stone crabs? Thirty-five dollars! Christ, I'm sitting on a fortune. Let me introduce to you the man who tickles my ivories every night and anything else he can get his hands on. Mr. Bobby Devine! *(Sings:)*

> "I'll be down to get you in a taxi, honey.
> You better be ready about half past eight
> We're going to dance off both our shoes
> When they play those jelly roll blues
> Tomorrow night at the—"

Tomorrow night? Tomorrow night! Oh, shit, I can't go tomorrow night. Bobby, can you go? Shit. Tomorrow. I want to go tonight! *(To us:)* How are you? Huh? How are you? This section looks like shit. Do we have any celebrities here tonight? Let me see the list. Oh, we have Francis the Talking Mule who's co-starring with me in my latest film *On Golden Blonde.* Oh, seriously, we have the congressman from Alaska. Where are you?

(The spotlight finds Reggie Kayak, the congressman from Alaska, who waves nervously. Fran sits on Reggie's lap.)

FRAN: *(Continuing.)* Oh, he's got little snow balls.

(Otis, sitting at another table, lowers a menu.)

OTIS: *(To us.)* Who is he waiting for? Whoever sits at that table is the source of all the drugs swarming into Alaska.

FRAN: Do I smell whale blubber? Is it true you all live in igloos and rub each other down with whale sperm? Fabulous. Bobby, play me some Eskimo songs. "Love To Keep Me Warm"? No. "Winter Wonderland"? That gets too wild. "Baby, It's Cold Outside"? I wish I was frigid. It'd make life easier for the band. We get all the politicians in here. Reagan was in here. He's a doll. We danced. He kept circling to the right. He sang in my ear. *(Sings:)*
"Seventy-six hormones did the trick for me
Nancy's feeling just like a bride to be."

OTIS: *(To us.)* Who is the Congressman waiting for? I faxed ahead for backup. Where are they?

(Osvaldo Munoz enters, all smiles. His lapels are covered with campaign buttons.)

FRAN: Look who we got here! Up for re-election! The Honorable Osvaldo S. Munoz, our own congressman from Hialeah! Talk about hung like a horse.

(Osvaldo Munoz takes Fran's mike.)

OSVALDO: *(To us.)* The friendship between the Jewish community and the Cuban world of Miami warms the cockles of my heart. Of all the candidates, I ask you, who else has got a Jewish mother and a Cuban father? I am proud to say to the people of Miami—*I am a Juban.* Miami, I love you. Please re-elect me! Vaya con Dios! Shalom! For a change Vote for Munoz.

FRAN: Gracias and mazel. Time for a change. Is that a hint? Thank God I got legs. Or else the floor would smell like tuna fish. A big hand for Congressman Osvaldo Munoz. You may be nowhere in the polls but we love you.

(Osvaldo is out of the room, waving, passing out campaign buttons.)

FRAN: *(Continuing.)* You believe these erections. I mean, elections. I'll vote for the first candidate to get me laid. Nothing personal, Bobby.

(Wilcox, a harried man in his 50s wrinkled suit, enters the Boom Boom Room, looking for someone. Belden follows. Wilcox and Belden examine each table. They reach Otis's table, stop and stare at him. Belden takes out a gun. Otis lowers his menu.)

OTIS: Four score.

WILCOX: Seven years.

OTIS: Hold these truths.

WILCOX: Self evident.

OTIS: Oh beautiful.

WILCOX: Spacious skies.

OTIS: Amber waves. Agent Presby down from Alaska. Thank God you're here.

(Belden puts away his gun. The three shake hands.)

WILCOX: Special Agent Walt Wilcox. Deputy Agent Belden. Welcome to Florida.

OTIS: There he is over there. The congressman from Eek. Don't look. He mustn't suspect. We have to catch him in the act of buying.

WILCOX: What is this place? My wife would love it here.

BELDEN: Would you stop talking about your wife!

(Shelley Slutsky and Giselle St. Just come into the Boom Boom Room and walk to their table. He is a large powerful force in a tropic shirt, gold chains and linen jacket. Giselle is fabulously chic.)

FRAN: Oh, it's not all politics. We have our regulars. A hand for Shelley Slutsky who gets more ass than a toilet seat. He's with his French pastry—what's her name, honey? Giselle. Isn't that a classy name? If she had every dick that's been stuck in her sticking out of her, she'd look like a porcupine. (Sings:)

> "Say there, you with the scars
> on your thighs."

(Shelley is not pleased to see Reggie sitting at his table. Reggie, groveling, stands up and shakes Shelley's hand as Shelley and Giselle sit. Giselle takes out a cellular phone and dials. Reggie leans into Shelley urgently. We don't hear.)

OTIS: There he is. This is the evil empire. Look at him. The source.

BELDEN: Oh, I know this guy.

OTIS: You know him!

BELDEN: Sheldon S. Slutsky. Continental Investors.

WILCOX: Investments, loan-sharking, laundering money, general extortion. They're harmless.

OTIS: Harmless? Like piranhas, they're harmless.

BELDEN: In Miami, these two are Little Bo-Peep and Tom Thumb.

(Reggie stands up from the table.)

REGGIE: Shelley, you can't cut me off!

SHELLEY: Who do you have to fuck to get a drink in this joint?

REGGIE: Thanks to me, you got into Alaska. I betrayed my own tribe, my own people, to do business with you.

SHELLEY: Waiter!

OTIS: Excuse me, sir. I'm about to become a waiter.

WILCOX: You can't moonlight.

(Otis goes off as Wayne Bentine, a distinguished congressman in his 60s, enters.)

FRAN: Look who's just come in! We are very honored to have the congressman from my favorite state—that is if you like them small. At my age, I like them any way I can get them—Rhode Island's own Congressman Wayne Bentine!

(Drum roll. The follow spot finds Wayne Bentine. He does not look amused. He's trapped in the light and bows.)

FRAN: So what brings the Chairman of the House Ethics Committee to the Boom Boom Room, Doll-face? Don't be shy.

BENTINE: *(To us.)* We're here in Miami holding the first annual World Hunger Conference asking the question: When does foreign aid become a crippling device designed to control countries that cannot afford freedom? Which brings up the issue of can we afford democracy?

FRAN: Sounds fucking fabulous. You'll make a real difference. *(Sings:)*
"What a difference a douche made."

BENTINE: Excuse me. I came in here thinking this was a supper place.

(He tries to escape. Fran keeps him in the spotlight.)

FRAN: I saw Congressman Bentine before the show. Wayne, I'm going to tell them this, and he said to me "Fran, do you know anything about real estate?" "Well, sure." Then he whipped out his shlong and said, "Is this a lot?" "Oh, my God, that is the ugliest dick I have ever seen. Quick put that in my mouth before someone else sees it."

BENTINE: I'm obviously in the wrong—

FRAN: Seriously, Cupcake. I want to wish you the best of luck on the World Hunger Conference. World Hunger. And God knows when I look at you I get hungry. So, *(Sings:)*
"Eat me, Daddy, 8 to the bar."

(Bentine, aghast, turns to Shelley.)

BENTINE: Who is this creature? She is absolutely disgusting.

SHELLEY: Listen, you fuck. You want your knees broken?

(Bentine flees.)

FRAN: My next song might be a little bit risqué. *(Sings:)*
"Missed the toilet last night
Shit all over the floor
Cleaned it up with my toothbrush
Don't brush my teeth much anymore."

(Otis appears as a Boom Boom Room waiter wearing a sarong, leis and head-

dress. *He wheels a food trolley with a video camera under a lobster. He stops by
Wilcox's table.)*

WILCOX: Waiter! Which is better? The Cajun shrimp or the lobster Bali hai?

OTIS: Sir. Four score.

WILCOX: Amber waves. First, bring me a Mai-tai, no, a Suffering Bastard. No,
a Samoan Fogcutter in the hula girl glass.

OTIS: Sir! I've got the videocam under the lobster. I'm wired. We are moving in.
Cover me.

WILCOX: Can't we do it after the show?

FRAN: My next story might be a little risqué. Mrs. Shapiro says to Mrs.
O'Rourke, "What does an uncircumcised shlong look like? I never seen
one." Mr. O'Rourke thinks a minute. "It looks like Yul Brynner in a turtle
neck."

WILCOX: Yul Brynner in a turtle neck!

BELDEN: I'll have—

WILCOX: You can't have anything. Waiter, can you get us a better table?

(Otis steers his food trolley over to Shelley's table and sets it in place.)

REGGIE: We made a deal.

GISELLE: I'm trying to talk to my mother. Oui, maman. Non, maman.

(Giselle speaks in an accent that is—is it French? Is it German?)

SHELLEY: Waiter!

OTIS: Take your order?

SHELLEY: Some prune Danishes to munch on while Mademoiselle and I peruse.

OTIS: Very good, sir. *(To us.)* I put a microphone under Shelley's table. *(Otis
retreats.)*

REGGIE: How am I going to get re-elected? I risk everything to come down here.
I have a campaign to finance. Why did I get hooked up with you!?

SHELLEY: You know why? You ever wonder where the center of the universe is?
You're in it.

REGGIE: I betrayed my own people. My wife is a junkie. My children are on the
nod. I've got my tribe on it to get money from you. To refinance my campaign, I've betrayed everybody.

GISELLE: Make him go away.

SHELLEY: Congressman, tell your story walking.

REGGIE: I'm going to destroy you. I don't need you.

(Shelley grabs Reggie by the throat.)

SHELLEY: You'll go down every alley in Miami and you know who you'll find? Me.

(Shelley flings Reggie away. Reggie goes. Otis returns with the Danishes.)

OTIS: *(To us.)* Follow him or stay here?

SHELLEY: Waiter! Asshole!

OTIS: Belden, don't let the congressman from Alaska out of your sight. If he leaves the building, come and get me.

BELDEN: I haven't ordered.

OTIS: Go!

(Belden goes. Otis puts the Danishes on the table.)

OTIS: *(To us.)* Slutsky, the hourglass is turned over. Count your last grains of sand.

FRAN: *(Sings:)*
> Gee but it's great
> After eating your date
> Brushing your teeth with a comb

(Otis stands over Shelley with his pad.)

SHELLEY: I'll try the water buffalo carpaccio, the fried medallions of barracuda, the squid tartar, leave the ink in, the flamingo sushi. How's the water moccasin tonight?

OTIS: Very good, sir.

SHELLEY: And a bowl of fries.

OTIS: Very good, sir. And Mademoiselle?

GISELLE: Why does it always have to be something. Can't there be a restaurant where you order nothing? Never. Because identifying the reality, naming the nothingness, is too painful.

OTIS: Very good. *(Otis goes.)*

SHELLEY: *(To Giselle.)* What the fuck is the matter with you?

GISELLE: All these political slogans. "Time for a change." Change this. Change that. Change terrifies me. Why must things change? If I could put a bullet in my mind, not to kill myself, just to silence the inner noise of my mind changing. What do I feel about you? I love you. I despise you. I must face another day of constant change. The sky. The sea. The menu. How do I survive a universe in constant flux? I want nothing to change. I hate these elections. I hate life.

SHELLEY: You don't vote, baby. You're not even in this country legally.

GISELLE: Oh, Shelley, I'm terrified! Take me out of Florida! Take me any place where the earth does not shift under my feet! Great change is about to occur!

SHELLEY: Baby, we can't leave. Our business is here.

(Otis appears for a moment.)

OTIS: *(To us.)* An illegal alien? Doesn't she know politics is how the people negotiate change. *(To Shelley and Giselle:)* Have you decided?

GISELLE: Caesar salad which I had last night and the night before that and the night before that and

SHELLEY: Caesar salad for the lady.

(Otis goes.)

GISELLE: I hear my body cry out "Giselle, you are a woman." My mother is getting married again and she is seventy-eight. My sister is having a baby. Marriage? A child? No. They are changes. I cannot change. But I cannot bear what I am. I hate myself. The only constant.

SHELLEY: What you are? I hear your body crying out you are a woman every minute of the day. Don't I make you happy?

GISELLE: No. You're always changing. Shaving.

SHELLEY: Everything changes.

GISELLE: No, Liebchen Cherie. There is one thing that never changes. The world of Michaelangelo. The world of Vermeer. Art is the only thing I can trust.

SHELLEY: Pussy pie, we *are* in art. Art is the best cover for laundering money. I learned that from you. Look at the masterpieces that have passed through our hands.

(Otis appears.)

OTIS: *(To us.)* Art? Is that the game? Wait! They buy stolen art to launder drug money. Of course! They want stolen art? This is how I'll get into their world. Icebergs crack! *(Otis goes.)*

GISELLE: I want to escape this rotting world and be part of the cool timeless world of Brancusi. Caravaggio. I don't need food. I need eternity.

SHELLEY: Giselle, I look at you—Baby, I look at you. Giselle, just to look at you. I've looked at people before, but I never looked at anyone the way I look at you.

(He dangles asparagus against her throat. She is aroused.)

GISELLE: You only love me for my mind.

SHELLEY: Fuck your mind. Everybody's got a mind. Even parakeets got a mind.

GISELLE: You swear you only love me for my body?

SHELLEY: Step on me, baby.

GISELLE: I don't want to ruin a good pair of shoes.

SHELLEY: —to look at you.

GISELLE: The asparagus. Lower.

(Giselle and Shelley go into a deep fevered clinch.)

FRAN: I want to leave you with one piece of wisdom. Look at the man sitting next to you. Now look on the other side. Remember this. Big man? Big

dick. Small man? All dick. Thank you, ladies and gents. I'll be back in twenty-five minutes. *(Sings:)*
"So park your carcass
On top of Fran Farkus
And let's all go down
To the Moon!"
(Fran is off.)

WILCOX: *(Writing down.)* Big man small dick. No. Big dick small man. If I could only meet her.

(Mambo music. Otis whips a tablecloth off a banquette table and looks at it.)

OTIS: *(To us.)* How hard can it be to come up with modern art? Look at the filth of this tablecloth. Ketchup. Mustard. I'll etch some squiggles on it. *(To Wilcox.)* Sir, I'm changing identities. You're the waiter. Keep the camera running.

WILCOX: I'm the waiter?

(Otis hustles Wilcox out. Bentine enters pursued by Osvaldo.)

OSVALDO: The great movie *Schindler's List*? Yo soy Schindler!

BENTINE: Get away from me.

OSVALDO: Congressman, one fucking photo op. Your arm around me discussing issues. I am in the race of my life. You have the prestige.

BENTINE: You have the worst attendance record of any congressman in the House.

OSVALDO: That is correct! You want no government, vote for Munoz. My slogan is "I am never there."

BENTINE: It would be political suicide to be associated with you.

OSVALDO: Oh, the little spick jew is not good enough for Congress. Prejudice spelled backwards is ecidujerp and either way it is ridiculous.

BENTINE: Let me talk to you straight. When you came into Congress, we all thought you might be great. You were talked about for vice president. What happened to you?

OSVALDO: I had to get re-elected.

BENTINE: You're a disgrace to the Congress.

OSVALDO: Your arm around me. One photo op.

(Bentine flees. Osvaldo, embarrassed, waves happily to the audience. He sits at Shelley and Giselle's table, interrupting their passion.)

OSVALDO: Hello? Shellito? Do you have my money?

GISELLE: Cherie, no business—

OSVALDO: *(All sunshine.)* I need my TV commercials. The primaries are three weeks away. I'm trailing by only ninety-two points. I can win. Do you like my new hairdo? Softer. And my new wardrobe? Forceful colors. My problem is I was wearing too much taupe. Confienza! Give me the trust.

SHELLEY: Waterlogged boat people don't trust you.

OSVALDO: The people of Miami love me.

SHELLEY: I wanted to build the Moon Bowl. A new football team to play in the Moondome. The Moonmen. You swore you'd get me government funding for the Moonarena. I gave you money for your last election. The legalized gambling in the Everglades. Where is it?

OSVALDO: I couldn't get the support. But next term—next term!

GISELLE: May I ask you a question, Osvaldo? Why would anyone spend a million dollars to get a job that pays one hundred thirty-five thousand dollars?

OSVALDO: The prestige! I see you talking to the congressman from Alaska. Are you giving him money?

SHELLEY: He's a close personal friend.

OSVALDO: Always the humoroso. Lend me money. For old times' sake.

SHELLEY: Cuanto? Twenty dollars?

OSVALDO: Three hundred thousand dollars.

SHELLEY: Get the fuck out of here. You wouldn't know what to do if you had a commercial.

OSVALDO: Wrong, Shelley. Tut tut tut. I would look into the camera and say: *(To us:)* Before you vote, ask yourself this. How stands Miami on this winter night? More prosperous? More secure and happier than it was before the election? We will make Miami stronger. We will make Miami freer. And when we leave her, we will leave her in good hands. And they will say "All in all, not bad. Not bad at all."

SHELLEY: You're a piece of shit, Osvaldo.

OSVALDO: Remember when I was first elected congressman from Hialeah? I was a hero. When all of Miami echoed with the cry of Munoz! Munoz! I might have been Senator. Then I met you. Why did I get mixed up with you to get re-elected? If I could only turn back time.

GISELLE: Turn back time? Time never goes back. Time laughs at us. Time is the poison that life forces us to drink. Time is a slave.

SHELLEY: Shut the fuck up, Giselle.

OSVALDO: Lend me the money. For old times' sake. We go back. The mambo teacher and the cabana boy. Those were the days! Getting laid left and right. Always the sunshine. Oh boy. Let the sun shine in. Like the immortal song from the immortal musical *Hair*. Oh, Shelley, let's drop some acid and pick up some chicks for old times' sake and drive up to Disney World. Let the sun shine in!

SHELLEY: Mickey Mouse sees you, he pukes. Give it up.

OSVALDO: I am magnificent! If I lose, I will sue the people of Miami. They deny me my constitutional right to be a congressman.

(The Sheik of Akbahran enters dressed in lavish robes over an English blazer, shirt and tie. He lights a cigar with a huge emerald and diamond encrusted lighter, shaped like Aladdin's lamp.)

OSVALDO: What a beautiful lighter. Vote for me November eighth.

(Osvaldo slaps a campaign button on the Sheik's robe and goes. The Sheik sits, setting the lighter down. Shelley sees the lighter.)

SHELLEY: Boy! Jose! We want nine piña coladas.

(Wilcox comes on dressed as a Boom Boom Room waiter in a sarong.)

WILCOX: Yessir.

(The Sheik turns to give his order to Wilcox. Shelley quickly takes the lighter and returns to his table. Wilcox goes. The Sheik picks up the menu and notices the lighter's absence. Pause. The Sheik goes to Shelley's table.)

SHEIK: *(An Oxford accent.)* In my country, if a man looks with lust at one of my wives, I rip his eyes out. If a man hears a secret, I rip off his ears.

SHELLEY: Oh, really.

SHEIK: If a man speaks evil, we rip out his tongue.

SHELLEY: You must give me the name of your country.

SHEIK: But when we catch a pickpocket, we cut off his hand.

SHELLEY: Which hand?

SHEIK: The hand that took my lighter. *(The Sheik takes a curved knife from his belt.)*

GISELLE: Don't hurt him!

SHEIK: Forgive me. I must obey Mademoiselle. Perhaps she is the reason I have traveled to Miami. *(The Sheik restores his scimitar.)*

GISELLE: I trust you did not come all this way to find her.

SHEIK: I traveled all this way to play polo—and to buy arms.

GISELLE: For personal use?

SHEIK: My father was the seventh son of a seventh son. His father was the seventh son of a seventh son. I am the eighth son of a seventh son.

GISELLE: People in your way.

SHEIK: I dislike anyone in my way.

(Giselle takes a business card from her bodice.)

GISELLE: Continental Investors occasionally sells arms.

(Giselle and the Sheik confront each other. Heat.)

SHELLEY: Look at us in the Boom Boom Room talking to a sheik. It's like fucking Camp David. I bet we could iron out the whole Middle East right here.

SHEIK: I have an idea for peace. I'm buying up portions of Miami and building

Israel here, stone by stone. I have nothing against Israel. I just would prefer it be someplace else.

SHELLEY: We don't do business with you.

SHEIK: This is your partner?

SHELLEY: I'm her partner. You want to buy some polo ponies, slightly used?

SHEIK: I want my lighter.

SHELLEY: Here it is. It must have fallen out of your sheets. *(Shelley tosses the
lighter to the Sheik.)*

SHEIK: Perhaps the gentleman wanted this not for himself. Allow me. *(In
Arabic.)* The sky would thank you if you would accept this lighter from my
hand, you Daughter of Love, you Daughter of Happiness, you Fish without Bones. *(The Sheik presses the lighter into Giselle's hands.)*

SHELLEY: The lady don't smoke.

GISELLE: Perhaps I'll start. Emeralds. Diamonds.

SHELLEY: Talk about bad taste. Get our of here, Lawrence of Arabia. You're like
Sunblock 29.

(Osvaldo enters and sees them together.)

SHEIK: *(To Giselle.)* It would give me great pleasure to see you. I am in
Penthouses A through M. *(The Sheik bows and leaves.)*

SHELLEY: Who's in N through Z? His harem?

OSVALDO: That was the Sheik of Akbahran!

GISELLE: To me he's just a friend who gave me a lighter.

OSVALDO: You know him?

GISELLE: Who truly knows anyone?

SHELLEY: Yeah. I know him. We're like fucking this.

OSVALDO: Emeralds. Diamonds. Do you know how many commercials I could
get just on that lighter?

GISELLE: It's such bad manners to pursue royalty.

OSVALDO: Maybe he has a cufflink.

SHELLEY: Get your shit together, Giselle. We're going upstairs.

OSVALDO: You could introduce me to the Sheik?

SHELLEY: He thinks you're scum.

OSVALDO: He knew who I was?

SHELLEY: Congressman? He couldn't care less.

OSVALDO: Perhaps I could be of help to him.

GISELLE: To somebody with a billion dollar a day income? Five million people
weigh him in rubies once a year. *(Mambo music begins.)* Stop talking and
dance with me.

(Giselle and Osvaldo fall into a very intricate mambo step. Wilcox in sarong

and headdress carries on a tray packed with Tahitian pineapple drinks to Shelley's table.)

WILCOX: My name is Bruce. I'll be your waiter all evening.

SHELLEY: Get the fuck out of here.

WILCOX: Very good, sir.

(Wilcox goes. Osvaldo and Giselle dance.)

OSVALDO: Your sheik must need something. Would he like to be a citizen? I could arrange it, for a price.

(Otis appears wearing a jacket, ascot and beret with his Bermuda shorts, carrying his tablecloth painting. He speaks with his idea of an English accent.)

OTIS: I'd like to sell a picture.

SHELLEY: You got me mixed up with Fotomat.

OTIS: Does the name "Moon Under Miami" mean anything to you?

(Osvaldo dips Giselle.)

GISELLE: *(To Shelley.)* Be careful.

(The mambo music stops. Osvaldo kisses her hand and goes off, waving to voters. Otis sits between Giselle and Shelley.)

OTIS: I understand you sometimes trade objects of art for—other objects of a different kind of art.

SHELLEY: Such as?

OTIS: I have borrowed some art works from the Anchorage Museum of Fine Art.

GISELLE: May I examine the materials?

(Otis unfurls his tablecloth painting. Giselle examines it.)

GISELLE: Exquisite detail. Note the brushstroke that betrays the essential insecurity of the times. The use of the obscene in the graffiti. This painting is like me. The beauty of the glaciers. Torn between ice and heat.

OTIS: *(To us.)* Is that an iceberg? Amazing! I didn't see that. *(To Shelley.)* There's a lot more art up there where this came from. How do I know I can trust you?

SHELLEY: Mademoiselle St. Just is an art expert.

OTIS: How do I know she's an art expert?

GISELLE: Modigliani. Watteau. Fragonard. Vermeer.

OTIS: I've never done business with you before.

SHELLEY: You want references? Billy "Pigpen" Lippert. Herman "Dog Days" Becker. "Bloodlust" Barone. "Deaththreat" Benedetto.

GISELLE: Velasquez. El Greco.

SHELLEY: "Snake Eyes" Castenada.

GISELLE: Monet!

SHELLEY: Spud Donegan!

GISELLE: Manet!

OTIS: I can call these people?

SHELLEY: Anybody vouches for Shelley Slutsky.

GISELLE: Matisse. Mondrian.

SHELLEY: "Machine-gun" Larry Pozzo. "Scissordick" Harry O'Rourke. "Scattershot" Bronfberg.

OTIS: "Scattershot" Bronfberg?

SHELLEY: "Scattershot" Bronfberg?

OTIS: *(To us.)* Even I had heard of "Scattershot" Bronfberg.

SHELLEY: "Scattershot" is a sensitive guy. And a close personal friend.

GISELLE: Can anyone ever be called friend?

(Belden runs in.)

BELDEN: *(Screaming to Otis.)* The Congressman is coming!

OTIS: *(Feigning ignorance.)* Who are you?

(Belden goes to Otis's table as Reggie returns to Shelley's table. Mambo music plays.)

REGGIE: Look, Shelley, maybe selling dope is not the best way to finance my campaign but it's what I've chosen. I'll take whatever you give me. You're like going into Tiffany's. You don't bargain at Tiffany's. Forgive me. I'll do business with you. I'm just a dumb Eskimo.

GISELLE: Make him go away.

OTIS: *(To us.)* We've got this on tape. I can arrest Reggie right now. Arrest Shelley. A clean sweep. I'll be back in Alaska before—

(Shelley produces an attaché case.)

REGGIE: You're going to make a lot of people happy. *(Reggie opens the suitcase.)*

SHELLEY: Don't open it here.

REGGIE: This isn't heroin. This is toilet paper. Hey—Everyone! I'm getting stiffed.

SHELLEY: Sit down.

(Reggie yells out. Shelley shoots Reggie in the head. The music stops. Silence for a moment. Reggie's body slumps over.)

OTIS: *(Horrified.)* Good God!

(The mambo music resumes.)

GISELLE: What other paintings do you have? Tell me more about icebergs.

(Otis stands, terrified. Wilcox comes to Shelley's table with a bottle of wine.)

WILCOX: Puligny Montrachet.

SHELLEY: Fill it up to the top.

WILCOX: *(Seeing Reggie.)* What about him?

SHELLEY: Let the fuck buy his own bottle.

WILCOX: Excuse me. Is your friend all right?

SHELLEY: He's got a little heartburn.

WILCOX: Can I get you some bicarb?

(*Shelley pulls up Reggie's body by the neck.*)

SHELLEY: (*Corpse's voice.*) I'm fine. I'm fine. I'm fine!

WILCOX: Sir, the bill.

SHELLEY: Charge it to Penthouses A through M.

(*Osvaldo passes by and slaps a button on the corpse.*)

OSVALDO: Do you vote in this district? I can register you.

(*Reggie's body slumps over.*)

OSVALDO: (*To Shelley.*) This maybe isn't a good time for you.

(*Osvaldo goes. Shelley props Reggie up.*)

OTIS: Let me—let me—I have some more iceberg paintings in my room. Excuse me.

(*Otis wheels the trolley away. Otis takes the tape out of the video. Wilcox appears weighed down with a tray of food.*)

OTIS: Sir, here's all the evidence we need. Make the arrest—

WILCOX: (*Furious.*) Can't you see I have a job? I've already made more money in tips than I have in six months—who has the water moccasin? You have the water buffalo—

SHELLEY: (*To Giselle.*) I'll get rid of our friend in the swamp. You go up to the suite. (*Shelley pulls a ring off Reggie's finger and gives it to her.*) To know you're waiting for me. Just to look at you.

(*Shelley picks up Reggie as if the corpse was drunk. Wilcox, Belden and Otis watch.*)

OTIS: Decision. Arrest him now and close the case or follow him with the body. Let him go and Shelley will lead us down every obscene alley in Florida. Arrest him now and settle for what we have. Follow him further into the black hole?

BELDEN: Pick door one!

WILCOX: Pick door two!

OTIS: Follow him!

VOICE: The Boom Boom Room of the Fountaine Moon Hotel proudly presents the one, the only, Fran Farkus.

WILCOX: Wait!

(*Fran appears in a spotlight.*)

FRAN: And that's why her pussy turned blue. But enough about me.

WILCOX: She's fabulous!

FRAN: (*Sings.*)

"Honey, but when you're queerly
I'm in the nude for love."

Good evening, Ladies and gentlemen. Welcome to the Boom—
(Shelley carries Reggie out of the room as if they're dancing.)

FRAN: Guy likes the show.

SHELLEY: Guy can't handle his liquor.

FRAN: I understand that. I'm feeling mellow myself. Yearning for the old days. Life was simpler. *(Sings:)*

> "Nothing could be finer
> Than your tongue in my vagina in the
> morning
> Nothing could be sweeter
> Than my lips around your peter in the dawning"

OTIS: *(Overlapping the song.)* Belden, don't let Shelley out of your sight! Wilcox, come on—

WILCOX: *(Overlapping the song.)* The show is still on. Can't we wait till—
(Shelley and Reggie are gone.)

OTIS: Belden, don't let Shelley out of your sight! Wilcox, come on—
(Otis drags Wilcox out of the Boom Boom Room. Giselle takes out her cellular phone and dials. Fran sings a torch song.)

GISELLE: *(Phone.)* May I have Penthouses A through N?

FRAN: *(Sings.)*

> A new kind of moon
> Hangs over Miami
> Controlling my soul

GISELLE: *(Phone.)* Would this be man who gave someone a lighter? It appears she needs a refill.
(Otis and Belden return and slide in on either side of Giselle.)

OTIS: This is an arrest. Please be quiet. Don't make a scene.
(Giselle tries to run. Otis grabs her. Belden blocks her. They arrest Giselle discreetly. Belden takes her away. The Mermaids draw a curtain of Everglades jungle vines over the Boom Boom Room.)

MERMAIDS:

> A substitute moon
> Singing a sensuous tune
> Bidding me follow
> Your life is hollow

(Otis, in his jacket and Bermuda shorts, and Wilcox back in his suit creep on into the everglades, their guns drawn.)

OTIS: *(To us.)* Inspector Wilcox and I drive out of Miami, following Shelley, deep, now deeper into the Everglades. Muscle power. Brain power. My heart is beating. *(Finds a label.)* Look! "Moon Under Miami!" The same wrapper from the lethal Chinese cut killing all the Eskimos. This must be the factory in there—

WILCOX: *(Takes wrapper.)* Shouldn't it be "Moon Over Miami?"

OTIS: Eskimos buy the contents of this package to support a traitor's re-election campaign. Housewives go to the supermarket and along with the milk and the peanut butter buy eight hours of oblivion.

WILCOX: Really?

OTIS: The horrible part is it's affordable. Fifteen dollars.

WILCOX: For eight hours of oblivion? Hmmm. What does heroin do for a man?

OTIS: Gives you an erection that lasts for hours.

WILCOX: Really?

OTIS: But you don't feel anything.

WILCOX: Well, you can't have everything. Let me see that.

OTIS: Sir! Focus on the enemy. If you could see the eyes of those corpses on ice floes clutching needles, dead of an overdose of snow. I hate how they desecrate the name of the purest element on earth. How many of Shelley's gang is in there?

WILCOX: It's so uncomfortable here.

OTIS: Remember what Mr. Hoover said? "Agents will do more work if they're uncomfortable!"

WILCOX: Mr. Hoover never went to the Everglades. Do your inner thighs make a scratchy noise when you wear wool? My wife says my trousers keep making a noise—

(Parrots squawk.)

OTIS: *(Wheeling around.)* What's that sound?

WILCOX: Oh, why bother. The DEA will come in, take all the credit. A dead Eskimo congressman? The Bureau of Indian Affairs will move in and take the credit.

OTIS: Sir! Cool! We don't want a replay of Waco!

WILCOX: And then Tobacco Alcohol and Firearms will swoop in. The CIA will barge in. And now this new one, the National Reconnaissance Office. Annual secret budget of six billion. Nobody even knows what they do. Let's pack it in. Let all of them have it. I give up. The FBI's over. Bring me a shot of rye.

OTIS: Sir, Mr. Hoover said "Fear is the enemy."

WILCOX: The Bureau used to be top dog. Where did we go wrong? When was our heyday? Was it all illusion?

OTIS: You want a heyday? July 22, 1934.

WILCOX: That's my birthday! Is this a surprise party? Is this why you've brought me out here? Is my wife here? Hello, honey?

OTIS: Sir, it's not a birthday party. While you were being born, a loathsome desperado named John Dillinger held America in fear. He took what he wanted, killed who got in his way. A new agency called simply the Bureau of Investigation got a tip that this gun-crazy lunatic had come out of hiding to go to a movie in Chicago.

WILCOX: *Manhattan Melodrama.* Clark Gable. Myrna Loy. I know it!

OTIS: A mysterious lady in red stayed with Dillinger so the agents could spot him. He came out of the movie. The lady in red pointed. Shoot out! Dillinger dead! America relaxed. The bureau captured the trust of the American people and became the Federal Bureau of Investigation. We can do it again.

WILCOX: America doesn't feel safe. Nobody votes.

OTIS: People only vote when they have an enemy. America needs an enemy. We have the opportunity to create a new Dillinger, a new Public Enemy Number One and destroy him. We have to bring America back to life. We can let America know that evil can be wiped out.

WILCOX: The FBI used to be able to handle the whole world. What happened, Otis? What happened?

OTIS: The world went international on us.

(*Otis cocks his gun. Corleen, a wonderfully capable-looking nurse in her 20s comes out of the infirmary, Shelley follows, dressed as a minister.*)

WILCOX: All bets are off. I'm not arresting any priest.

OTIS: Wait—

(*Otis and Wilcox crouch behind a bush.*)

CORLEEN: You're home! Stay a good long while!

SHELLEY: I have to go.

CORLEEN: You just got here.

SHELLEY: I'm guiding a poor lost lamb named Giselle back to the fold.

CORLEEN: Giselle?

SHELLEY: Do you want Giselle to die and spend the rest of her life in hell because you wanted me for your own selfish purposes?

CORLEEN: My purposes aren't selfish!

SHELLEY: Now you've upset me. Have you taken your medicine today? Give me your hand. Oh God, forgive this fragile creature. Do you hear me, God? Forgive Corleen!

(*Corleen kneels and takes Shelley's hand. Vibrations pass from him to her.*)

SHELLEY: Feel it! His love is passing to you.

CORLEEN: I feel it! I'm sorry! God? Please forgive me. And God help—

SHELLEY: —Giselle—

CORLEEN: Giselle. Thank you for bringing Shelley back. Amen. *(She stands.)* Did you sell lots of Bibles? How was New Orleans? Did you eat?

SHELLEY: I eat only loaves and fishes. Let me turn on the radio and dance very quietly.

(The Mermaids appear in the trees. Shelley and Corleen dance.)

MERMAIDS: *(Sing.)*

> "Jesus has the hots for you
> That's all that he knows how to do
> Jesus has the hots for you
> And he hopes you have the hots for him
> Holy, holy, holy"

(The Mermaids fade.)

SHELLEY: I must go. I only have time for the sinner.

CORLEEN: I only have time for the wounded.

(Corleen waves and goes. Shelley starts to leave. Wilcox sneezes. Shelley stops, suspicious. Otis makes a bird sound. Shelley turns to go and sees Otis and Wilcox with their guns drawn.)

OTIS: Sheldon S. Slutsky. I arrest you for the murder of Congressman Reggie Kayak of the sovereign state of—

(Corleen comes out. Otis puts his hand over Shelley's mouth. Shelley struggles. Corleen doesn't hear anything and goes back in.)

OTIS: —Alaska. Take him to headquarters. Did I advise you of your rights? *(Knees Shelley in the groin.)* There. I did. Dump Shelley in the trunk of the car. Take him back to Miami. Book him.

WILCOX: We have our Dillinger.

OTIS: Simple as that. You go along. May I have permission to stay here in Seminole City for? I want to sniff around this operation. I'll hitch a ride back.

(Wilcox drags Shelley off. Then, the enormous weird sound of an iceberg cracking.)

OTIS: *(To us.)* Icebergs have the innate need to cleanse themselves, to rid themselves of the debris they've accumulated. They make an enormous sound in discharging the past. That sound of change is called calving. When an ice glacier cleans itself, a new iceberg is born. God! I'm calving.

(Corleen appears, testing a hypodermic needle. She goes back inside.)

OTIS: She only has time for the wounded.

(Otis takes out a pen knife and gingerly cuts his finger. He screams. Corleen appears.)

OTIS: I had a little accident.

CORLEEN: Suck on it. *(She shoves Otis's finger into his mouth. She looks into her kit. She reads from a first aid manual and takes out a long strip of surgical gauze. She wraps his finger.)*

OTIS: What a view! To see all those expensive boats out there.

CORLEEN: *(All business.)* Sport fishing.

OTIS: Are those children unloading bags off the boats?

CORLEEN: Seminole day care center.

OTIS: Are those Lamborghinis and Masseratis parked alongside all those fishing shacks?

CORLEEN: Yes.

OTIS: Are those swimming pools behind every fishing shack?

CORLEEN: Yes. The frugal people of Seminole City know how to budget their money.

(Otis's finger is wrapped.)

OTIS: *(Looking at her.)* It is beautiful here.

CORLEEN: You think so? I wish my husband was here to enjoy it with me.

OTIS: Your husband?

CORLEEN: Shelley's gone back off on the Jesus trail. He's a Bible salesman.

OTIS: *(To us.)* Shelley is a Bible salesman!

CORLEEN: My husband sells Bibles. The condensed version. They leave out the sad parts. Jesus doesn't die or anything. It's what the Moonies call Heavenly Deception.

OTIS: Were you a Moonie?

CORLEEN: No. Were you?

OTIS: No.

CORLEEN: Wow. Two people not Moonies!

OTIS: Heavenly Deception, I like that.

CORLEEN: Your voice has such a nice pitch to it. You don't go in for singing, do you? I don't mean country western. I mean real singing like fat Italian opera stars on TV.

OTIS: You like music.

CORLEEN: Music is my life.

OTIS: I'm—a composer.

(Corleen gasps in happy disbelief.)

OTIS: Yes! A great composer. Come to write an Everglades Symphony. The first movement: Getting Into the Swamp. The second movement: Getting Out of the Swamp.

CORLEEN: Would I have heard of anything you've written?

OTIS: My Symphony Number One. My Symphony Number Two.
> *(They look at each other. Then:)*

CORLEEN: I'd better be going. I have a sick Seminole I have to tend to.

OTIS: *(Waving his finger.)* Well, thank you—

CORLEEN: You wouldn't like to join the Everglades Light Opera Association? Of course, you'd have to audition.

OTIS: Everglades Light Opera?

CORLEEN: The Everglades is a lot more than ten thousand islands. I'm trying to bring culture into these people's lives. I'm trying to keep the tiny shreds of their souls alive. It must be nice being an artist. Are you straight?

OTIS: Yes. I'm from Alaska.

CORLEEN: The North. Snow. How beautiful.

OTIS: The South. Heat.

CORLEEN: I'm unfortunately drawn to the he-man type.

OTIS: Thank you.

CORLEEN: But I'm not surprised. Jesus was a real he-man.

OTIS: You think I'm like Jesus?

CORLEEN: Around the eyes.

OTIS: I've been told that before.

CORLEEN: Is Alaska nice?

OTIS: Suppose you're driving along and you see someone stranded on the side of the road, if it's more than 20 degrees below zero, it's against the law not to stop and help that person. I love a land where it's a crime not to help someone.
> *(Corleen pulls her hand away.)*

CORLEEN: I've got to be strong, I've got to be strong. I'm a married woman. If Shelley knew the thoughts I had out here alone—please, you must leave. Good-bye. Good luck.

OTIS: How does one get accepted into the Everglades Light Opera?

CORLEEN: Only one way. T.A.L.E.N.T. Your money cannot buy you a part in the ELO.

OTIS: Look, I better be honest with you. I do have a problem.

CORLEEN: Oh God, I knew it.

OTIS: Do you have audiences?

CORLEEN: I hope so.

OTIS: If I even have to give a speech in front of two or three agents—I mean people—

CORLEEN: Do you break out in a cold sweat?

OTIS: Yes!

CORLEEN: And get horribly nauseous?

OTIS: Yes.

CORLEEN: And feel like you're getting appendicitis? And your eyeballs are like ice cubes in your head?

OTIS: And your ear lobes are like—

CORLEEN: Cement!

OTIS: Yes! Yes! And your knees feel like broken soda fountain straws.

CORLEEN: You have stage fright too.

OTIS: You mean, you too? It's such a problem.

CORLEEN: Don't call that a problem. Call it an obstacle. A problem is something you're stuck with. An obstacle is something you can overcome.

OTIS: But aren't you still terrified to sing in actual public?

CORLEEN: Listen. *(Corleen sings "Ave Maria" in a clear, beautiful soprano.)*

OTIS: But you're astonishing.

(She takes a recorder out of her pocket as the voice continues singing.)

CORLEEN: I'm pre-recorded. I wait for days when my voice is rested and I'm feeling very confident and I sing into my little recorder. Afterwards I just sing along with myself.

OTIS: But you have such confidence.

CORLEEN: My terror was only an obstacle.

OTIS: Not a problem.

CORLEEN: Never.

OTIS: Could I try? So you can judge if I have any T.A.L.E.N.T.?

CORLEEN: G.O.O.N.

OTIS: Goon?

CORLEEN: Go on.

OTIS: *(Sings: A sudden Elvis!)*

> By day, I'm Mr. Nowhere
> By night, I'm Captain Moonlight!

(The Mermaids appear and supply backup.)

OTIS:

> I sneak in through your window
> Land upon your bedspread
> Creep beneath your blanket
> Boo! What a fright!
> It's Captain Moonlight!

CORLEEN: And a ballad.

(The Mermaids sing barbershop.)

OTIS: *(Sings tenderly.)*

> "We were sailing along

On Moonlight Bay
You could hear the voices singing
They seemed to say"
(To us:) As I sang the Infirmary faded away and flamingos soared in sudden flight, exotic birds dove into the water, extraordinary fish leapt into the air to nip at fabulous iridescent insects. *(Sings.)*
"You have stolen my heart
Now don't go away
As we sang love's old sweet song
On Moonlight Bay"

MERMAIDS: "On Moonlight Bay"

CORLEEN: You're hired.

OTIS: Thank you.

(Blackout.)

(Shelley, handcuffed, sits beneath a harsh, crude light in a chair. Wilcox circles him. Belden has his gun drawn.)

SHELLEY: *(Screaming.)* I cannot be put behind bars! It is medically impossible for me to be held! I want my lawyer! I can pay any amount of fucking bail you set up. I have *Cash!* Where is Giselle! I want to see Giselle.

WILCOX: Giselle is in Krome Park where all the illegal aliens are held. *(Giselle appears in wrap clinging to a wire fence. A hand appears behind her and pulls her down.)* You want Giselle out? You cooperate.

SHELLEY: I got lawyers.

WILCOX: But we have tapes. Let me refresh your memory.

(Wilcox puts on Otis's tapes from the Boom Boom Room. Mambo music. Reggie appears and opens the suitcase.)

REGGIE: This isn't heroin. This is toilet paper. What are you doing to me?

(Gunshot. Reggie dies.)

WILCOX: Murder in the first. For starters.

SHELLEY: Wait a minute. Let's see that again. Play that back.

(Reggie in rapid reverse sits up from his murder and cries out what he said in reverse. Reggie exits in reverses as Giselle and Osvaldo enter in reverse.)

SHELLEY: Further! Further!

(Osvaldo and Giselle mambo in reverse. Shelley pulls the remote control from Belden and clicks it forward. Again. Again.)

SHELLEY: There!

(Giselle and Osvaldo mambo.)

OSVALDO: Your sheik must need something. Would he like to be a citizen? I could arrange it, for a price.

SHELLEY: Freeze frame.

(Osvaldo and Giselle freeze their dance.)

SHELLEY: You want a crime? Look at that. You want the wrath of America? Give the people something they can hate even more than me. Everybody knows I'm a scumbag. Where's the surprise in that? Get a politician. I'm just a simple pimp panderer procurer drug dealing serial killer pervert. Can't you assholes even recognize the better crime when you see it? The congressman from Alaska may be dead, but the congressman from Hialeah has three things going for him. He's guilty, he's alive and he's yours.

WILCOX: He only said it on a dance floor. That's not a crime.

SHELLEY: With my know-how, I can make it a crime. Give me a chance.

WILCOX: Hold it. Belden, play that part of the tape again.

(Osvaldo and Giselle reverse their mambo and then dance.)

OSVALDO: Your sheik must need something. Would he like to be a citizen? I could arrange it, for a price.

WILCOX: Again.

(Giselle and Osvaldo reverse and repeat their dip.)

OSVALDO: *(To Giselle.)*

For a price.

WILCOX: You can make that a crime?

(Shelley takes the phone and dials.)

SHELLEY: *(Phone.)* Osvaldo? I talked to my friend, the Sheik of Akbarhan. He really wants that citizenship. He's appointed me his agent to set up the deal. You can do it? Come to my suite. At the Fountaine Moon Hotel. The offices of Continental Investors. Yes. In one hour. *(Shelley hangs up the phone.)*

WILCOX: Wow!

(Blackout. An empty theater. Otis comes on stage.)

OTIS: *(Calling.)* Corleen?

(Corleen appears on stage in a hoop skirt, carrying a costume.)

CORLEEN: *(Proudly.)* Otis? This is our theater.

OTIS: It's very nice. Where are the other members of the ELO?

CORLEEN: We're the only members of the Everglades Light Opera Association. But I pray there will be more. Now, here is your costume.

OTIS: Already? Did you make it?

CORLEEN: Yes. Yes, I did. And here is your button. *(She helps him put on his golden robes.)* And here is your button. *(She pins a large badge on Otis bearing the initials ELO and hands him a Bedouin headdress.)* This is called a burnoose. Can you say burnoose?

OTIS: Burnoose?

CORLEEN: Very good.

> *(Otis is entranced with his new image.)*

OTIS: What operetta is it that we are going to be doing?

CORLEEN: It's called *Broad Moonlight* and it is a really outstanding operetta about this girl who loves this mysterious bandit called the Desert Mirage who steals from the rich and gives to the poor. But, at the end, she finds out the shy boy who loves her is really the Desert Mirage.

OTIS: Is that my part?

CORLEEN: Yes, it is.

OTIS: It pays to get here early.

CORLEEN: Yes, it does. Now let's rehearse the title number again.

> *(Corleen turns the tape recorder on. She lip-syncs and Otis sings along tentatively, following her instructions: "Turn to me." "Lift your hand." "Hold my hand." "Hand over Heart." "Arms out." "Big finish.")*

CORLEEN AND OTIS: *(Sing.)*

> "Broad moonlight
> Makes blue shadows
> Giving us no place to hide
> We were both dying of thirst
> I simply got to the oasis first
> Broad moonlight
> Makes two shadows
> Broad daylight never can part
> You cannot fake your thirst
> Come slake your thirst in my heart
> Beloved
> In Broad Moonlight
> Broad Moonlight
> Come slake your thirst in my heart"

CORLEEN: Then we bow and everybody will applaud.

> *(They bow to us.)*

OTIS: Did you say "slake?"

CORLEEN: It's operetta for "come drink your fill."

> *(Otis rips open his costume and points to his heart.)*

OTIS: Come slake your thirst in my heart.

CORLEEN: Please! Please!

> *(They fall into each other's arms. Suddenly, out of Otis's jacket, Wilcox's voice blares.)*

WILCOX'S VOICE: Dimsby! Dimsby!

(Wilcox appears in another part of the stage in a harsh light. Otis reaches into his pocket and tries to shut off Wilcox's voice.)

CORLEEN: Did I hear voices?

OTIS: I do a ventriloquist act.

CORLEEN: You could be a ventriloquist for Jesus! You could play a sinner and then your Jesus doll could come and save you.

OTIS: Excuse me for a moment.

WILCOX: Is this Goddamned thing on? Can you hear me?

OTIS: Mr. Wilcox, I must have a certain amount of privacy. I'm in the middle of an investigation.

WILCOX: Feel free to go back to Alaska. Shelley Slutsky is working for us.

OTIS: We have a bad connection.

WILCOX: No, we don't. I hear you perfectly. We're here in his suite at the Moon.

OTIS: Sir, he murdered a congressman.

WILCOX: So what? We don't need you anymore. Good luck in Alaska. Thanks for your help. Have a nice day.

OTIS: What are you saying? Have you gone mad? Don't hang up!

(Wilcox goes. Corleen sings "Broad Moonlight" with the appropriate gestures. Otis starts to go back to Corleen, but hesitates. Without taking off his costume, he runs out of the Everglades Light Opera Theater. Corleen is drowned out by violent bongo drumming. Fran appears, backed up by the Mermaids.)

FRAN:

> Every evening at Cape Canaveral
> All the astronauts
> Line up on the launching pad
> Got to get it up
> Got to get it up
> Got to get it up tonight!

(Congressman Bentine appears, followed by the Hotel Manager, dressed in dinner jacket, headdress and sarong.)

BENTINE: Don't tell me she's an institution! I think America is a more important institution! I want her closed down! This will be some people's first glimpse of America! Do you want me to take the World Hunger Conference to another hotel?

MANAGER: No!

BENTINE: Then close down that thing in the Boom Boom Room!

FRAN:

>All their wives
>Are waiting for the astronauts
>To finally blast off
>And send them into outer space
>Got to get it up
>Got to get it up
>Got to get it up—

(The Manager wrests Fran's mike away from her.)

MANAGER: *(To us.)* Excuse me, everyone—

FRAN: What the hell are you doing?

MANAGER: *(To us.)* The Boom Boom Room will shortly re-open with its new revue, "Broadway Goes Christian!"

(The Manager drags Fran off, protesting violently.)

FRAN: You weenie dick congressman! I'll get you if it's the last thing I do!

BENTINE: Now that that's taken care of, perhaps we can resume our next panel focusing in on human rights violations in Bolivia—

(The Mermaids advance on us.)

MERMAIDS:

>On this evening
>Out of the Everglades
>All the elements
>Rise into a hurricane
>Got to get it up
>Got to get it up
>Get it up tonight!

(The Sheik of AkBahran appears.)

SHEIK: Giselle! Where are you? Giselle?

MERMAIDS:

>Up comes wind
>Down comes the thunderclap
>Down comes rain
>And up comes the lightning bolt
>Got to get it up
>Got to get it up
>Get it up tonight!

(Belden drags on Giselle, holding a gun against her head, forcing her to kneel. She has a number around her neck for her prison photo. The Sheik appears,

searching. Osvaldo appears, waving victoriously. Shelley and Wilcox appear in great camaraderie. They all freeze.)

MERMAIDS:

> Mother Nature
> Turns into a poltergeist
> Father Time
> Moves in like a juggernaut

(Otis in his operetta costume appears between the Mermaids.)

OTIS: *(To us.)* I am an iceberg sailing majestically into southern waters. Deeper and deeper I go, tilting, turning!

VOICE: We interrupt this program to bring you a special bulletin: A hurricane—repeat—an unnamed hurricane of deadly force sweeps down on the Florida coast!

MERMAIDS:

> Got to get it up
> Got to get it up
> Got to get it up tonight!

CURTAIN

ACT TWO

The Mermaids lovingly pack an attaché case with stacks of cash.

MERMAIDS:

> A new kind of moon
> Hangs under Miami
> A new kind of moon
> Controlling my soul
> A substitute moon
> Singing a sensuous tune
> Bidding me follow
> Your life is hollow
> I have a life
> Safe in Miami
> Why do I cry and plead to the moon:
> Tell me what you want me to be
> And I shall be it

Yes, I shall be it
No matter the cost.
(The Mermaids snap the attaché case shut.)
A new kind of moon
Hangs under Miami
Darling, hang onto me
Or else I am lost.
(The Mermaids reveal Shelley's suite in the Fountaine Moon Hotel. The living room and the bathroom are divided by a wall containing a two-way mirror. The bathroom sink contains a video camera pointed into the mirror. The Mermaids open the door to the suite and lead in Wilcox and Shelley.)

SHELLEY: —Easy. I sell the boat people fake permissions to get into America for a thousand dollars a head. Hard cash. I take the money. We dump them.
(Wilcox sits at Shelley's feet.)

WILCOX: So that's how it's done!

SHELLEY: Look, they'd drown out there anyway on those little rafts.

WILCOX: Absolutely. How do you make money?

SHELLEY: I pry the gold out of their teeth.

WILCOX: And this is not part of the drug deals?

SHELLEY: Separate.

WILCOX: How do you keep it all in your head! Tourists keep getting murdered. Are you in any way involved with—
(Belden, wearing a headset and dressed as a lifeguard, runs in.)

BELDEN: Sir!

WILCOX: We don't want CPR.

BELDEN: Four Score!

WILCOX: Amber waves. Belden?

BELDEN: I'm in disguise! Sir, the hurricane is scheduled to hit in seventeen and a half minutes! Congressman Munoz is entering the pool area on his way up here. *(Belden runs out.)*

WILCOX: Let's get the swearing-in over. Wait— *(Wilcox wheels in a large shrine.)* Let me get this opened.

SHELLEY: What the fuck is this?

WILCOX: A shrine. I had it delivered. Belden and I brought it up here to the suite of Continental Investors which you're so sweet to let us use. Besides, I thought he'd want to be here. Get out of the office.

SHELLEY: Get who out of the office?
(Wilcox pulls the curtain aside: A glowering portrait of J. Edgar Hoover.)

WILCOX: He'd come down once a year to the races. I'd drive him around. We'd laugh. Sweet, funny guy. God, I miss him. See how his eyes follow you around the room.

(Wilcox dances back and forth across the room under the fierce stare of Hoover. Shelley follows.)

SHELLEY: Amazing.

(Otis, still in costume, rushes in and grabs Wilcox by the lapels. Belden, as lifeguard, follows.)

WILCOX: Who are you!

BELDEN: You can't come in here! *(Belden grabs Otis in a hammerlock and bangs his head against the table.)*

OTIS: Four score.

BELDEN: Beautiful for spacious skies. *(Belden releases Otis.)*

WILCOX: Grimsby? What holiday are you dressed for?

OTIS: Inspector. Have you gone mad?

BELDEN: *(Listens to his headset.)* Wait! Munoz is leaving the pool area.

WILCOX: Back to your post!

(Belden goes. Otis aims his gun at Shelley. Shelley retreats.)

WILCOX: Thanks to Shelley, Munoz is going to come up here. Shelley will then get him to repeat his offer to sell the Sheik of Akbahran a citizenship. I'm in the toilet taping away.

OTIS: I cannot believe you have made a deal with Slutsky.

WILCOX: Are you suggesting I don't know my job?

OTIS: I regret it if it comes out that way but this is illegal entrapment and Slutsky, who, when I last saw him was a criminal under arrest, would seem to lack the authority—

WILCOX: He has all the authority in the world. He's about to become an agent.

OTIS: Sir, it takes years to become an agent. You become an accountant. You train, you take psychology.

WILCOX: I want to destroy Munoz.

OTIS: Osvaldo will destroy himself at the ballot box.

SHELLEY: Then you better hurry while he's still in office.

WILCOX: A crooked Cuban congressman selling a citizenship. It makes my blood boil. *(To Shelley:)* Raise your right hand.

(Otis starts to pull off his burnoose.)

SHELLEY: Wait. Leave that on—

OTIS: Don't give me orders.

SHELLEY: We promised Osvaldo a sheik.

WILCOX: You said you didn't need a sheik.

SHELLEY: I didn't need a sheik when we didn't have a sheik. Now we got a sheik, I'll use a sheik.

OTIS: I look about as much like a sheik—

SHELLEY: Osvaldo is so desperate you could nail his dead grandmother to a stuffed camel and he'd call her sheik. You got the fish on the hook, why not decorate the bait?

WILCOX: Fish! Hook! Decorate the bait! I like it. Keep your clothes on.

OTIS: No!

WILCOX: You want to stay with the Bureau?

OTIS: The Bureau is my life.

(Wilcox steers Otis into the bathroom.)

WILCOX: I ran a check on you. You came down from Alaska on your own. Is this true?

OTIS: Yes, but—

WILCOX: You're whale blubber. Is that true?

OTIS: For the moment it's my post—

WILCOX: You're a vigilante!

OTIS: One way to look at it, sir.

WILCOX: I can have your career destroyed.

OTIS: Sir, I implore—

WILCOX: Shelley has given us a wonderful idea. I want you to thank Shelley.

OTIS: Thank Shelley? He's the enemy!

WILCOX: Say "I'm sorry" as loud as you can.

OTIS: You can't make decisions that humiliate and trivialize the Bureau—

WILCOX: *Say it. (Wilcox steers Otis back to the living room.)*

OTIS: I'm sorry.

WILCOX: I can't hear you.

OTIS: I'm sorry.

WILCOX: I still can't hear you.

OTIS: *(Screams out.)* I'm sorry! What do you want me to do?

WILCOX: Be the sheik. Nab Osvaldo. You're back to Alaska. God provides.

SHELLEY: Can we trust this guy?

OTIS: Of course you can trust me.

WILCOX: He's an agent. Like me. Like you're about to be. Raise your right hand. I, Shelley Slutsky—

OTIS: Wait—what did you promise Osvaldo?

SHELLEY: He needs three hundred.

OTIS: Three hundred thousand!

SHELLEY: Offer him two fifty. We only have to hand over ten percent.

OTIS: Where do we get $25,000?

WILCOX: We'll wire Washington. They'll send forms to fill out. Tell Osvaldo he'll get his money the first of the month.

SHELLEY: You got the fish on the hook, you don't tell the fish to wait till you got the recipe.

WILCOX: *(Very impressed.)* Fish hook! Recipe! Wow!

SHELLEY: Don't the FBI keep petty cash handy?

WILCOX: About twelve dollars.

OTIS: This man has a fortune.

SHELLEY: No way. No no no no no.

WILCOX: Don't you have any cash we could borrow?

SHELLEY: No. No no no no!

WILCOX: Please please please please please?

SHELLEY: What can I get for it?

OTIS: A receipt.

SHELLEY: I want Giselle freed!

OTIS: Giselle is an illegal alien.

WILCOX: That label only applies to dark people who travel on rafts. Not to white people of elegance like Giselle.

SHELLEY: After that, I want to renegotiate.

WILCOX: Sounds fine to me.

OTIS: Sir!

(Shelley opens the attaché case and spills out bundles of cash.)

SHELLEY: I hereby donate $25,000 on loan to Operation Moon.

WILCOX: Omygod! Look at this booty!

OTIS: *(To us.)* Oh Christ, the blood of Eskimos. The blood of Haitians.

WILCOX: Belden!

(Belden opens the door dressed as a French maid.)

WILCOX: Go to Krome Park Prison Facility and prepare Mademoiselle St. Just for immediate return.

BELDEN: Yes sir!

WILCOX: Belden, nice tits.

BELDEN: Yessir! Hubba hubba! *(Belden goes. Storm clouds begin to form outside the window.)*

WILCOX: CIA! Eat your heart out! Raise your right hand, Shelley. No, over here. Let him see you.

(Shelley stands in front of the shrine. Wilcox opens another curtain and takes out a velvet pillow containing mysterious relics. Otis looks at it.)

OTIS: What is this, sir?

WILCOX: It's Mr. Hoover's toupee. And little eyelashes. I had it brought over from the office.

OTIS: Mr. Hoover wore a toupee? And little eyelashes?

WILCOX: No one knew. This was his spare. After he died, we were supposed to return all personals. But I couldn't give it up.

OTIS: I can understand that. *(Amazed.)* Little eyelashes?

WILCOX: Don't touch them!

OTIS: I'm sorry.

WILCOX: See how the eyes follow you around the room.

(Wilcox repeats his dance across the room under Hoover's watchful eyes. Shelley and Otis follow.)

OTIS: Amazing!

WILCOX: Smell the toupee. If anything happened to them, I don't know what I'd do. *(To Shelley:)* Raise your right—

(Belden as a French maid opens the door.)

BELDEN: Munoz has stopped by the gift boutique to shake hands. Sir, winds are rising to gale force—

SHELLEY: Hey, Belden, nice tits!

BELDEN: Thank you, sir.

WILCOX: Go to Krome Park!

(Belden curtsies and leaves.)

WILCOX: Do you, Shelley Slutsky, swear to uphold the Constitution of the United States and obey the demands of the Bureau no matter where it leads you.

SHELLEY: I do.

(Wilcox gives Shelley an envelope.)

WILCOX: Welcome to Operation Moon! Here are your poison pills in case of capture—

SHELLEY: Here, Odious, take two before bedtime.

OTIS: The name is Otis. Sir, Operation Moon is my creation—

(Wilcox sits at Shelley's feet.)

WILCOX: Now that you're an agent, I can play you the secret Hoover tapes. Pat Nixon was one of Kennedy's girls. Pat Nixon set Nixon up for Watergate. Mamie Eisenhower. Bess Truman. They were all Kennedy's girls. They were sluts. Kennedy took what he wanted when he wanted. Marilyn Monroe? Now she was a Russian agent—

(Belden as the French maid runs in.)

BELDEN: Congressman Munoz is pacing in the lobby nearing the elevators. Sir, the rain is flooding in—

WILCOX: Belden!

(Belden curtsies and runs out. Wilcox runs into the bathroom and puts on a headset.)

WILCOX: Quick! Quick! Set up the cameras. I'll handle the taping.

OTIS: I'll handle the taping.

WILCOX: You can't be two places at once. I think I know how to operate this kind of camera. You just turn it on and point, right?

OTIS: "Just turn it on and point." Would that life were so simple. Is the two-way mirror set?

WILCOX: Right here.

SHELLEY: To think I used to be afraid of you guys. *(To Otis.)* What you need is a beard. Look like a sheik. You're about to become a citizen.

WILCOX: God is in the details! Oh, Shelley! You think of everything! Presley, get facial hair!

(Shelley and Wilcox go into the bathroom to set up the camera.)

OTIS: *(To us.)* Where am I going to get facial hair in Miami with a hurricane coming? Is Corleen safe? If only there was someone I could talk to—wait, there is! *(Otis approaches the J. Edgar Hoover shrine. Variations on the FBI theme play. Now light, now serious. Mr. Hoover responds musically to Otis. To the Portrait:)* Mr. Hoover, I hate to bother you. The Bureau has asked me to participate in an illegal setup. It means working with a criminal. This is the problem. I'm in love with the criminal's wife. Corleen. Her name is Corleen. Yes, it is a nice name. Mr. Hoover, if it wasn't for the Bureau, I never would have met Corleen. What should I do? I have to put the Bureau first. Is that what you're saying? And all the Bureau is *is obeying.* So what I must do is obey Wilcox. And if I'm ordered to play the sheik, then I must find a way to be the sheik. Is that right? Thank you, sir. They want me to get facial hair? Check the yellow pages. Under what? *(Otis pulls back the curtain. He reaches in. Otis puts his hand over Mr. Hoover's eyes. He takes out the pillow containing Hoover's toupee.)* Mr. Hoover, I don't mean any disrespect. I only want the Bureau to be magnificent. *(Otis takes a pair of scissors. He cuts a strip off the toupee and holds it under his nose. Rumbling of thunder.)* I hear the icebergs crack. Deeper and deeper I go.

(Wilcox and Shelley come out of the bathroom. Belden runs in dressed as a Chinese coolie.)

BELDEN: Congressman Munoz in hallway approaches the suite. *(Belden runs out.)*

SHELLEY: Greetings, your highness.

(Shelley tries to kiss Otis's hand. Otis, trying to affix the mustache, snatches his hand away.)

WILCOX: Snap to!

(Shelley puts the cash into an attaché case.)

OTIS: Yes sir.

(Shelley rushes to place the chairs.)

SHELLEY: Osvaldo will sit here. I'll sit in this chair. Otis will sit in the middle.

(The door to the suite opens. Osvaldo stands in the doorway.)

OSVALDO: Your Excellency! Right on time! Punctuality is the politeness of princes.

(Otis, trying to affix his mustache, slams the door on Osvaldo.)

BELDEN'S VOICE: Congressman Munoz has stepped into the elevator.

(Wilcox screams into his headset.)

WILCOX: You nitwit, he's outside the door!

OTIS: Battle stations! Do we have video go?

OSVALDO'S VOICE: Shellito? I'm counting to ten.

OTIS: Do we have audio go?

(Otis screams into the mike hidden in the flower pot on the table to test it. Wilcox screams and rips out his earplugs.)

WILCOX: Roger. A.O.K. Ten four.

OSVALDO'S VOICE: Ten. Nine. Eight.

(Otis runs into the bathroom.)

OTIS: *(To Wilcox.)* Sir, I feel I'm going insane. We came here to get Shelley—

WILCOX: *(Confidentially.)* Godammit, Pitsby, I know he's a criminal. What I'm doing is using Shelley to nail Munoz. The minute that's done, we run in Shelley. It's all betrayal. Wheels within wheels.

OTIS: You swear?

WILCOX: By Mr. Hoover's eyelashes.

OTIS: I feel better. *(Otis runs back to the living room and leans by the window to affix his disguise.)*

OSVALDO'S VOICE: Five. Four—

(Shelley answers the door as Wilcox rushes into the bathroom.)

SHELLEY: Osvaldo. You're late.

(Osvaldo strolls into the room.)

OSVALDO: So the little mambo teacher and the cabana boy turned out all right.

(Otis turns out from the window. The mustache and goatee have transformed his face into Arabic plausibility.)

OSVALDO: *(Dazzled.)* Excuse me, Your Highness. I thought you were a curtain.

(Wilcox operates the camera.)

SHELLEY: Shall we get down to business?

OSVALDO: Your Excellency is sweating. May I cool your brow?

SHELLEY: Don't touch him! In his country he is a god.

OSVALDO: Like me. Tell the Sheik, he and I got a lot in common. I am the god of Miami. I got fucking *halos* shining out of me.

(Otis bows. The three of them sit down. Shelley sits in the wrong chair. Osvaldo sits down with his back to the two-way mirror that conceals the camera. Wilcox signals for them to move. Otis stands up. Osvaldo stands up. Otis gracefully gestures for Osvaldo and Shelley to change chairs.)

OSVALDO: Oh. Protocol.

WILCOX: *(At the camera.)* That's better!

OSVALDO: Your Highness! You are a member of the ELO—I love the ELO

SHELLEY: Don't touch him!

OSVALDO: Forgive me.

SHELLEY: My client is very impressed that I know you in spite of the fact that you're an uncircumcised dog.

OSVALDO: *(Standing.)* I am a Juban!

(Otis pulls Osvaldo back down.)

SHELLEY: His Highness says that will be unnecessary.

OSVALDO: I just want him to know that in America, we are all equal. Which is what's wrong with this country. You're crowned for life. I have to get re-coronated every two years.

SHELLEY: So why won't America let his Highness in here? What do they have against royalty?

OSVALDO: I apologize for my country. Look. A few terrorists make it bad for all of you. You help me get re-elected, I'll pass a law where not only you but every ancestor you ever had becomes an American citizen. But you must understand, your Excellency—for all this to work, I need my TV commercials.

SHELLEY: My client needs to become an American citizen.

OSVALDO: Osvaldo Munoz cannot be bought. But he can be borrowed.

(Shelley places the attaché case containing the cash on the table.)

OSVALDO: Tell him he would honor our country by his presence, not to mention you won't go on no food stamps.

SHELLEY: The Sheik understands you need three hundred thousand dollars for your TV commercials. As much as he likes America, he feels the citizenship is not worth three hundred thousand.

OSVALDO: No! I need three hundred thousand for my TV commercials.

SHELLEY: He thinks it is worth only two-hundred and fifty thousand dollars.

OSVALDO: *(Stunned.)* He will give me two-hundred and fifty thousand dollars?

SHELLEY: His Highness likes a bargain as much as the next guy.

OSVALDO: I can understand that.

SHELLEY: If you agree to start work for his Eminence, you get ten percent now.

OSVALDO: Twenty-five G's? I could start my commercials today and have them on the air tomorrow! Tomorrow! It's like the beautiful song from the movie *Annie. (He sings.)*

> "Manana Manana
> Te amo
> Manana"

Osvaldo Munoz will see that you're a regular Yankee Doodle Dandy. You have the money?

(Shelley takes out the attaché case and holds it up for the camera.)

SHELLEY: In my client's country, because all things come from God, God must know what the fuck is being done with his money.

OSVALDO: It's very simple. He buys my commercials. I get him a citizenship. Tits for tats.

SHELLEY: I think his god can buy that.

(Shelley hands the case to Otis. Otis passes the briefcase to Osvaldo. Otis and Shelley duck to make sure they don't block the cameras. Wilcox lifts his fist in triumph, then:)

WILCOX: *(At the camera.)* Shit. I was out of focus.

(Shelley, Otis and Osvaldo shake hands. Behind Osvaldo's back, Otis sees Wilcox, waving frantically. Wilcox holds up two fingers.)

WILCOX: *(Desperately mouthing words.)* Take two!

(Otis triumphantly flashes back the two-finger victory sign in response.)

WILCOX: No, take two!

(Otis runs to Wilcox.)

WILCOX: We screwed up. You've got to give him the money again.

(Shelley shakes Osvaldo's hand at the door. Otis speaks to Osvaldo in his idea of an Arabic accent.)

OTIS: My American friend, in my country, we say no gift is given until it is given twice.

OSVALDO: You will give me twenty-five thousand more?

SHELLEY: *(To Otis.)* What the fuck are you doing?

OTIS: Take two. *(To Osvaldo.)* If I may have the present I gave you back again—

(Osvaldo holds the attaché case to him.)

OSVALDO: No!

OTIS: I will give it to you back again and then it will be yours forever.

OSVALDO: That's more like it.

(Osvaldo gives Otis the attaché case. Otis steers Osvaldo back to his seat. They

all sit in the wrong seats again. Realizing the mistake, they get up, laugh and move to the correct positions.)

OSVALDO: Ah. Protocol!

OTIS: Now say what you said before.

OSVALDO: What did I say?

OTIS: *(To Shelley.)* First you said, "God must know what is being done with the money."

(Shelley leans into the mike in the flowers.)

SHELLEY: God must know what the fuck is being done with his money.

OSVALDO: He buys my commercials. I get him a citizenship. Tits for tats.

OTIS: Tits for tats. I love that.

(They return the case to Osvaldo, leaning back to make sure Wilcox has caught it on camera. Osvaldo stands and clutches the case.)

OSVALDO: *(To us.)* I am going to give a small portion of this money to the orphans of Cubans who have died swimming to America.

SHELLEY: Tell your story walking.

OSVALDO: Your Excellency, come to Washington. I'll introduce you to all my pals in Congress.

SHELLEY: Get re-elected first.

OSVALDO: I will! With my TV commercials, I will! *I am charisma!*

(Osvaldo goes. Shelley slams the door. Otis pulls off his burnoose.)

SHELLEY: That was fun.

(Wilcox runs out of the bathroom.)

WILCOX: Be careful with this tape. This is our future.

OTIS: I wish he hadn't said that about the orphans.

(Wilcox places the tape on the shrine.)

WILCOX: Mr. Hoover, the Bureau will rise! The wheel of fortune spins around and around. Our time is here! Shelley, you were a marvel!

OTIS: I was good too!

(Belden, dressed as a jaunty bellboy, runs in.)

BELDEN: Osvaldo ran out of here dancing on air!

SHELLEY: I want Giselle!

WILCOX: Get Giselle.

BELDEN: Sign the order.

(Wilcox signs the pile of forms Belden holds out.)

SHELLEY: You're keeping your word?

WILCOX: That's the way we are.

BELDEN: Just one more form. Sign sign sign.

(Wilcox signs the last form.)

SHELLEY: Nobody ever kept their word before.

(Belden goes.)

WILCOX: And now presenting direct from Krome Park Prison facility for Illegal Aliens, the one, the only, Mademoiselle Giselle St. Just!

(A crack of lightning. Belden brings in Giselle, in prison garb, soaking wet, a wreck, wearing only one high heel.)

SHELLEY: Giselle! To look at you!

GISELLE: Palm trees bend over into epileptic arches. Solid automobiles tumble into the sea like Lucifer's game of croquet. The never changing sky is the color of dead chewing gum that a furious god has spit out. The clouds are the yellow of a bed pan. Blown down electrical lines writhe on the cracked streets like neon cobras. Alligators crawl out of the canals with pet dogs and infants struggling in reptilian jaws. Dead Cubans, dead Haitians, wash up, tongues bloated, on the streets of Miami. Everything is changing. I don't want to be deported. Marry me, Shelley. Make me safe.

OTIS: Tell her, Shelley. He's married.

SHELLEY: I'm married only technically—

GISELLE: Oh.

OTIS: He married the most beautiful pure creature in the Everglades to use land that she owned as a base.

SHELLEY: How do you know about Corleen?

WILCOX: Shelley is now an agent of the FBI.

GISELLE: You became one of the people who arrested me? Betrayal is the only drink that life ever offers. Pass me my rouge. *(Giselle goes to the bathroom and begins beautifying herself in the two-way mirror.)*

SHELLEY: If I thought you even talked to Corleen—

OTIS: I've done more than talk. I've auditioned.

SHELLEY: Auditioned!

OTIS: Where do you think I got my burnoose?

(Shelley strangles Otis. Wilcox separates them.)

WILCOX: Boys! Boys! Giselle, I'll marry you.

GISELLE: Whoever.

BELDEN: You're going to a marriage counselor to save your marriage.

WILCOX: Okay. You marry her.

BELDEN: Sir, I'm married.

OTIS: Sir, look at the storm out there—

WILCOX: *(To Otis.)* Wait. Are you married?

OTIS: I plan to marry somebody rare and pure and—

SHELLEY: Giselle, Otis will marry you.

GISELLE: Are you American?

OTIS: You bet I am!

(Giselle prepares herself for her wedding, stripping her prison garb and putting on a proper frock.)

WILCOX: As head of the Miami Beach Bureau, I can perform the ceremony. We have to celebrate. Belden, go to the Boom Boom Room and get us a ringside table! Otis, are we still waiters in the Boom Boom Room? See if we can get a discount! I want to see Fran.

(Belden starts to go.)

WILCOX: Wait! Do we still have that list of prostitutes we used?

BELDEN: Sir, that convention was twenty years ago.

WILCOX: Shit. They were wonderful girls.

(Belden goes.)

SHELLEY: *(Offering a card.)* You want girls? Call this number.

(Wilcox takes the card and weeps.)

WILCOX: Shelley, my wife ran off with a CIA man. I've never told that to anyone. She said I didn't have enough balls. Aren't one and a half enough? God, Shelley, I open up to you! To talk to a criminal. I've been talking to people like me for so long. No wonder people hate politicians. Politicians represent people. People hate themselves. Oh, Shelley, thanks to you, I'm in touch with my inner woman.

(Giselle steps out of the bathroom, miraculously transformed.)

WILCOX: "Here comes the Bride."

OTIS: I'm not marrying a criminal.

(Wilcox puts flowers in her hair and improvises a veil.)

WILCOX: You're about to be married to a piece of ass the likes of which I have never seen and you're complaining?

(Shelley marches Giselle around the room humming "Here comes the Bride." Wilcox bids Giselle and Otis to kneel.)

WILCOX: By the power vested in me, do you, Otis Mosby, take Giselle St. Just?

OTIS: This can't be legal.

WILCOX: This marriage will hold up forever. Do you, Giselle St. Just, take Otis Putzby as your lawful—

OTIS: We don't have a ring.

GISELLE: I have a ring.

WILCOX: *(Looks at the ring.)* I love ethnic art. Is that a polar bear?

OTIS: You took this ring off a dead congressman's hand.

WILCOX: Something borrowed. Something blue. *(Wilcox puts the ring on Giselle's finger.)* Giselle, I pronounce you by my phenomenal authority wife to Otis Slursby and forever an American citizen. You may now kiss the bride.

(Giselle kisses Otis passionately. Corleen enters, soaking wet.)

CORLEEN: Bride?

OTIS: It isn't what it looks like! I arrested Giselle—

CORLEEN: Giselle? The poor sinner?

OTIS: Corleen, Giselle is an illegal alien. That's why it only appears I'm marrying—

CORLEEN: It looks like a marriage.

OTIS: No, you see, I'm an agent. We all are.

CORLEEN: Where are the Bibles?

SHELLEY: No Bibles.

CORLEEN: *(To Shelley.)* You're not a minister?

OTIS: He's lied to you as often as—

CORLEEN: *(To Shelley.)* An FBI agent! Praise God! I was so afraid you were involved with those drug boats.

OTIS: He's been one for about twenty seconds—

SHELLEY: I want you to go back home. It's not safe for you—

CORLEEN: I can't go back. The infirmary washed away.

SHELLEY: Seminole City?

CORLEEN: Gone.

SHELLEY: All the Lamborghinis and Masseratis?

CORLEEN: Gone.

SHELLEY: All the fishing shacks, the fishing boats?

CORLEEN: The fishermen. Gone.

SHELLEY: Everything I buried?

CORLEEN: Gone. It's all gone. The storm has destroyed the Everglades. A dead body washed up out of the swamp. A congressman from Alaska.

OTIS: Justice rising out of the grave! Shelley murdered that congressman—

CORLEEN: The police said the dead congressman was last seen in Miami with you. I said it can't be true. Shelley's not in Miami. That's why I came and I arrive and everything is out of focus.

SHELLEY: I'm bankrupt? We're bankrupt?

(Shelley collapses. Corleen rushes to him to revive him.)

GISELLE: Bankrupt? Life has made me destitute? Typical.

OTIS: *(To Corleen.)* Not mouth-to-mouth.

CORLEEN: Please. This is my husband.

WILCOX: Shelley, if you want to move in with me, I have bunk beds.

SHELLEY: *(To Corleen.)* Oh, baby. To look at you—

(Corleen tries to revive Shelley.)

OTIS: Corleen, look at me. We can go to Valdez, the Switzerland of Alaska, and see how nature has healed the oil spill.

CORLEEN: Do you write symphonies? Can you even play the piano?

OTIS: We can clean off seals.

CORLEEN: That's the worst kind of lie.

OTIS: Heavenly deception.

CORLEEN: Don't throw my words back at me.

OTIS: You learn your husband is an agent and you're happy. You learn I'm an agent and—

CORLEEN: May I have my burnoose?

OTIS: I thought I could keep it as a member of the ELO

SHELLEY: *(A challenge.)* Corleen, my heart feels weak—

OTIS: Good! Let him die!

SHELLEY: *(A challenge.)* You know how to take care of it. I need to get my ashes shoveled. Do you mind, Giselle?

GISELLE: It's my wedding day. Someone should make love. God knows we don't have any money.

SHELLEY: *(Gets up.)* Fucking light bulbs! Osvaldo has my last twenty-five thousand. All I have to do is get that money back. I can turn it back into a fortune. I've been down before. I'll be up again.

WILCOX: Get Munoz. Your first assignment.

OTIS: Sir, we have to catch Osvaldo in the act of spending that money in order to make it a crime.

SHELLEY: He's not spending one fucking red centavo of my money. Sir, Agent Sheldon S. Slutsky requesting permission to pursue Congressman Munoz and get my money back!

WILCOX: Permission granted. I'm proud of you, lad. *(Wilcox tosses Shelley his gun.)*

SHELLEY: Do I have a license to kill?

WILCOX: A permit. That's all I can offer.

(The Sheik enters, waving his knife over his head. Giselle runs into his arms.)

GISELLE: You came!

SHEIK: Who took my woman away?

GISELLE: *(Pointing to Otis.)* He did.

SHEIK: Who is he?

OTIS: I don't know her.

WILCOX: He's her husband.

SHEIK: Husband! *(He puts a knife to Otis.)*

OTIS: *(Backs away.)* She's not my wife. What do you say in your country? I divorce you I divorce you I divorce you. *(Spits.)* Tui tui tui. There! She's free.

SHEIK: *(To Corleen.)* But who are you?

CORLEEN: I'm the wife.

GISELLE: I'm the mistress.

(Osvaldo, carrying the attaché case, opens the door followed by a video operator filming him.)

OSVALDO: I'm the congressman. Vote for me November Eighth.

(Osvaldo puts his arm around the Sheik for the camera. Shelley grabs the attaché case. Osvaldo hangs on to it for dear life.)

OSVALDO: Voters of Miami, Osvaldo Munoz counts as his close personal friends many international leaders such as the Sheik of Akbahran who I affectionately refer to as Spike.

(Shelley falls back as the Sheik lunges at Osvaldo with his sword drawn. Osvaldo sees the two Sheiks.)

SHEIK: Out!

(Osvaldo and the cameraman run out. The Sheik flings Otis down, his knife against Otis's throat.)

SHEIK: You insulted my woman. You will pay.

GISELLE: Abdul, he's an agent of the FBI. He's an agent of the FBI. He's an agent of the FBI. You're in the underground headquarters of the FBI. They're entrapping congressmen.

WILCOX: Right here!

SHELLEY: You want power? This FBI thing—this is the power.

SHEIK: Is it very difficult to become an agent?

WILCOX: No! These days we're having so much better luck with amateurs. Let me swear you all in! Corleen! Giselle! Your Excellency! Everybody! Raise your right hand—

(Belden in civilian clothes runs in.)

BELDEN: Sir! The Boom Boom Room is closed!

WILCOX: The Boom Boom Room is what?!!!

SHELLEY: The Boom Boom Room is closed?!

BELDEN: Congressman Bentine had it shut down for obscenity!

WILCOX: What about Fran Farkus? Is she safe?

BELDEN: Fran Farkus is missing! No one knows where she is!

SHELLEY: *(To us.)* The Boom Boom Room closed? I feel a grief I've never felt. I never had any family. I never had anything. The Boom Boom Room is the only place I've ever known warmth, ever known love, that ever gave me oxygen. I'll tell you a secret. It's the only place I've ever drunk milk. And now it's closed? By Wayne Bentine? I want to destroy him!

WILCOX: And then another congressman and another! And then a senator! And then the President! Close the Boom Boom Room? I'll put a guillotine on the steps of the Capitol!

OTIS: Operation Moon was my idea.

WILCOX: And a damn good one, Pizbee. Thanks to you, we can make anyone a Dillinger. Munoz. Bentine. Even you. Now everyone! Raise your right hands— (*Wilcox reaches into the inner part of the shrine to remove the velvet pillow.*)

OTIS: Sir. Don't open it up.

(*Wilcox lets out an unearthly howl when he sees the pillow containing the shredded toupee of Hoover.*)

WILCOX: Who destroyed the only thing I love! Not since Pearl Harbor! Arrest everyone in Miami! Communists! Negroes! The Cubans sailing over here! The Haitians! Arrest all the Jews! I want revenge! This is war!

OTIS: Sir, don't go overboard. It's not a desecration.

WILCOX: This? Not a desecration?

OTIS: There's only a little bit snipped off. (*He rips off his mustache.*) Here. I can paste it back together. It's sort of like a hairy jigsaw puzzle. Sir, I needed it for my beard. Sir, you said to get facial hair. I had nowhere to go—

WILCOX: You? Those little hairs on your face belonged to Mr. Hoover?

(*Otis takes the Osvaldo tape.*)

OTIS: This tape has everything on it. You murdering Reggie. Entrapping Osvaldo.

SHELLEY: Give me that tape.

(*Otis cocks his gun against the tape, holding the tape hostage.*)

OTIS: I came here to do a job and I'm going to do it! I'm getting this tape to Washington to the proper authorities and then I'm going back to Alaska where everything is sane. Corleen, will you come with me?

SHELLEY: He's a liar, Corleen.

CORLEEN: (*To Otis.*) You're a liar. Are you?

OTIS: One day you'll learn who I am. This shy boy becomes the Desert Mirage! Good-bye! (*Otis runs out. The storm mounts.*)

CORLEEN: Otis!

SHELLEY: That tape is government property! Am I right?

WILCOX: Kitsby is an enemy of the state. Kill Otis!

SHELLEY: (*Shaking Wilcox.*) Sir, listen to me! You have to stay calm. Everyone! This is what we have to do! First—Get the money from Osvaldo—

ALL: Right!

WILCOX: Kill Otis!

SHELLEY: Find Fran Farkus.

ALL: Yes!

WILCOX: Kill Otis!

SHELLEY: Entrap Bentine.

WILCOX: Kill Otis!

SHELLEY: And then what do we do?

ALL: Kill Otis!

SHELLEY: Partners? Are we all partners?

ALL: Partners!

WILCOX: Now let me swear you all in. Raise your right hands! Do you solemnly swear...

(The storm blows the room apart. Bongos.)

MERMAIDS: *(Sing.)*

> Pink flamingoes crash into the Fountaine Moon
> Pelicans are trapped in an apocalypse
> Got to get it up
> Got to get it up
> On this evening out of the Everglades
> All the elements rise into a hurricane.

(The stage is bare. People run by holding parts of the scenery blown by a ferocious wind. Otis appears.)

OTIS: My own men trying to kill me. The iceberg cracking. The voices leading me on.

(Osvaldo swirls on in the hurricane, filming his commercials.)

OSVALDO: I come poolside to remind you of the Cuban Missile Crisis. I am a veteran of the Bay of Pigs. Battalion 2056 and a half. I came the second day.

(Otis appears behind him, trying to stay upright in the wind.)

OTIS: Don't turn around. I'm warning you.

OSVALDO: Who is it?

OTIS: I'm a friend. Get rid of that money.

OSVALDO: *(Turns.)* You are the Sheik!

OTIS: I'm not any sheik! There were cameras in that suite. It's all recorded here! You've been entrapped!

OSVALDO: I'm not giving any money back.

(Shelley appears in the wind.)

SHELLEY: Give me that money!

(Osvaldo runs in one direction. Otis runs in another. Shelley runs in another. The storm roars. The Mermaids appear.)

MERMAIDS:

> Crocodiles crawl onto a catapult

Alligators arch into an avalanche
Cows and ducks and geese flee on water skis
Barracudas swim into the loony bin

(Wilcox appears, carrying a shattered portrait of Hoover.)

WILCOX: Mr. Hoover, is this storm your rage? Blow winds and crack your cheeks! You will be avenged! Otis Figsby just sealed his own death warrant. I'll kill that dog in the streets.

(Wilcox is off, howling. Shelley chases Osvaldo. Elements of the Boom Boom Room, the suite, the Everglades fly by forming what will be a Colossus.)

MERMAIDS: *(Twisting.)*
Alte Kaches start shooting heroin
No old timer saw such calamity

(Bentine comes on in the wind addressing the Hunger Conference.)

BENTINE: *(To us.)* Don't worry. The Fountaine Moon is strong enough to weather—this can't be the first hurricane to hit—

(Otis runs in.)

OTIS: Sir, beware of any sheiks offering you money.

BENTINE: Sheiks? Money?

(Otis and Bentine are blown away in separate directions. The bongos play violently.)

MERMAIDS: *(Sing.)*
Mambo classes drown down in the swimming pool
Mah jongg players crushed beneath a tidal wave
Got to get it up
Got to get it up

(Shelley and Wilcox enter with their guns drawn.)

WILCOX: Hugsby?

SHELLEY: Otis? Here, pussy cat? Otis! Otis!

(Shelley and Wilcox blow off. Bentine swirls on, Giselle and the Sheik on either arm.)

BENTINE: I need money! That's why this World Hunger Conference means so much to me. I'm trying to make the people aware of the issues, to let them see I'm valuable. Anything to get re-elected!

(Giselle lights a cigarette with the Aladdin's lamp lighter.)

BENTINE: What a beautiful lighter. Are those jewels real?

GISELLE: I'm insulted.

(The Sheik hands the lighter to Bentine.)

SHEIK: Keep it.

BENTINE: *(Taking it.)* No. Well—I did want a souvenir of Florida.

SHEIK: Now about those fighter planes—

BENTINE: I think something can be worked out.

> (*Blackout. Lights up. Belden appears, carrying the video camera.*)

BELDEN: Holy Christ, this isn't Operation Moon. This is foreign policy.

> (*The moment is repeated. It is being taped.*)

BENTINE: I think something can be worked out.

> (*They are off.*)

MERMAIDS:

> Sarasota ruined by suicide
> Coral Gables total catastrophe
> Lightning bolts destroy Collins Avenue
> Devastation on Tamiami Trail
> On this evening out of the Everglades
> All of nature rises in a hurricane
> Got to get it up
> Got to get it up
> Get it up
> Tonight!!!

> (*Shelley drags Corleen in by the wrist.*)

SHELLEY: Get him. You have to lure him out—

CORLEEN: No.

SHELLEY: If you want your "Moon Under Miami"—

CORLEEN: Not that. I'm trying to be good.

> (*Shelley holds up a packet of white powder.*)

SHELLEY: Here it is, baby.

CORLEEN: Don't let it blow away.

SHELLEY: Bring us Otis. He loves you.

> (*Shelley takes out a hypodermic needle.*)

CORLEEN: No. I've said good-bye to that. No more—

> (*Shelley injects Corleen. Belden runs on.*)

BELDEN: Otis is here somewhere. I can't get him out of hiding—

> (*Fran comes on carrying an orange dress.*)

SHELLEY: Fran!

WILCOX: Thank god you're safe!

FRAN: Put this on her. No guy can resist a red dress. It'll be easier to spot Otis with her on his arm.

WILCOX: That's how they caught Dillinger—

FRAN: That's right. Dillinger.

WILCOX: This dress is orange.

FRAN: It was an orange dress. The neon lights under the Biograph Theater that night in Chicago made the dress look red.

WILCOX: How do you know this? No one knows this.

(The "FBI in Peace and War" theme plays. Lights stream out of Fran.)

FRAN: I am who I am.

(Fran stands on pieces of Florida blown apart by the hurricane, all golden. The Mermaids appear beneath her and speak in a choral chant, their words echoing each other.)

MERMAIDS: *(Choral chant.)*

> She was there that night
> She was the lady in red

WILCOX: Who are you?

MERMAIDS: *(Choral chant.)*

> She is Fran Farkus
> Yet she is not Fran Farkus
> As Otis was a waiter
> And then an art dealer
> And then a sheik
> As Shelley was a minister
> And is not a minister
> And as Shelley is an agent
> And is a criminal
> As Giselle was illegal
> And is now legal
> As she is Otis's wife
> And not Otis's wife
> Fran is also J. Edgar Hoover

(Fran's clothes and wig peel off her. Fran is in a suit. Fran is J. Edgar Hoover. Wilcox and Shelley fall.)

FRAN/HOOVER: This is who I am.

WILCOX: But J. Edgar Hoover died in 1972.

MERMAIDS:

> She only put out the news of his death.
> She announced his death in the land of
> Ponce de Leon. She has always been alive.
> She touched the fountain of youth.

FRAN/HOOVER: This is who I am.

SHELLEY: You were a transvestite?

FRAN/HOOVER: Cupcake, I was always a woman. *(Very simply.)* I went to work as a secretary for this new outfit called the Bureau. I was a funny chick. I liked to tell jokes. You know, to fit in. Even I could see what was wrong with this new outfit. I tried to speak up but the Agents pinched my ass and whistled and said "Fran, keep telling your jokes." One day as a joke I came into work in a suit and told everyone what was wrong. Everyone listened to me. They didn't know who I was. I was a man. "Who are you?" I looked at the vacuum cleaner and named myself for that. I wanted to suck up everything wrong in the world. The secretary vanished. Hoover was born. America relaxed. I conquered evil. We became the Federal Bureau, thanks to me.

WILCOX: You killed Dillinger?

FRAN/HOOVER: I took control. America needed me to stay tough. Tougher than tough. I had to suppress my womanness. I gave up my child. I became the most powerful man in America. *(She laughs wildly, then is quiet.)* But the years went by and I began to miss the girl in the red-orange dress who whispered in John Dillinger's ear and made him laugh. I started to wear the dress on my vacations. Jesus, I needed to relax. I would come and perform and then go back to my suit. Come and perform. Back to the suit. Come and perform. Back to the suit. And then Clyde... died.

(The Mermaids sigh mournfully.)

FRAN/HOOVER: Fran performed more and Edgar performed less. Finally I had to give up the Bureau. I had to live the life I was meant to live. I was a mother. Yes. I didn't die. I retired. I had to find the child I gave up. I had to follow him.

WILCOX: Who is that?

FRAN/HOOVER: I looked and looked—

WILCOX: Is it me?

FRAN/HOOVER: When I learned Shelley was an agent, I said Blood tells.

SHELLEY: Mom?

(Fran/Hoover nods happily. The Mermaids weep with joy and applaud.)

SHELLEY: *(To us.)* I don't know what shocks me more, my mother is Fran Farkus or my mother is J. Edgar Hoover.

FRAN/HOOVER: Son, I pass on the torch! Get Otis for me.

SHELLEY: *(Saluting.)* Yessir. Mom! Sir!

(They go off. Bongos. Otis appears.)

OTIS: Where is safe? Protect the tapes. I'll leave Miami. Go to Washington. Keep my sanity. If I can keep my sanity—

(Corleen appears in a red dress, singing shakily.)

CORLEEN: "Broad moonlight"

OTIS: Don't respond. It's a trap.

CORLEEN: "Giving me no place to hide

We were both dying of thirst"

Otis, I love you. Don't hide from me. Are you there? Otis?

(Otis comes out of hiding. He takes Corleen in his arms.)

OTIS: I'm not a composer. But I could start. How hard can it be? Together we can start again. We build America on our shoulders. We are the future. I love your red dress. *(Pause.)* Why are you wearing a red dress?

(Corleen holds up a hypodermic needle.)

CORLEEN: I've betrayed you.

(Lightning bolt. Thunder crash. A full moon with the face of J. Edgar Hoover descends onto the heap of hurricane wreckage. Huge arms extend out forming a Colossus.)

COLOSSUS: Agent Presby.

OTIS: You look like—you look like Mr. Hoover?

COLOSSUS: Give back the tape.

OTIS: No! You're going to be so proud of me. On this tape, I've got the new Dillinger!

COLOSSUS: We don't need a Dillinger. We're a nation of Dillingers. We need a Hoover. Criminals are a dime a dozen. We need more Hoovers. More repression. More fear.

OTIS: I came into the bureau to do good. Shouldn't I bring Shelley to justice?

(Fran/J. Edgar Hoover appears from behind the Colossus.)

FRAN/HOOVER: Wrong, Agent Presby. Politics. Everything is politics. Give me the tape.

OTIS: No. Mr. Hoover?

FRAN/HOOVER: Do you want to go to Butte?

OTIS: I want to go to Washington. And take Corleen with me—Corleen?

(Otis sees Corleen is slumped at the base of the Colossus. Shelley appears.)

SHELLEY: She's dead. Another unfortunate drug overdose.

(Otis leaps at Shelley who shoots Otis. Otis stumbles at the base of the Colossus. He takes Corleen in his arms.)

OTIS: We'll go to the Mantanuska Valley, the breadbasket of Alaska, and see giant tomatoes in bloom. We'll climb Mount McKinley which is called Danali in the Athabaskan language. It means Great One. We will pan for gold...

(Otis dies. Wilcox takes the tape out of Otis's hand.)

WILCOX: He's dead. That'll teach him.

SHELLEY: Go down our checklist. Entrap Bentine.

WILCOX: Done that.

SHELLEY: Kill Otis.

WILCOX: Done that.

SHELLEY: Last item on the list? Get Osvaldo.

FRAN/HOOVER: Good man.

(Shelley salutes and goes.)

WILCOX: You're back.

FRAN/HOOVER: You remind me of Clyde. You were always a good scout when I'd come down here.

WILCOX: Together we could run the Bureau. Will you come out of retirement?

MERMAIDS: Don't leave us!

(Fran/Hoover hesitates, then shakes Wilcox's hand firmly and turns to the Mermaids.)

FRAN: Don't worry, girls. My home is now and forever the Boom Boom Room.

(The Mermaids pull off Hoover's suit and transform him back into Fran.)

FRAN: Wilcox, honey, how would you like a permanent ringside table?

WILCOX: Fran, let me confess. I have a—

(Belden appears.)

BELDEN: Sir! Your wife was lost in the hurricane.

WILCOX: I'm free!

FRAN: Happiest day of my life!

(Wilcox and Fran embrace. Blackout. Osvaldo enters, drawing the curtain closed.)

OSVALDO: *(To us.)* I hate to interrupt but I wanted to tell you I was dead. They set me up. I'll go down in memory as Munoz the bribe-taker. You think it's easy taking the bribes? Everybody always says "Oh, the bribe-taker. Sit by the pool. Eat the bonbons. Polish the nails." You realize how hard it is to take bribes? You have to call up all the people, remind them over and over. People want all the favors in the world from the politicians. But they never make it easy. So I make one last stab to rescue my campaign. I take the Sheik's money and charter a plane to fly to Havana. I will personally capture Fidel and bring him back to trial. The people of Miami will coronate me. I speed over the Caribbean, back to Havana, looking down at the people sailing to America on their little boats. *(Sings:)*

"I can see the ships at sea
Mariel to Miami
Why do they come?
They keep sailing here in droves
Multiplying fish and loaves

Why do they come?
All my life I've dreamed of green
Precious green I've never seen
And still they come.
They come here and when it's dark
Fiesta in Flamingo Park
Why do they come?"

I see a giant eye staring at me. It is the eye of the hurricane. The tail of the hurricane unfurls and very gently wraps around my airplane and whips me down into the sea. My money floats. The news cameras fly over and film the wreckage to show on the evening news. Ola! I ended up on the TV.

(Sings.)

Ved de cuan poco valor
son las cosas tras que andamos y corremos
que, en este mundo traidor,
aun primero que muramos las perdemos:
dellas desfaze la edad
dellas casos desastrados que acaescen,
dellas por su calidad,
en los mas altos estados desfallescen.
Ved de cuan poco valor
son las cosas tras que andamos y corremos
(Osvaldo blows a kiss. Blackout.)

(Pool-side. Bentine appears.)

BENTINE: *(To us.)* —all the flags of Miami lower to half mast to mourn the tragic death of my honored colleague, Congressman Osvaldo Munoz, over the water separating America and Cuba.

(Wilcox comes out in pool togs.)

WILCOX: What a shame. He was such a good dancer.

BENTINE: *(To us.)* Osvaldo Munoz was a man I was proud to call friend. But democracy must go on. The field opens wide and a new candidate has consented to step in. A candidate who has come to politics by the most original route. A candidate who brings the breath of fresh air we need in that arrogant empire called Washington.

(Shelley appears in pool togs.)

SHELLEY: *(To us.)* My qualifications for office? On my TV commercials, you will see me murdering a drug-dealing congressman from Alaska. How many of my opponents can say this? I will kill for you.

(Cheers.)

WILCOX: The polls are in. You're ahead! Congressman Slutsky. What is your platform?

SHELLEY: *(To us.)* My image advisor, Mademoiselle Giselle Presby, the grief stricken widow of a murdered FBI agent, will answer that.

(Giselle appears in a black mourning bikini and enormous black hat.)

GISELLE: *(To us.)* This is a painful time for me. To have my husband snatched away from me on our wedding day—but this is what gave me strength and why I want you to vote for Shelley. The world is in a constant state of flux. This is my vision. It is time for "Time for a change" to stop. Elect Shelley because he will never change. Once he gets into office he will never leave. He is up there with the cockroach and the oyster. He is beyond evolution. He is Miami.

WILCOX: Like most people in Miami, you lost everything in the hurricane. How will you finance your campaign?

(The Sheik of Akbahran stands beside her.)

SHELLEY: *(To us.)* Madame Presby's new husband has become my financial advisor. The Sheik of Akbahran is not only investing in me. He is investing in America.

SHEIK: *(To us.)* This is what I propose. We invest in a future war. Start planning it now. I will get America in on the ground floor.

SHELLEY: *(To us.)* If elected, I promise you I will assign you all marketing rights to the next war. Gulf Storm 2.

SHEIK: I want the missiles.

GISELLE: I would suggest you get the rights to the caps and T-shirts.

(Cheers. Everyone begins to hum "America the Beautiful" with an inspiring bongo accompaniment.)

SHELLEY: *(To us.)* Before you vote next Tuesday, ask yourself this: How stands Miami on this winter night? More prosperous? More secure and happier than it was before the election? Miami, still a beacon, still a magnet for all who must have freedom, for all the pilgrims from the lost places who are hurtling through the darkness toward home. My friends, we shall do it. We aren't just marking time. We will make a difference. We will make Miami stronger. We will make Miami freer. And when we leave her we will leave her in good hands. And they will say "All in all, not bad. Not bad at all." Vote for me. Our campaign headquarters will be the newly reopened Boom Boom Room starring the one, the only, my Mom, Miss Fran Farkus.

(Everyone cheers. Fran comes out in full regalia and embraces Shelley and Wilcox.)

FRAN: My boy!

WILCOX: Baby, what can I do for you?

FRAN: Make love to me until dawn and then turn into a pizza.

WILCOX: Sing the song.

SHELLEY: Our campaign song.

(Shelley, Wilcox, Bentine, Giselle, The Sheik, The Mermaids join in.)

FRAN: "Missed the toilet last night..."

(Fran leads a sing-a-long which fades away into darkness. An iceberg carrying Otis appears. He wears silver white robes. Otis is lost, desperate.)

OTIS: *(To us.)* I love the way Alaska feels... all the dark at once. All the light. Look! A caribou... Some people say the lonely quiet drives you mad. But, no, I have all my icebergs for company, tilting, turning, casting a blue light. The icebergs must have magnets in them, the way they hold me in their thrall. I understand the Titanic. The Titanic didn't just collide with an iceberg. The Titanic plunged into the iceberg on purpose, trying to crack it open, trying to identify the voices within. *(There is a great cracking noise.)* I hear the voices... the calving. Hello?

(Otis is terrified as the iceberg splits open. Corleen steps from it. She wears a white ball gown and tiara.)

OTIS: Corleen!

CORLEEN: Places. Otis?

OTIS: How can we do good?

CORLEEN: Keep trying and hope that one day... one day...

OTIS: What do we do till then?

(Corleen removes a silver white burnoose from inside the iceberg and hands it to Otis.)

CORLEEN: Keep rehearsing. *(To us.)* The Aurora Borealis Light Opera Company proudly presents the opening night of their premiere production *Broad Moonlight*.

CORLEEN AND OTIS: *(Sing.)*

> You cannot fake your thirst
> Come slake your thirst in my heart
> Beloved
> In Broad Moonlight
> Broad Moonlight
> Come slake your thirst in my heart!

(Otis and Corleen embrace passionately. Curtain. Everyone appears on the iceberg.)

ALL:
>So stay in Hawaii
>If all you want's a lai
>Or else come to Miami
>And park your carcass
>On top of Fran Farkus
>And let's all go down at the Moon!

END OF PLAY

Rich and Famous

ORIGINAL PRODUCTION

Rich and Famous was first presented by the New York Shakespeare Festival, Joseph Papp, producer, at the Public Theatre, in New York City, on February 19, 1976. It was directed by Mel Shapiro; settings were by Dan Snyder; costumes by Theoni V. Aldredge; lighting by Arden Fingerhut; the music and lyrics by John Guare. Musical direction and arrangements were by Herbert Kaplan; the associate producer was Bernard Gersten. The cast was as follows:

Bing Ringling . . . . William Atherton
Dante Alighieri, Beatrice, Virgil, The Spirit of the Entire Divine Comedy, The People of the Inferno, Purgatorio and Paradisio, Black People, White People, Straight People, Gay People, Actors, Actresses, Producers, Directors, Composers, Mothers, Fathers, Boy Friends, Girl Friends, Old Friends, New Friends, Failures, Fans,
Stars . . . . Ron Leibman, Anita Gillette

An earlier version of the play was produced by William Gardiner and the Academy Festival Theatre, Lake Forest, Illinois in August 1974. The cast was Charles Kimbrough, Linda Lavin and Ron Leibman and directed by Mel Shapiro.

The events occur on the night of the first preview of Bing Ringling's new play.

CAST LIST
Male
Bing Ringling
Aphro
Anatol Torah
Hare Krishna
Dad
Tybalt Dunleavy
Female
Leanara
Veronica Gulpp-Vestige
Allison
Mom
Actress

RICH AND FAMOUS

The play begins as if it were a musical. A glittering overture from any terrific Broadway musical plays. The curtains swing open. A young playwright in a rented tux stands on a street corner in Manhattan. Lights all around him. He clutches his script to his heart. His girl friend, Leanara, runs after the young playwright, carrying two shopping bags. The young playwright's name is Bing Ringling.

LEANARA: To walk to the theater with the playwright on opening night!

BING: Oh, Leanara, we're going to have the best life. A life you'll want to read about. A life they'll write musicals about in twenty years. John and Yoko. Scott and Zelda. Dante and Beatrice. Bing and Leanara.

LEANARA: Oh, Bing, I'm so honored to be in your play. All those years wasted on Shakespearean comedy. Lovers in the woods. All that Chekhov crap. Chopped down cherry trees.

BING: Wait. Don't say that about Chekhov.

LEANARA: I hate people like Chekhov.

BING: He tried.

LEANARA: But people like that are so good they don't leave room for the new people. For the Bing Ringlings. I want to do Ringling for the rest of my life.

(The music swells into this terrific Bossa Nova. Bing embraces Leanara.)

BING: *(Sings.)*
> I. I. I will always love you
> Don't Be Sure
> I. I. I will never leave you
> Don't Be Sure
> I promised I could be relied on
> Remember the shoulder you cried on
> Well, here is the Bible I lied on
> When I swore
> Forevermore
> I. I. I will drive you crazy
> Don't Be sure

I. I. I cannot be trusted
Don't Be sure
Darling, if you're into trust
Possibly I might just
Surprise you
If you want surprises
Like a love that's pure
Can I deliver?
Will I deliver?
I will deliver!
Don't Be Sure.

I went into that little all-night bookstore over there on the corner to see where I'll fit in and I'll be between Rimbaud and Rin Tin Tin. Beloved Hollywood dog reveals all in touching memoir.

LEANARA: Do you like me in your play? Honest. I mean, really honest.

BING: As simple as this. If you were not in it, it would not be worth doing. As if you stepped out of my brain right onto the page.

LEANARA: Recite my favorite part. Right from the playwright's mouth.

BING: "I ran down into the subway. In a panic. I'll go anywhere. Trains rush past me. E trains. F trains. As. GGs. RRs. Cs. Pursued by the entire alphabet."

LEANARA: I love it. I love you. Are you in as much pain as the play says?

BING: Oh, yes. More.

LEANARA: How do you stand it? How do you live?

BING: Well, no, not really. You see I make up bad things about myself so I'll be more interesting. I read about O'Neill and I think, Christ, I could have been a great playwright too if my Mother was a junkie and my father was a miser who ran around playing the Count of Monte Cristo all the time. So I write my autobiographical play, based on Dante's *Inferno,* and it's close enough to the way I'd like my life to be. With a few songs thrown in. Oh, God!

LEANARA: What is it?

BING: *(Pulls a small box out of his shopping bag.)* I bought these cufflinks at a little magic store on Fourteenth Street. One set has the initial R and the other set has the initial F. I mix them up and wear them R and F. For rich and famous. Sometimes I wear them the other way around. F and R. for famous and rich. I don't care which one comes first. But if my play stinks. If my play flops. I'm going to be wearing them D and B. For dead and buried. O and O. For over and out. I'm not going to be the World's Oldest Living Promising Young Playwright.

LEANARA: Your first produced play. After 843 plays. My God, the typing alone. What those fingers have been through.

(Bing get his cufflinks set in his cuffs.)

BING: Sorry, Aeschylus. Sorry, Brecht. Sorry, Chekhov. Sorry, Molière, Feydeau. Racine. Sorry, guys, but I got a machine gun attached to my typewriter and you haven't seen the plays I've got in my head.

LEANARA: *(A gun moll.)* Ratatatatatatatatatatatatatata!!!!!!!!!!!!

(An ominous chord plays. Overhead an enormous billboard appears in the process of being painted. It is a billboard dominating all of Times Square. It announces a new film: Gangland, *and the music plays again and a face appears on the billboard and it's the face of that hot young actor, none other than Tybalt Dunleavy. The music plays again Tybalt smiles malevolently down at us. Bing looks up at the billboard. Leanara takes his arm.)*

BING: There he is again. My old friend, Tybalt Dunleavy, on a billboard at the crossroads of the world. Here I am, my play opening in a toilet on Lower Death Street and my boyhood chum up there like a plague—

LEANARA: Bing, calm down. Will you stop it with Tybalt Dunleavy already? I hate to say it, but sometimes people become stars because they're very good and Tybalt Dunleavy happens to be very good.

(Kinder music plays. The street has revolved away and backstage at the theater appears. Bing pulls himself together. Leanara runs into her dressing area and changes.)

BING: *(Sings.)*
 Success
 Is a Yes
 From a Bess or a Tess
 In a dress
 Which she removes
 Thereby proving
 Success
 Is a Yes.
 Success
 Is the cress
 That you fress
 At Lutece
 Where they stress
 That they buy you dinner

Cause you're a winner

Gobble up Gobble up Gobble up

(And the song is picked up by Aphro, a black actor of indeterminate age and sex who is getting dressed in a costume that will represent Dante Alighieri. Aphro places silver laurel wreaths on his head.)

APHRO: *(Sings.)*

Fail

Rhymes with jail

Without bail

Slow as snail

Hit the trail

Fail!

(Leanara finishes dressing as Beatrice, beloved of Dante, and she's all in white and silver stars around her head.)

LEANARA: *(Sings.)*

Unless

You've success

You're a mess

Under constant duress

LEANARA AND BING AND APHRO: *(Sing.)*

And I guess

Cleanliness

Next to it maybe godly

But, darling, I say hardly

Success is successful

It's not penniless-full

It is phosphorescefull

Yes! Yes! Yes! Yes! Yes! Yes!

Success!!!!!!!

(Champagne is opened. Opening night greetings and presents and kisses are exchanged. A voice booms out.)

STAGE MANAGER'S VOICE: Places!

(Panic. Aphro and Leanara make a good luck gesture and very grandly march out onto stage. Music plays. Bing sits at the curtain through which they've departed and hangs on every word.)

BING: Come on, Aphro. You can do it. This part will make you a star. Oh, Christ, if only I told him that. Jesus, Buddha, Mary Baker Eddy, which ever one of you got cast in the role of God up in heaven, please help me???????

(The music soars up. Aphro runs breathlessly through the curtains into this backstage area. Bing is terrified.)

APHRO: B-2. B-2. I was marching through the audience during your beautiful procession number and a man pressed a note into my hand. I started to slap him and say fresh, but then I thought it might be a critic so I looked down to kiss him and oh my heart! Oh my asthma! Oh, my teeth! It was Tybalt Dunleavy!!! Right in B-2. He pressed this note into my hand. It's for you. He's gorgeous. He's got block-long teeth.

(Bing takes the note that Aphro gives him. He opens it very suspiciously. Overhead the billboard changes. Tybalt glows.)

APHRO: Just tell me what he say? Does he love my performance? I've got a cue. *(Exits.)* The P Train. The T train. *(Aphro is gone.)*

BING: *(Reads.)* "Bingo, voice out of the past. Got into town. Looked in the ABCs to see what was playing. Saw the opening night of a new play by my old friend. Long time no see. The actor playing you is all wrong. Why didn't you ask me to be in it? Did you notice I became an actor? Ha. Ha. Since I became a star, nobody asks me to do anything. I'm not doing anything right now. The adventure might be thrilling. I love your play. The beauty of it is shining through. God, *Gangland* played to five hundred million people in movie theaters and I envy you tonight playing to ninety-nine live ones. Love to see you. Hate to bother. Call at the Algonquin. Tybalt..." Move Aphro out of the play. Move Tybalt into the play. Oh yes. Oh yes. Tybalt would make a wonderful me. My parents would get a kick. They always loved Tybalt. Tybalt Dunleavy as me! He'd even make a better me!

(Bing sings.)

> Success
> Is a Yes
> From a Bess or a Tess
> In a dress

(The music turns into a waltz and Veronica Gulpp-Vestige enters. She's that legendary lady producer who's been in the business at least since the opening night of Macbeth. She is held together fantastically. Scarves swathe her aged chins. A cane supports her but she is all energy and fire. She is quite elegant and everything we thought the theater would be when we grew up.)

VERONICA: Hello, Bing.

BING: Veronica, wait till you hear the news I have for you.

VERONICA: You've given me all the news I need. It's going perfectly.

BING: You're the producer's producer! God, to take all those musicals—*South Pacific, Carousel, Gentlemen Prefer Blondes, Wish You Were Here*—to revive all those musicals and take the music out. *(He sits adoringly at her feet, his head in her lap.)*

VERONICA: *The Sound of Music.*

BING: To do *The Sound of Music* on a bare stage without the music, the actors all in grey rags, their faces painted the white face of death.

VERONICA: To show the bleakness behind American joy, darling boy. It's as simple as that.

BING: The clarity, the honesty with which you speak about your work.

VERONICA: Bing precious, if the musical is America's only indigenous art form, then that puts us on a par with Switzerland and the cuckoo clock.

BING: The honor that you would do my play and leave the music in. A first.

VERONICA: Yes, tonight is a first...

(Bing impulsively shows her Tybalt's letter.)

BING: Tybalt Dunleavy wants to do the play.

VERONICA: *(Scanning the letter.)* Typical. So typical.

BING: Yes, it is, isn't it! Typical of the beauty of the future. God, he can learn Aphro's part in a second. In school we used to call him Polaroid Brain.

VERONICA: Bing, come here. Sit by me. Sit by Veronica. Let me tell you why I wanted to produce your play.

BING: Because it's ripped out of my guts?

VERONICA: Did you ever hear of the musical of the Ten Commandments? Remember the musical version of the Encyclopedia Britannica?

BING: I remember that review in the *Times!* "A celebration of learning becomes a salute to illiteracy!" *(Bing laughs.)*

VERONICA: "A salute to illiteracy." The *Nude Hamlet on Ice?* Did you know Aphro skated the role of Ophelia? The one-man show where the man with the cleft palate dangled his little feet over the footlights of Palace Theater and chanted *Moby Dick* cover to cover? "Call Me Ishmael." I produced them.

BING: No. You only do hits, Veronica.

VERONICA: Secretly. All my flops I did in secret. My hits I produce under my own name, but my flops I always did in secret. Bing, I have everything. I have all of Bergdorf's. All of Bloomingdale's. All of Bendel's. Ten traffic-clogging triumphs currently littering Broadway. I have it all. Hits. Hits, hits. What's the one thing I don't have? A comeback. I studied all the great comebacks. Nixon. DeGaulle. New York. Judy Garland. How did they do it?

BING: They failed...

VERONICA: Of course they failed. In order to have a comeback, one must fail. But Veronica Gulpp-Vestige fail???? I've flirted with failure. God knows I've been a closet failure for years. But to move in with failure? The idea was ludicrous. Preposterous. Ridiculous. Exhilarating. I've never had the courage till I met you. My beautiful young playwright. And tonight I'm ready, finally ready to sign my name to a flop. Your first play. My first failure. We make our debuts together. I feel so close to you.

BING: Veronica, only this afternoon I had this dream where the whole world died except for me. Only it wasn't their bodies that died, but their minds. But luckily I had stored up in my shopping bags all the great books and paintings and music the world had ever produced. The world was lost and confused and there I am with my shopping bags, doling out the art, dealing out the magic, parcelling out the joy. And I woke up to come to the theater and it was all true. I had this play. I had you. And now the whole world wants Tybalt Dunleavy and he wants us.

VERONICA: He's not there anymore. I had him sent away. I didn't want his success cluttering up my failure. I'm so excited. So nervous. I think you should move in with me, Bing. You write them and I'll produce them and together we'll become synonyms for stupidity, waste and anguish. Then, in ten years, when we're on the bottom, you write a turkey and I'll turn it into the Nobel Prize. I'll give us such a comeback.

(And she is gone. Bing runs to the pay phone backstage. He dials.)

BING: *(Ferocious.)* Hello??? Algonquin Hotel?? I'd like to leave a message for Mr. Tybalt Dunleavy. Tell him that Bing Ringling called. That's B.I.N.G.-R.I.N.G.L.I.N.G.

(Hangs up. Picks up his shopping bags. Leanara in a daze wanders from off-stage into her dressing area.)

LEANARA: I'm not into Zen, but I think I finally heard the sound of one hand clapping. I heard all this writing during my big number and I looked out and it was the critics like the Last Judgment and they were all writing and nudging each other and snoring and glaring at me and I froze. I just froze. I forgot all my lines. The Ice Age descended. But don't worry. The miracle can happen. *My Fair Lady* was a famous disaster on opening night.

(The scene has revolved away and Bing is all ready running out of there to get to the Algonquin and Tybalt. The billboard flashes. Tybalt Dunleavy smiles down at us. The stage revolves and reveals outside the fabled Algonquin Hotel. A black hooker in a red miniskirt and feather boa anxiously looks around for customers and police. Bing strides on.)

THE HOOKER: Hi, sailor! Want to take a walk on the wild side?

BING: The Algonquin. I'll have to be witty walking into the Algonquin. Do they still have all those old wits there? Or do they have new wits?

THE HOOKER: *(Embarrassed.)* Mr. Ringling?

(Bing stops startled. The Hooker shifts from one foot to the other tugging at her long red curls.)

THE HOOKER: Hi! I hear you say Tybalt Dunleavy was staying at the Algonquin and I thought I'd better mosey my old buns over to get a closer look, but that old Irish mick doorman, he call me cheap old hooker and he throw me out.

BING: Aphro?

APHRO: That's me, honey. C'est moi. When that curtain come down tonight and I heard that bravo of silence, I was so embarrassed I didn't know what to do. So I put on my old working clothes and headed down here. This is what I do betwixt and between theatrical engagements.

BING: But, Aphro, you're an artist.

APHRO: Thank you, kind sir.

BING: This is so degrading.

APHRO: Degrading? No! It's like being a Kelly Girl, only on the outside. I was on my way down to work at the mouth of the Lincoln Tunnel and I get thinking maybe I stop off and see Mr. Tybalt Dunleavy he might consider me for a part in his next masterpiece, seeing how he saw me performing tonight. But that big old Irish mick doorman, he call me cheap old hooker. Maybe if you could escort me in on your arm—

BING: Aphro, Tybalt won't be doing any films for a while. He's going to be doing a play.

APHRO: What play? You got a new play?

BING: *Spreaded Thin.*

APHRO: *Spreaded Thin* is our play. Which part he be playing?

BING: He'll be playing your part. I hesitate to call it your part as you never even cast a shadow on it.

APHRO: But it's my part. *(A threat.)* You Mother Jumper. *(Lunges at Bing.)*

BING: You couldn't cut it. *(Bing uses his shopping bags to defend himself.)*

APHRO: *(Circling Bing.)* I was on the outskirts of it.

(Aphro smashes Bing with his purse. Bing retaliates with his bags. The fight is suddenly interrupted. The morning edition of the papers is thrown in. A pile of papers all bound up. And another bundle flies in. Bing and Aphro cling together in fear.)

APHRO: Hold in, honey. That could be the reviews.

BING: No. It couldn't. So soon. No.

(Aphro takes a knife out of his garter. He slices open the wire. He takes the top copy.)

APHRO: Don't worry, honey. Maybe the miracle happen. You take the *Times*. I take the *News*. That's my paper.

(Bing and Aphro are down on their hands and knees in the street with the papers open in front of them looking for the notices.)

BING: *(Reads.)* "Ringling Play Opens. The next time you read that name I hope it's on the obituary page." Oh my god. Oh my god. *(Bing's hands clutch his stomach. Then they go to his mouth, He runs/crawls offstage.)*

APHRO: *(Reads.)* "Bing Ringling. Sounds like three Chinese restaurants." *(Looks off at Bing.)* I don't think it's too witty to be throwing up in front of the Algonquin. Over at the Dixie, maybe. That's another matter. *(Reads.)* "When they write the history of stink, this shall be the Plimsoll Line."

(Bing wanders back on.)

APHRO: I'm sorry, honey.

BING: *(Glancing casually at the papers.)* They don't print these reviews in every copy of the paper, do they? That would mean there'd be, oh God, two, three million copies of these reviews. Why can't I stop reading these reviews!!!!!!!!

APHRO: 'Cause you get all the mention. I can't even find my own damn name. Oh, here's a mention. Sheeee, they spell it all wrong again. I ain't no hair-do. I am A.P.H.R.O. for Love. Well, back to work. Don't be too depressed, Bing.

(Bing is at a pay phone out on the street. He dials.)

APHRO: Things aren't too bad for you. You still got that musical with Anatol Torah. If you get a part in it for me, you can find me at the mouth of the Lincoln Tunnel... or if it's raining, I'm across the street from the Port Authority Bus Terminal. Accent on the terminal. Buck up, Bing. You got another project. *(Aphro goes off.)*

BING: *(On phone.)* Algonquin? This is Bing Ringling again. I want to talk to Tybalt Dunleavy. Yes, I'll hold.

(Veronica Gulpp-Vestige drifts on in a state of shock, trailing the reviews behind her.)

VERONICA: After stocking Broadway with hits like a trout stream for twenty-five years, this is the treatment I get.

BING: *(Still holding on the phone.)* Have you finally come to the remnants of your senses? Tybalt is right through those doors. Friday's flop can become a triumph by Sunday.

VERONICA: The greatest comeback since Easter? No, thank you, Bing. All the triumphs I've had and I've never experienced the degree of intensity I'm feeling right now. Failure at such an early age. I hope you can appreciate it.

BING: *(Phone.)* Yes, I'm holding. Checked out? No forwarding address? *(Hangs up.)* Oh, Christ, he read the reviews.

VERONICA: Hits. Hits. Hits. My hits linger year after year. Failures are these beautiful youths who died before their time. Juliet. Joan of Arc.

BING: *(Dials.)* Operator? Area code for Alaska? 907. Thank you. *(Hangs up. Dials 907-555-1212.)*

VERONICA: I think I'll become a bag lady. One of those charming old ladies who plow through the garbage with their shopping bags. The relaxation of failure. Better than meditation. Better than success.

BING: *(Phone.)* Alaska? Fairbanks? Do you still have that Homestead Act where they give you free land if you just show up? What about Nome? Do you have scholarships to bring future hopeful Alaskans up to Alaska? I don't know who I want to talk to. Sometimes you call Information to see if there's any numbers you should call, any numbers you don't know about. That North Pole must be plugged right into your heart, operator.

(Hangs up. Veronica searches through a garbage can. She begins singing.)

VERONICA:

Lonely Again
I walk the empty rooms of my mind
A zoom lens on the brooms of my mind
I find I can't sweep it away
Better sleep it away.

BING: Aphro's right, this isn't the end of the world. I still have another project. Get to work. That's the answer. Parachuters go right back up again. Come on, face. Up you go. Face, do your stuff.

(He pushes his face into a smile. He looks at Veronica. She has climbed into the garbage can. She sits there quite happily, her legs hanging over the edge of the can. She sings.)

VERONICA:

Lonely again
Open up the med'cine chest of my mind
Sweep the *Clairol* and the *Crest* from my mind
Till I find *Valium*
Librium
Vacuum!!!!!

(Bing shakes his head and walks away from her. The stage revolves away. Veronica vanishes into oblivion singing.)

VERONICA:

> Lonely no more
> I'm closing all the doors of my mind
> Retracting all the claws of my mind
> Till God knows when
> Until I'm Lonely Again…

(Veronica is gone and we are now in the fabulous pink and white satin apartment of the legendary Anatol Torah high in New York City. An enormous pink bed takes up most of the space and where there isn't bed there is every conceivable musical instrument. Pianos. Xylophones. Marimbas. A set of snare drums and trap drums. Guitars. Trumpets. Anatol plays them all. And where there isn't every musical instrument under the sun, there are frames filled with Anatol's nearest and dearest friends: Greta Garbo. Charlie Chaplin. Indira Gandhi. Harry Truman. All signed with love and kisses. Fabulous ferns and plants grow in profusion and Anatol even has stone white garden statuary under the plants: Flamingoes. Dwarves. An enormous statue of Buddha wearing an eye mask is over there in a corner. A few tanks of oxygen. Reams of composition paper, all blank. Phones. Phones. Phones. Head sets. Stereos. Recordings. All in all, fantastic, but it all dims somehow when Anatol is in the room. As he is now, Anatol is still the most fantastic thing in any room. His long silver hair is tied in a pony tail by a lavender silk ribbon. And his lavender silk caftan robe with a beautiful music staff embroidered on the back. At the moment, he is adjusting a red ribbon around a contract. A doorbell rings from far off.)

BING'S VOICE: Mr. Torah? Mr. Torah?

(Anatol hides the contract and himself is transformed into a little kitten. He hides coyly under the harpsichord. Bing enters the room all smiles. He sees no one in the room. Anatol throws a pillow at him.)

ANATOL: Bingele, my Ringele. *(Anatol leaps up and covers Bing with kisses. Anatol's wife, Wanda, screams from offstage.)*

WANDA: What's going on in there?????

ANATOL: Nothing, Wanda darling. It's Creation Time. Bing Is Here. *(Sings to the tune of "Spring Is Here.")* "Why doesn't my heart go dancing? Bing Is Here." *(Secret.)* Have you got it? Did you bring it?

BING: You think I'd let my collaborator down? *(Bing smugly and coolly rummages through his shopping bags.)*

ANATOL: *(A wreck of anticipation.)* What is it this time?

BING: *(Takes out a joint.)* It's Acapulco Aqua, Mr. Torah.

ANATOL: *(Sings to "Fascinating Rhythm.")* "Acapulco Aqua/Got me on the Go/Acapulco Aqua/I'm all a-twitter!"
(He grabs for the joint. Bing hides it behind him.)

BING: First let me hear what you composed.
(Anatol leaps for the joint.)

ANATOL: No! no! First let me have—what do you youngsters call it?—a Tokyo?

BING: A toke, Mr. Torah. You didn't compose today?

ANATOL: I did!! I did! I didn't. All right. I'll play you something. But first I have to hear the story again from your lips. Carbonate the air with your genius. I've missed you so much. *(Anatol kisses Bing fervently, a big wet kiss on the mouth.)*

BING: *(With great pride.)* Homer, the blind poet, has gone mad because he has nothing to write about.

ANATOL: I love it. I love this beginning. *(Anatol sits at Bing's feet.)*

BING: Now not only does Homer, destined to be the world's greatest poet, have nothing to write about, since paper and pencils have not been invented yet, he has nothing to write it on.

ANATOL: Bravo. The logic of it. Love it.

BING: Now, in my metaphor, I've tried to sum up the entire artistic problem. Ulysses as a male nurse in an ancient Greek insane asylum makes up stories to entertain the Blind Poet and he calls it the *Odyssey.* Calls it the *Iliad.* Homer listens. His inner eye is opened. His imagination is stirred.

ANATOL: All thanks to a younger man. Darling cookie pants, it's our story. You've brought me this story and given me back creative life.

BING: My pleasure. Your music has meant so much to the world.

ANATOL: Youth! Talent! I had it all once. I'll have it again.

BING: You have it now! Your music's beautiful. I grew up with it. Symphony Number One.
(Anatol is stirred by the memory of his work. He's written an enormous amount of music and it all sounds pretty much the same. He begins to sing his hits. His voice sounds like the muezzin's chant from the minaret on a burlesque house. He sings all his music with a breathtaking gusto in what should only be described as Yiddish double-talk: Moloch Mosai, Mallaca Mazoy.)

ANATOL: *(Tragically.)* Moloch Mosoi.

BING: Concerto Number One.

ANATOL: *(Sings even more tragically.)* Mallaca Mazoy.

BING: Sonata Number One.

ANATOL: *(Sings yet more tragically.)* Moloch Masai.

BING: Your Musical comedy: Uno.

ANATOL: *(Joy! Sings to tune of "Black Bottom.")* Malacca Mazoy Macca!

BING: Your ballet: Primo.

> *(And Anatol's Charleston becomes a lyrical ballet leap across the room. He belts out a high note and pirouettes.)*

ANATOL: Thank you, Bing! You've inspired me! *(Throws open the windows.)* I'll be back on top. You hear me, New York???? These terrible days are over. *(Slams window shut.)* Filthy city! Clean it up! *(Goes to harpsichord.)* Are you ready? This is Ulysses meeting Circe. *(He plays wildly on the harpsichord. Sings.)* Maloch Masai Mallaca Mazoy. *(Shakes Bing by the shoulders.)* Do you love it? Tell me you love it.

BING: I love it!

ANATOL: *(Picks up guitar.)* Here's something more your beat. A younger beat. For the young people. Ulysses being turned into a swine. Soo-wee! Soo-wee! *(Strums with great intensity like a gypsy. Sings.)* Moloch Mozoy! *(Throws down the guitar. Desperately to Bing.)* Do you love it?

BING: I love it!!!!

ANATOL: *(Goes to the drums.)* In this theme, I think I've captured the entire Trojan War. Wish me luck, dollface.

> *(Almost like a prayer, he takes the drumsticks and plays a drum riff of dazzling dexterity. He pounds the kettle drums in a fever of real pain. It goes on and on and on. Anatol finishes. Grabs his oxygen mask and collapses. Bing in terror runs to help him. Anatol inhales deeply. Drops the mask.)*

ANATOL: Can I have the Acapulco Aqua now?

> *(Bing hands him a joint and lights it for him. Anatol takes a deep drag. He falls back in Bing's arms.)*

ANATOL: Success. It's been so long since I've connected in my work. Thank you, Bing.

BING: *(Cradling Anatol.)* Oh, God, the privilege of working with you. Of hearing these melodies for the first time. Of being in on this part of the creative process.

ANATOL: When one's work is wet with pubescent dew.

BING: I want to be so good, Mr. Torah. I hear you, work with you, and I say yes, being an artist *is* the only thing in the world. You've been such an inspiration to me. I read about you and I say God, if Anatol Torah can come out of the Bronx, then I can too. You were like me once. You ushered in

Carnegie Hall every night. You learned opera by being an extra in *Aida* every time it was performed for five years.

ANATOL: *(Sings.)* "Celeste Aida…"

BING: Working in record stores. Always practicing. Mr. Torah, you're my hero and if you hadn't been the one to tell me that reviews didn't mean anything, that it was the work that counted, I would have gone cuckoo.

(Anatol reaches for the papers. He shows them to Bing. Bing falls back. Rolls away in shame.)

ANATOL: I know about the reviews. What do openings mean? I never even go to my own. Wanda threw these reviews in because Wanda wanted me to hate you. She's poisonously jealous of you. *(Screaming so she'll hear it.)* Wanda wanted my muse. Wanda wanted to inspire me. *(Softly.)* But how could she inspire me? Only a mirror can inspire. And how could a woman be a mirror to me? A woman could be a mirror to another woman, but only a man could be a mirror to another man. Put down those reviews, my mirror? *(He takes the papers from Bing. Anatol makes a funny, tender gesture circling his hands in front of his face.)* I'm not too big for you, am I? I can mirror you.

(He continues the gesture. Bing copies it. He makes the circling gesture, his hands in front of his face.)

BING: I hope so!

(Bing and Anatol mirror each other's gestures.)

BING AND ANATOL:
You can mirror me.
Cause that's the way collaborators ought to be

ANATOL: My thoughts end. Yours begin. Bing, I kiss those evil, wicked reviews. I wanted your play to close. I can now tell truths. I resented your play for taking you away from me. Your play didn't need a production to convince me of your brilliance. I have readers out reading every new play. When I read your play, *Spreaded Thin,* I said here is a mensch, a kindermensch, I must work with. I brought you here that fabulous day. My mirror. *(They make the mirror gesture.)* Young man, do you have any ideas for a possible musical?

BING: And I said, Well, I always thought the *Iliad* and the *Odyssey* would go nice together.

ANATOL: Perfection he calls nice together.

BING: You really don't mind these reviews?

(Anatol throws the reviews over the wall out of the set.)

ANATOL: Bing, darling, can we please get to work? Always with your little nose buried in the papers. The only thing deader than yesterday's news is today's news. The only news is the news of the future. So you had a little opening tonight? Isn't that an evening when presents are ordinarily exchanged?

BING: You really don't have to. You've given me so much all ready.

ANATOL: It's only a little piece of paper. *(Anatol produces the contract he had tied with ribbon at the beginning of the scene.)*

BING: The contract???? The contracts finally came through????
(He grabs for it. Anatol dangles it in front of Bing.)

ANATOL: *(Sings.)* "The contracts are here! the contracts are here!" Bingo, you've been working on speculation so long, I could have taken all of your ideas and thrown you out anytime I so chose.

BING: You wouldn't do that, Mr. Torah.

ANATOL: Anatol. Anatol.

BING: *(Sings.)* Anatol!!!!!

ANATOL: Your trust. Like the trust I had when I was young.

BING: Do you really really think we're alike?

ANATOL: Could we work together if we weren't? Your thoughts end. My thoughts begin. You start. I finish. A team. *(Hands Bing one of the contracts.)* Mazoltov, beloved. One for you. One for me. Let's get to work. Oh, I almost forgot! *(Hands Bing a few dollar bills.)* A little advance. You've also made me remember the realities of youth.

BING: I sure could use a few bucks. I can't get a grant because I haven't had a hit, but if I had a hit, I wouldn't need a grant.

ANATOL: One thing I know for sure. You can't make anything working in that ferkachte restaurant. Your poor dishpan hands.

BING: I hate working in that restaurant so much.

ANATOL: *(Looks in phone book. Dials.)* Board of Health? Do you speak English? Good! I'd like to report—

BING: The Ristorante Rigoletto—

ANATOL: The Ristorante Rigoletto in Greenwich Village. Dirty. Filthy. Bugs!!!! Close them down! Bugs right now crawling all over my lasagna.

BING: *(Leaping up and down.)* Yes! Yes! Yes!

ANATOL: *(Hangs up.)* Now can we get back to work?

BING: Anatol, would you do one favor for me? I've told my girl so much about you. Would you sing part of the opening number for her over the telephone?

ANATOL: No! I shall sing an original composition for her. What's her name?

BING: Leanara. *(Bing dials.)* Leanara? Hello? Wait. Wait.

(Bing holds the phone in front of Anatol who takes up his guitar. Anatol sings in a burst of gypsy passion.)

ANATOL: "Ohhhh, Leanara. Moloch Masai. Mallaca Mazoy."

BING: That was Anatol Torah!

ANATOL: Did she love it? Did she love it?

(Bing puts the phone to Anatol's ear. Anatol listens. Pushes the phone to Bing.)

ANATOL: She sounds very charming.

BING: *(To Leanara.)* What? You're packing? You got discovered tonight? An agent was in the audience and saw you? No. No. There's a lot of good work being done on TV series. You can rise above the material. No! No! I understand. Write as soon as you know where you are. Fine. Yes. It's all right. Sure. Sure. *(Hangs up. Very embarrassed.)* Let's get to work.

ANATOL: Good! Get rid of the baggage. Artists and revolutionaries should never have families. Never have connections. The world is our battlefield and our works of art are our only survivors.

BING: Mr. Torah? Could you tell me how to live my life?

ANATOL: Certainly.

BING: In the movie *Limelight,* Claire Bloom says to Charlie Chaplin, I can't wait to grow up and be a professional like you. And Charlie Chaplin says but we're all of us amateurs. We never live long enough to be anything else but amateurs. Is that true?

ANATOL: Olympian bullshit. I have lived long enough to become only a professional. My craft is all I have. Now you must make a phone call for me. I have had a very bad setback tonight.

BING: You? Mr. Torah?

ANATOL: I went to 21 tonight and I walked into that loathsome establishment, but where else can you go, and there I saw my spiritual double. I saw sitting there in front of me, by himself, at a table, swirling ice cubes in a glass, slow, legato, lento, serioso, Tybalt Dunleavy. I said I must have him for our show. I must have him for *The Odiad.* I felt I was seeing my true self sitting there. My pacemaker heated up and broiled my lungs, but I didn't care. I ran to him and I said Hello, Tybalt. What have you seen this evening? And he said he had been downtown to see a play by a friend of his in a toilet on Lower Death Street. I said a friend? He said Bing Ringling. I said but Bing Ringling is collaborating with me! Tybalt said he is my oldest friend. We grew up on the same block. I said, aha! Lightning is the only thing that does strike twice. Of course you'd know each other. All the brilliant people know each other. Reinforce each other. I noticed that my knuckles were white as I grabbed the snow white tablecloth.

Please, I blurted out. Be in my musical. Play Ulysses. It's a role based on me. Unabashedly autobiographical. My hopes. My dreams. And you are the only person big enough to play, whom I would entrust with the role of me. That's when he said it. Tybalt said that if I did anything, I'd do my friend's play. I'd save it. I'd salvage it. That's where I first saw the reviews. Tybalt had the reviews in front of him. He said I will only do my friend's play. But Bing, darling, your play, I'm sorry but *finita la comedia,* eh? Bing, make him do *The Odiad* for us. But first, I have to know. What is Tybalt Dunleavy really like?

BING: I knew him very well. We grew up on the same block together. I knew him as well as anyone. We were like Siamese twins growing up. We were very close.

ANATOL: On what side does Tybalt Dunleavy wear his keys? That's how you can tell all you need to know about a person. On what side does Tybalt Dunleavy wear his keys?

(Bing is puzzled.)

ANATOL: Sit down, puppycakes. Anatol has something to tell. You're my collaborator, my partner, I tell you everything. If you wear your keys jingling jangling on this side of your belt, that is a signal when you go into certain bars that you like to be hurt.

BING: Like to be hurt?

ANATOL: If you wear your keys on the other side of your belt, transfer them to that side, that is the signal that you like to inflict the wound.

BING: Tybalt's not into any scene like that.

ANATOL: In to. In to. I love that expression. What scene is Tybalt into, man?

BING: I don't think he has a scene.

ANATOL: Everybody has a scene.

BING: I don't have a scene.

ANATOL: I don't believe you. What bars do you go into? There are bars for everything. Bars where boys go to meet girls. Where boys go to meet boys. Where dwarves go to meet dwarves. Firemen to meet other firemen. I even heard there's a bar in the East Eighties, shhh, don't let her hear, she'll want to go there, where they prop up dead people on stools in booths. Where you can go to meet dead people, which is a very hard thing to do socially. Drink with them. Talk with them. Dead people can be very cheery, if you happen to be frightened, as some people are, of living people. Kiss them if you're shy. Try out the latest or the oldest dance steps. One nifty thing about dead folks, they can't say no.

BING: But it's so desperate.

ANATOL: I know, darling, but look at the world. But seriously, everybody wears keys of one sort or another to inform the world of their wants so their spiritual double will see those keys and recognize those wants. Now I want Tybalt, but he rejected me. Anatol Torah is not rejected. Anatol Torah wants Tybalt Dunleavy. Bring him to me now. Finito.

BING: Well, I haven't seen him in years. I really don't know him anymore. We were kids together, but he hasn't seen the enormous strides I've made.

ANATOL: What are you saying? You don't know him well?

BING: I know him but I don't know him now. Why don't we get back to work?

ANATOL: I'm not too big for you, am I Bing? I mean, you're working at full capacity?

BING: I hope so.

ANATOL: My fame doesn't diminish your capacity to give me your very best?

BING: It thrills me.

ANATOL: Anatol Torah, legend that is he, doesn't frighten you?

BING: Could we get back to work?

ANATOL: If you were working with someone of less renown, would you be freer? Sometimes people like you are intimidated by people like me. People like you can't operate at full capacity in the presence of people like me. Are you sure I'm not too big for you?

BING: You're not too big for me!!!

ANATOL: Tybalt Dunleavy wouldn't be too big for me, but he thinks he's bigger than me and that's what I want! That's what I need! Someone bigger than me!!! God, I had an amusing experience the other night, very much to the point. Listen and learn. (*Anatol begins a slow mounting roll on the kettle drum.*) Jesus appeared in my room. In the dark. All lit up. Inner light. Looking great. I said, Jesus, what are you doing here? He said, I hope I haven't bothered you, but I just wanted to meet you once before you died. He, Jesus, wanted to meet me. I'm not even Christian. His light shown up the dark. Now that's big! (*The drum roll hits its crescendo.*) Also a lovely compliment. But now you see, Bing, I've lost myself. I had myself so firmly in my hands but now I've lost myself. I met you and I thought I was you. You were me... I was you. A team. Perfect collaborators. But no, I'm not you. I'm Tybalt! So don't lie to me and keep Tybalt for your own measly little show. Get him for me. Give Anatol back his body. Give Anatol just one last success. One little success-ette? All right, I'll tell you my scene. What I do, once or twice a year, is fly to Germany, to a little bar I know in Hamburg. A death bar. Where people go to kill or be killed. Depending on which side you wear your keys, on which arm you wear your mourning band. I sit at the bar, buy a drink, and size up the crowd, looking for a man who looks vaguely like me, for my vague double. It doesn't take much—a jawline, a nostril, an eyebrow, for someone who wears his keys on the opposite side from mine. Who has come there to be killed. By the way, Bing, there's nothing illegal in this. Death between consenting adults is hardly illegal. And when my vague double enters, I buy him a drink and then take him into the back room specially provided and I take a length of piano wire and turn that man's throat into a Steinway, a Knabe, a Yamaha, and I squeeze a symphony out of that man's body and I pretend it's my own body and I squeeze the evil out of it, squeeze death out of it, squeeze the fear out of it, squeeze the failure out of it, and he slumps to the floor with the others. I pay my check—charge it, really, it's a deduction—then fly back to this country, so full of life. Better than a face-lift. Better than art. What I hate most about art is it's on the side of life. I have to go to reality for the one thing art can't give me. I have to go to reality for death. Yes, death. I must fill myself with death in order to feel life. I fly back here, across oceans, safe on Central Park South, watch the moon rise over the reservoir, hear the sounds from the zoo, write notes for my Symphony #2, Concerto #2, Rhapsody #2, Capriccio #2. I am filled with life. Then I can begin my search for a collaborator. A double on the side of life to give me life. It's the only way we can grow. We find someone we love and become them. I became Mozart that way. Verdi. Stravinsky. I thought I'd become you.

BING: Mr. Torah, yourself plus myself—not since $E = MC^2$.

ANATOL: Bing, darling, you don't have enough self for yourself. Tybalt will be my new collaborator. Read the contract. The large print. I haven't hidden anything away in small print. It says Bing Ringling will produce Tybalt Dunleavy for me or he has no further value for me. Bing, don't hate me. I feel weakness in me. I feel age in me. That's why Tybalt rejected me. He saw my weakness. He saw my fear. He saw the death in me. All the life in him was frightened by all the death in me. That's why he said no to me. All right, I see what I must do. I will fly to Germany. Have a quick kill. A good death douche. Get all the death vibrations out of me. Fill myself with life. Jet back here rosy cheeked. Have Tybalt standing by the sunrise when I return to these rooms. Bing, you're still here? Get Tybalt. Find him. Bind him. I will be Tybalt. Tybalt will be I. I will be Tybalt. Tybalt will be I.

(Bing has picked up his gear. He looks at the contract. He throws it down. Anatol has begun a drum crescendo over his last lines. Bing picks up his shopping bags. He leaves. Anatol doesn't even notice. The bedroom revolves away. An art gallery swings into place. A beautiful very large picture of a turn of the

century woman in a white flowing dress is painting a field of poppies. The painting is done in an American Impressionist style: Hudson River School. The painting is in an elaborate gold frame. A girl sits in front of the picture looking at it. She's dressed in the style of, say, ten years ago. Her name is Allison. Lots of paper cups, plastic champagne glasses litter the floor. Bing passes by. Bing looks in.)

BING: A gallery opening tonight? The world is littered with openings. The world of art. Clear my head. Peace. Clean. Cool. Green.

(He goes into the gallery. The girl looks at him. Bing looks at the painting.)

ALLISON: *(Tentative.)* Hello?

(Bing looks at her, but looks back at the painting.)

ALLISON: Hello? Bing?

(Bing looks at her.)

ALLISON: Do I look so different? I read your play was about to open and I said, my God, Bing did what he really always wanted to do. I was thinking I'd get into town again and I'd go see it because it'll be running forever and we'd see each other at the play and I'd tell you how much I liked it.

BING: I have a great memory. I mean, I am noted for my memory. People in memory courses sleep with pictures of me under their pillows. You're not going to tell me who you are?

(Allison does a cheerleading routine.)

BING: That's a hint?

ALLISON: I was thinking I'd get all dolled up, wear a veil. You'd lift up the veil and I'd say: Do you remember your old friend now that you're rich and famous?

BING: Allison.

ALLISON: Yeah!

BING: Allison de Mears. I'm talking to Allison de Mears in front of her grandfather's painting.

ALLISON: I used to laugh at you. The theater. It all seemed so childish. But now I'm so happy to read about you. I cut the ad for your play out of the paper and I keep it right over my Washomatic. To know somebody's life turned out the way they wanted it to.

BING: I can't believe I'm seeing you, Allison. The geometry of life. That I'd come here today.

ALLISON: We came in for the opening night of the gallery. We never come into town, but seeing it's my grandfather's painting… he's having a revival.

BING: It's been a long time.

ALLISON: When you left me, Bing, after I found I wasn't pregnant. That's how long ago it was. Wow. Remember the days when kids had to get married if you thought you were, you was... my syllables get all mixed up talking to a writer. You see, I always knew you'd be a writer. Your Christmas story about the juggler who goes to the cathedral and the Kings and Emperors all bring gold and diamonds, but the Blessed Mother only comes alive when the juggler juggles because he had a talent and gave what was closest to him.

BING: That was a cute story. I'm remembering a time I went to confession.

ALLISON: Do you go anymore?

BING: I said bless me father for I have sinned.

ALLISON: Me neither.

BING: I forgot all this! How could I have forgotten all this? I said Father, there was this girl. We didn't mean to. *(Mock torture.)* I. Her. We.

ALLISON: Was that me?

BING: Us! I said, Father, please forgive me. I'll never commit that awful sin again.

ALLISON: That sounds like Father Caiphus to me. I never went to Father Caiphus. I always went to the deaf priest.

BING: Father Caiphus exactly. And Father Caiphus said I will give you absolution my son, if you promise on the breast of the Virgin Mary or her shoulder or her neck that you will never see this tool of Satan again.

ALLISON: Tool of Satan!

BING: I said Father, I can't do that. I've invited her to the Fall Festival next weekend.

ALLISON: Me, a tool of Satan! Wow!

BING: Father Caiphus looks at me through the grill. Is that you, Bing? Yes sir, Father. Bing, this is Father Caiphus. Let me talk to you man to man. Sure, Father. Bing, what is more important? The Fall Festival or your immortal soul? I said Father, you're talking about eternity and I'm just trying to deal with next weekend.

ALLISON: The Fall Festival... I still have the corsage.

BING: It's nice to see you, Allison.

ALLISON: They transformed the whole gym into Camelot. *(Sings.)* "The winter is forbidden til December. And exits March the Second on the dot." You know where I was before you came in here? I was in the picture. Walking around. It was very nice.

BING: In the picture?

ALLISON: Look at you. A show playing Off-Broadway.

BING: Who did I hear you married?

ALLISON: And you're working on a new musical with Anatol Torah to open the new Washington Theatre Center in Washington, DC based on the *Iliad* and the *Odyssey* called *The Odiad*.

FRANCIS: *(Offstage.)* I'll rip every hair out of your head, you fruitcake. It's her grandfather and her grandmother and you're selling it for fifteen grand. And she don't get a Buffalo nickel.

BING: That yelling is awful.

ALLISON: That yelling is Francis.

BING: You married fruity Franci… Francis Schreibertoni?

ALLISON: He heard about the sale of my grandfather's painting and he's in there trying to get us a share.

BING: The captain of the cheerleading squad was Francis.

ALLISON: At least you're doing what you want to do.

BING: Well, it's a choice. It's a life commitment. Like anything.

ALLISON: At least you're not selling toupees.

BING: Is that a wig? I'd never have known.

ALLISON: No. It's what Francis is studying to do.

FRANCIS: *(Offstage.)* If I had the Mona Lisa's granddaughter out there you'd be singing a different tune. You'd be inviting the Mona Lisa's granddaughter's tooshie in here.

(Allison cannot bear Francis's screaming. Music plays. Allison becomes quite happy. She simply steps through the frame into the picture.)

BING: Allison? Get out of the picture. That is a fifty thousand dollar painting.

ALLISON: Come on in, Bing. This is our past.

BING: Allison, they can arrest you for walking into a fifty thousand dollar painting.

ALLISON: It's so safe in here. This is our past.

BING: You know that story. Chinese story. Man sees moon. Picture of moon. Over a lake. He reaches in to get it and he drowns.

ALLISON: But how could we drown, Bing? This is my past. It's so safe. You must do it all the time. Walk into the past. You're a writer. You see a movie you like, don't you just walk right into it? I take out snapshots and I walk right into them. I take my car and drive into the yearbook. Tool around. Hi, Donny. Hi, Kenny. Hi, Grandma. I used to think you were so old. She's the same age then as me right now. All these dreams in my head. It must be wonderful to have a talent like you do. Like my grandfather. A place to put your dreams. My dreams are just wandering around in my head. Some go here. Some go there. Hey, there goes Tybalt!

BING: Where?

ALLISON: In my head. And there you are. You're always there.

BING: You look very pretty in that picture, but I think you should get out of it. Hopefully, we've grown, Allison. Developing. Stretching. Our body cells change every seven years, Allison. There's probably none of the old of us left. Now, get out of the painting, Allison.

(Bing offers his hand. Allison steps out. The music stops.)

ALLISON: I want to tell you a secret. You're a writer. You'll understand.

BING: I shall.

ALLISON: I'm thinking about leaving Francis.

BING: Now that's what I want to hear.

ALLISON: Get a job. Maybe working with emotionally disturbed children. Jobs nobody else wants. I'm not qualified to be a dogcatcher's assistant, Bing. This is what I keep trying to tell Francis. It's so hard to get started in your life. To pull yourself together just to begin. You're a mind reader, Bing. No wonder you're a writer. I'm thinking of going to night school. Is it too late?

BING: Never!

ALLISON: I don't care! Am I too old?

BING: No!

ALLISON: I don't care! You did it. Tybalt did it. You really can invent your own life. This is the speech I'm going to make at our Sweet Sixteenth reunion. I'll never be rich and famous like you are, but I can have a life. I'm so frightened. Give me courage. I want to thank you. What a wonderful bump-into. See my grandmother looking at you? She's not painting the poppies. She's painting you. She likes you very much.

FRANCIS: *(Offstage.)* Hey Allie! Come on! We have to get the car out of the garage.

ALLISON: I've got all these dreams. You're so lucky. You're doing what you want to do. Talent. A place to put your dreams. You must be raking in the cash, Bing. All the wonderful things you can do for people. Your parents must be crazy with joy. A passport to freedom. Dreams. Money.

FRANCIS: *(Offstage.)* Allie! Move your ass!

ALLISON: Bing? Write about me changing? You could call it *Tool of Satan.* Give me a beautiful life and then send me a copy. Second thought, don't. Francis don't like me getting mail. I'll remember today for the rest of my life. Hey, remember the way Tybalt used to pronounce it? He had the most beautiful accent. Au revoir, he'd say. Au revoir, Bing. Au revoir. *(The scene revolves out.)*

A very clumsy Hare Krishna boy wrapped in robes dances on rapturously until he steps in dog dirt.

HARE KRISHNA: *(Scraping his foot.)* May I read to you from the Bhagavad Gita?

BING: No. Not now. Please. Go away. Don't bother me.

HARE KRISHNA: Please, mister, I'm new to the organization and they won't feed me if I don't do this. "When the mind leaves behind the dark forest of delusion, you shall go beyond time past and time that is to come. When in recollection he withdraws all his sense from the attractions of the pleasures of the sense, even as a tortoise withdraws all his limbs, then his is a serene wisdom." *(He dances off, stumbling.)*

BING: What? Are you some Westchester kid on vacation? I have a headache. My feet hurt. I didn't tell my parents the show was opening. I didn't want them there. I didn't want them part of my triumph. I didn't want them. I wanted to surprise them. But I want comfort and I want to go home. I want my head rubbed. I want my feet pulled. Home. Home. I want to go home. Home. Home. Home. Home.

(Bing steps into his parents' living room. The house is decorated like a shrine to Bing as a baby with sleds and roller skates and baseball bats and footballs. Balloons and streamers garner the walls. Mom and Dad are all dressed up in party clothes with confetti in their hands and party favors. Dad wears an American legion cap and slippers. Mom has a paper party hat over her grey hair. They're both old and asleep.)

BING: Mom? Dad?

MOM: *(Joyously snapping to attention.)* Charlie! The baby's home!
(They throw the confetti, blow the horns.)

DAD: *(So happy.)* Bravo, author! Give me your laundry. Ah, Mother, smell that laundry.

MOM: Why don't you write?

DAD: Orville Wright! Wilbur Wright!

MOM: Call anytime of the day or night.

DAD: Dennis Day. Fuzzy McKnight.

MOM: Either one of us is always here in case you want to come home. Twenty-four hour devotions at the phone in case you want to call.

DAD: Alexander Graham Bell.

MOM: Do you have a temperature? Dear God, get right into bed. Why do you leave home? It's not safe out in the streets. Sick. Hungry. *(Exits.)*

DAD: Do you need any money?

BING: Dad, about the tux…

DAD: Are you hurting for cash? You making out great? How's the girls? Show business. You must be getting laid like crazy.

MOM: *(Enters.)* What are those veins under your skin?

BING: They're veins under my skin.

MOM: You're not into drugs! Oh, God, Charlie, my worst fears. He's a junkie. Look at those veins.

BING: Mom, we all have veins.

MOM: Thank God. I have so much to tell you. Your father has been awful. Terrible. Unspeakable. Let me look into your eyes.

DAD: How's the play going? I got my tuxedo all rented for the opening.

MOM: I got my dress.

DAD: How's it going?

(Bing makes an "O.K." sign.)

MOM: Celebration! Celebration Charlie! Want a bottle? He wants a bottle! *(Exits.)*

DAD: Your mother's having her third complete menopause.

BING: I wouldn't mind a drink.

DAD: The old prostrate's acting up, but screw it. That's what I say.

(Mom enters with a baby bottle.)

BING: Mom! I don't want it anymore.

DAD: Don't get too big for your mother.

MOM: Yeah. Outgrow us. Go ahead. Spit right on us.

BING: Mom. Dad. I'm so unhappy. Believe it or not, I came home to be somewhere familiar. I don't have a nickel to my name. I can't get a grant because I haven't had a hit but if I had a hit I couldn't get a grant because then I wouldn't need one. I want life to begin for me and I think maybe I picked the wrong profession. The wrong dreams got tattooed on me. I'm dreaming somebody else's dreams. My head hurts. My feet ache. I want my head rubbed. I want my feet pulled. *(He sits on both their laps, stretching out.)*

MOM: Give me that head.

DAD: Give me those feet. Wow, Mother, smell those socks.

MOM: Better than Chanel.

DAD: Coco Chanel.

BING: It feels good.

DAD: Goodman's noodles. Benny Goodman. Bing, I know there's a silver bullet called greatness with your name on it. I used to think the bullet had my name on it, but I looked closer and the bullet said Junior.

MOM: Bing, look at all the men who've tattooed their names on life. They are your guides. They are your mottoes.

DAD: To be fancy is to be—

MOM: Putting on the Ritz.

DAD: Who is it? Who is it?

MOM: He knows this. Monsieur Cesar Ritz. Who owned a glorious hotel. Not a Hilton. That's Conrad.

DAD: Conrad Nagel.

BING: Couldn't you just rub my head and feet. It feels so good.

DAD: More. More. More. More.

MOM: Gregorian Chant.

DAD: Julian Calendar.

MOM-DAD: Pope Gregory. Pope Julian.

BING: Mom. Dad. I know all this. My whole life you'd wake me up in the middle of the night crying "Don't be like us."

MOM-DAD: Be somebody. Be great.

MOM: Be like the men who've tattooed their names on life.

DAD: Who've put their names in the Dictionary of life.

MOM: The Webster's Dictionary of Life.

DAD: Noah Webster.

MOM: And such love.

DAD: Bessie Love.

MOM: We never minded if you had an Oedipus complex because Oedipus was a King.

DAD: A Dennis King. Billy Jean King. That's my girl. My Ziegfeld girl.

MOM: Oh, Bing, you're so blue.

DAD: So who? Do it for your Mother.

BING: So Ben Blue.

MOM: Now you're coming to life.

DAD: Miller's *High Life*.

MOM: Go with it, Dad. Bing's on the track again. Getting his John Brown's body into a Lionel train...

DAD: H. L. Lionel.

MOM: ...into his own little Pullman car.

DAD: Who?

BING: George Pullman!

DAD: Go with it, boy! We're giving you values. Shake that Richter scale of greatness.

MOM: Charles Richter.

BING: I'm home! I'm home! I'm so happy! I'm so hungry!

MOM: What do you want?

BING: *(Thrilled to be home!)* Hershey Bars. Pasteurized milk. Louis Pasteur. Graham Crackers. Billy Graham. Caesar salad. Orange Julius. Julius Caesar. Napoleon Brandy. Brandy Alexander. Alexander's Ragtime Band.

MOM-DAD: *(Sing in vaudeville style.)* "Come on and hear/Come on and hear/Let me take you by the hand! Up to the man/Up to the man/Who is the leader of the band!"

DAD: The whole world wants their name in lights and—

MOM: Claude Neon.

DAD: Made them lights.

MOM-DAD: *(Sing to "Light of the Silvery Moon." A soft-shoe.)* By the Light of the tiffany Lamp/I got a cramp!

DAD: Louis Tiffany!

(Mom digs in the toy chest and takes out an enormous penny. She hands it to Bing who smiles like a horrifying child performer and goes into a baby specialty that he sings for us in the audience.)

BING:

> I Found a Penny
> It was the brightest I've ever seen
> I Found a Penny
> And Mr. Lincoln
> Was winkin' at me.
> You know what that means!
> No more trouble
> No more woe
> Mr. Lincoln gonna free us
> From the bad luck we know
> You're not broke anymore he seems to say
> Cause I found a penny
> A shiny penny
> And I'm on my way. *(Stops singing.)*

Dad, where is the spirit of Chartres? Those men built this great cathedral because they wanted to celebrate. All this grappling after me me me. Don't you ever want to rub a big eraser over yourself? I do. Don't you ever dream that you don't want anything? I do. Don't you ever dream that you don't dream? I do. What went so wrong in your lives that you have to take it out on my life?

MOM: We love you, Bing. No one will ever love you like we love you. Would people who didn't love you never throw away your diapers? Six thousand

bronzed dirty diapers kept right here in the bookcases. We'd take them off
you. Dad would run them right over to the jewelers.

DAD: Horace Harding Blvd.

MOM: Your bath water stored in Mason jars.

DAD: Jackie Mason.

MOM: Never flushed any of your tinkle away.

DAD: Terry Tinkle. Frankie Flush.

MOM: Left over dinners kept in the oven.

DAD: Metal oven. Christopher medal. Saint Christopher.

MOM: Twenty-five years of Christmas trees kept in the basement.

DAD: Christopher Columbus. Columbus, Ohio.

MOM: Every chicken pox. Every measle wrapped in Reynold's wrap. You're our
baby.

DAD: Baby Snooks.

MOM: You're our second chance.

DAD: John Chancellor.

MOM: We're mesmerized by love for you.

DAD: Igor Mesmer.

MOM: Shut up, Charlie, I know.

DAD: Then you had to grow up and leave us. God, the wonderful times we had
when you were a kid. They were the happiest days of my life. Why did you
have to grow up? Look! Another whisker. I suppose you got a pubic hair.
Suppose you got hair under your arms. You think you're pretty hot stuff,
don't you. Let me tell you. No one ever got as much love as we gave you.
What a childhood you had. We had. I'd ride you. Push you. Swing you.
Put dreams in your head. Look at the sky. Look at the ground. Look. Look.
Look. That's right. I'd kiss your feet. Don't be like me. I know the truth
about myself. But you. The world. And then you had to grow up and leave
us. I wish sometimes we had the Gagliardis' luck.

(Dad puts an old teddy bear on his lap.)

BING: But their son is mentally retarded.

DAD: I watch Mr. Gagliardi pushing little Antonio around.

BING: Little Antonio is forty-six years old.

DAD: But what a sweet kid. His Daddy plays with him. Looka up, Antonio,
Looka uppa!

MOM: How's the play going, Bing?

BING: Mom. It might not be very good.

MOM: Did you hear that, Charlie? Movie offers. Look, Bing, here's the dress I'm
wearing to your play.

DAD: All the movie offers in the world can't bring me back my little baby boy.

MOM: I'll wear this to your musical and this to your play.

DAD: Throw you the ball.

MOM: Maybe I should wear this to your musical and this to your play.

DAD: Show you the words.

MOM: Your father's wearing the tux to the musical and this to your play.

DAD: Teach you the dreams.

MOM: Maybe I'll wear the suit and Dad will wear the dress.

DAD: Read you the back of old cereal boxes.

MOM: Which do you like better?

BING: Take them back. Save your money. The play might not be very good.

MOM: What do you mean the play might not be very good?

BING: The man playing the lead is terrible. The producer is crazy. And it might not be very good.

DAD: What kind of shit is this you're hurling at us?

MOM: But I've made presents for the critics. I knitted a scarf for the *Herald Tribune*.

BING: Mom, there is no *Herald Tribune*.

DAD: Everything comes back. Nothing goes away.

MOM: Slippers for the *Times*. Scarves for the Sunday *Times*. Necktie for the *News*. Look at the gift wrapping. I'm going to stand at the door opening night and introduce myself and hand each critic his present.

DAD: I didn't straighten your teeth to hear words like your play might not be very good.

MOM: The Brooklyn *Eagle*. The *Mirror*. The *Journal-American*.

DAD: Open your mouth. Let me see those teeth I broke my ass to straighten.

MOM: Candy for Channel Two. Gift Certificates for Channel Three. English lessons for Channel Forty-Seven.

DAD: Let me see my trip to Europe. Let me see my season tickets to the Yankees. Let me see my color TV. There it is. All hanging out of your gums. That those teeth should hiss such shit at me. And where the hell is your orthodontist? Probably got a villa in Acapulco or on the moon and here we sit in two and a half rooms freezing our asses off waiting for you to take us the hell out of here. What do you think we had you for? God! Take me! Strokes hit one of every six men. Where the hell is my stroke? Where is my heart attack? Hit me with it now!

BING: It's a flop. A flop. A flop, Pop. It opened tonight. For all time failure is tattooed on my name like a tattoo on the arm of an Auschwitz inhabitant. An equal sign burning between my name and failure. Ringling equals fail-

ure and Ringling is my name and our name and my failure is your failure
for all time.

(He takes the reviews out of his bags and assaults Mom and Dad with them.
Mom and Dad each read the reviews. Then.)

MOM: Thank God for the musical.

BING: That is over too.

(Dad takes out a gun and shoots at Bing.)

MOM: Charlie! He's only kidding!! What a kidder!!!

BING: Mom. Dad. I'm sorry. I'm sorry about the dresses and the tuxedos. I'm
sorry. You got the wrong son. I'm sorry. You should have had Tybalt for a
son. I always felt in my stomach that what you liked best about me was I
had Tybalt for a friend and you wished he was your son. And you could be
living in Tarzana, California.

MOM: And we could read in the papers how the Ringling boy—what was his
name? Bing? How Bing's show was a flop. And we were glad our son Tybalt
was a star. Wouldn't that be nice?

(Mom and Dad turn their couch into a pull-out bed. They ignore Bing. Mom
and Dad climb into bed. Bing takes out a gun and shoots Mom and Dad.)

DAD: Under normal circumstances, we would die, but you know why we won't.

MOM: They don't give Pulitzer Prizes to boys who kill their parents.

DAD: Your play is going to be wonderful, Tybalt.

BING: I'm not Tybalt.

DAD: Yes, you are. You're our success.

MOM: How is your friend, that Ringling boy… what's his name? Bing!

BING: I'm Bing. (Bing climbs into bed with them to get their attention.)

DAD: Get rid of Bing, Tybalt. You're a star. Bing's a real loser.

BING: (In bed between them.) I wanted to write a play based on Dante's Divine
Comedy. This poet going through hell to get up to Paradise. But the first
section couldn't work because that's the Inferno and there's no escape from
that. The last part is the Paradisio and I couldn't make that work because
there's no place to go from there. All that left me with is Purgatory and the
prime sin of Purgatory is people not seeing reality for what it is. But I only
gave that part of the play one page. Let me see life the way it is so I'll know
what to do with it. Let me see reality for what it is. Let me see things the
way they are so I'll know what I have to do. Tell me how to live my life and
then get out. I want you out of my life. I want me out of your life. I want
my own life.

MOM: Your play will be wonderful, Tybalt.

DAD: We'll see you at the opening, Tyb.

MOM: Isn't he beautiful, Dad?

DAD: Can you believe he's ours?

MOM: We did good, Dad.

DAD: Love.

(Bing crawls out of bed. Mom and Dad go to sleep serenely.)

MOM: Perfect.

DAD: Ours.

MOM: Our son.

DAD: Our life.

(Bing comes to the edge of the stage. He tries to sing to us, to get our attention, affection, approval. He puts on the big smile again but it is all crooked and forced and off-key.)

BING: *(Sings.)* I Found a penny/It was the brightest I've ever seen?/I Found A Penny? And Mr. Lincoln was winkin' at me/You know what that means/No more trouble/No more woe/Mr. Lincoln will free us from the bad luck we know/You're not broke any mo'/he seems to say! I Found a Penny/A shiny shiny Penny/and I'm on my way! *(The smile turns into a grimace. Tybalt's face flashes high above him.)* I want to see life once through Tybalt's eyes. That poster of *Gangland* over Times Square. Looking down at me from that great eye. Looking up at a great eye. Me. A kid watching my father shaving. Looking up at his face. I'm going to see life once through Tybalt Dunleavy's eyes. I'm going to find a secret staircase. Here's a secret door. Climb up the secret staircase behind the secret door. Up more secret stairs. Higher. Higher. Secret stairs. Higher. Up. Up. *(Bing is lost in darkness. The wind howls. Tybalt's billboard fades because we are now in front of it. This enormous eye with a painter's scaffolding in front of it swinging in the wind. We are high over Times Square. A door in the eye opens. Bing steps out gingerly. He almost falls over the edge. He hangs on. A man wrapped in an army blanket, wearing dark glasses, steps out on the scaffold behind Bing. He runs to the far edge of the scaffold. Bing runs to the other edge to get balance. This new fellow who is roughly Bing's age sees Bing and screams in terror. This new guy is shaking so badly that Bing is calmed as if Bing were confronting his own fear. The fellow is, of course, Tybalt.)*

TYBALT: I'm sorry, fella. There isn't supposed to be anyone else up here. They told me I'd be the only one up here.

BING: *(Hanging onto the ropes.)* Tybalt? Tybalt!!!!

TYBALT: *(Hanging onto his ropes.)* Bing?

(They try to cross the scaffolding to get to each other but they're too afraid to let go of the ropes. The scaffold swings in the high wind.)

BING: What is this, geometry? Is this astral projection? Three-dimensional wish fulfillment? Tybalt. I would love to give you a hug, but I'm afraid to walk across this scaffolding. The wind. I tried to call you. You were never in. They wouldn't put me through. I said here is my oldest and dearest... what is wrong with the world when I can't get through? Can you hear me? My mind is racing like the Allied Chemical Tower. Where the news goes round and round the building. The part where one sentence ends. Another begins. The lights jumble. My head is breaking open. Tybalt. Hello.

TYBALT: Look at them lined up down there.

BING: To see you.

TYBALT: Loew's One. Loew's Two. Loew's Three.

BING: Loew's Four. Loew's Five.

TYBALT: The DeMille One. The Gable Two.

BING: All lined up. Money in hand. *Gangland.* Tybalt Dunleavy. The whole world walking like you. Talking like you. It must be very gratifying.

TYBALT: Did they send you up here?

BING: Who sent me where?

TYBALT: Are you in on it?

BING: In on what?

TYBALT: They haven't changed the plan, have they?

BING: Tybalt, what plan?

TYBALT: You're just up here?

BING: I was just wandering by.

TYBALT: Oh. That's nice.

BING: Don't you think it's strange I'm up here? I think it's very strange you're up here.

TYBALT: Strange? No. You being here? It's a shame I didn't think of you before, Bing. We could have worked something out.

BING: I don't want anything from you.

TYBALT: Where you took over my life. I didn't know till last night you wanted to be rich and famous. That you wore the cufflinks. That you went to that little magic store on Fourteenth Street and bought the R & F cufflinks. I have the R & F cufflinks too. Last night I met Anatol Torah at 21. A charming man. He had the cufflinks too. The R & F cufflinks. Anatol wears his on a chain around his neck. I wish we'd kept in touch, seen each other. If I'd known you wanted to be R & F, I'd have given you my life. You could have had that. I'd have left you my money. My house. My name. The key to the Maserati hanging on a hook as you come in the garage. You could have had that. But everything is worked out now. You better not be here, Bing. Norman hasn't planned it this way. That I should meet an old friend.

BING: Norman?

TYBALT: Norman Mailer. Actually a group of lawyers and agents. That's why I've come back to New York. That's why I'm up here on this billboard in front of my eye. They've bought the rights to my death.

BING: Tyb, this has been a hard day for me. What do you say we go downstairs and have a drink? Catch up on old times?

TYBALT: After *Gangland*, I got all these offers. I said to my lawyers and my agents as a joke really—I said it's a shame I have to go and try to top *Gangland*. I'm a legend now. I don't want to do any parts that'll hurt my legend. Protect myself. Lucky Jimmy Dean. Lucky Marilyn. Lucky people like that. Jesus. Lucky Jesus. Never get old. No work. No sweat. No reality getting in the way of my immortality. The lawyers and the agents looked at each other. As a matter of fact, Kid, we were thinking of approaching you. It can be arranged.

BING: What can be arranged?

TYBALT: My death.

BING: You've sold the rights to your death?

TYBALT: Don't jump to any conclusions. I'll be a multimillion dollar industry. I've posed for nude photos that'll be released in a year. I've written, had written for me, a beautiful book with all my hopes and dreams. I wish I'd known you wanted to be a writer. You could have done some of my ghost work. I've shot scenes that are going to be inserted into Marilyn's old movies so we can seem to appear together. They think we'll make a great team. They're making a movie of my life. Cameras hidden down there filming my leap. Norman then is doing a beautiful, had done it already, picture book, you know, for coffee tables, a book of my life and death and why. Why. That's the title. Then they'll make a play out of it. Then a movie version. Then a stage musical of the movie. Then a movie musical of my life. Then a TV series. Then a spin-off. They'll be looking for someone to play me. They'll be starting a major search to find me. Maybe you could go up. Audition. I could give you the names of the top people in the industry to see. Or maybe you could write my life and sell it to the magazines. The small ones. The big mags have already been contracted. The early Tyb. I hadn't planned on that. God, I wish I had known you wanted to be a writer. That you found that little store on Fourteenth Street. That you wore the cufflinks. Just before I came up here, I went back to Fourteenth Street. Returned the cufflinks. Let somebody else use them. Tybalt's boyhood. We had fun, didn't we? Did we? I can't remember. I always thought about the future so much, I never remembered the past. I wanted to be rich and famous so badly. But we're afraid to grow. I was so afraid to take the plunge into immortality. To settle for the old rich and famous. I'll never have to work again. The most returns for the least outlay. No sweat. I'm lucky. Always have been lucky. No strings. No ties. *(Looks down.)* That's my signal. Two minutes to go. *(Throws off army blanket revealing blinding saffron robes.)*

BING: Why the saffron robes?

TYBALT: Why? Why? A good question further deepening the mystery surrounding his death. Had Tybalt been investigating the mysteries of the East before he died? Or were there political implications we will never understand in this action that denied the world its greatest icon of a star. These are very bright guys. Very bright guys.

BING: Tybalt, I don't know who's advising you, but…

TYBALT: Oh no. They know what they're doing. They've done it so many times before. They've got it down to a science. These people are experts. They've got a new F. Scott Fitzgerald novel coming out next week. I'll be bigger in death than I ever was in life and I just do—did—what they tell—told—me to do—did. Bing, for your protection, you'd better not write about anything I've told you today. Norman, the others, they might sue. Put you away.

BING: Don't you ever think for yourself?

TYBALT: My lawyers and my advisers advised me that…

BING: Don't you see what they're doing?

TYBALT: Yes. So clearly.

BING: Make your own decisions. Hey! You saw my play last night.

TYBALT: I loved it.

BING: It's cute, huh?

TYBALT: It was beautiful. The hell with what the critics say.

BING: How about being in my play? A new career.

TYBALT: I'd love to do your play but they told me I couldn't do it. It's not big enough. It doesn't fit the legend.

BING: Look. The doors of the movie theatres are opening. The people are coming out. Dazed. Walking like you. Talking like you.

TYBALT: That's my cue.

BING: We have to live.

TYBALT: It's too late for me now. If I decided to live, I'd be spending the rest of my life in lawsuits. No, it's better this way. Believe me. Hey, Bing. Write about me. I'd like that.

BING: No. I'm going to write about a guy. A fella. A boy really. Who keeps seeing life through everyone else's eyes.

TYBALT: That's a beautiful thing to write about. If I'd known you wanted to be rich and famous... God, it'd been so easy.

BING: Will the guy make it? This fella. This boy. He can fail. He could win. It's a tightrope act. You can't tell. And it's a play. In a theatre. And this fella, the boy, comes to the edge of the stage and asks the audience to see the fella. See the boy without any illusions. And this fella, the boy, the man, looks back at you. The man has clear vision. Potentially clear. I look at you with my vision, he says. You look at me with your vision. And the room is crisscrossed with this network of private visions. Sharing. And we see life with our own eyes.

(Tybalt steps to the edge of the scaffolding and pitches himself off, all in an unbearably slow motion as if time had stopped and we could explore and examine every frame of a man's plummet to his death.)

TYBALT: *(At his last moment.)* Au revoirrrrrrrrrr...

BING: Tybalt!!!!!!

(And Bing digs his hands into his eyes as if to dig out these old eyes. Tybalt is like the amputation of some terrible part of himself. The stage quickly revolves taking Tybalt's body and Bing on the scaffold with it. The Actress is revealed. She is dressed in Bing's tuxedo. She looks like some bizarre version of Bing. Music plays. She sings.)

ACTRESS:

> Before I was Born
> Angels fluttered down
> And promised I'd be
> Rich and Famous.
> Then I got born
> To earth I sputtered down
> Now I'm not Rich
> And I'm not Famous.
> Where are those angels with their broken promises?

Do I fall in line with the other doubting Thomases?
Where are those angels? What do they think they're doing?
If they don't show up soon, I'm suing.

(Bing appears, lost. Dazed. The Actress confronts him. She sings to him. They do the mirror images Bing did with Anatol.)

ACTRESS:

Before I was Born
Other angels came
And said we offer
Peace and Quiet.
Then I got born
And it's like I'm dead
I don't want Peace.
I don't want Quiet.

(The Actor who played the other parts appears. He is dressed as Bing is. He confronts Bing. They all play the mirror images.)

ACTRESS:

Where are those angels? The ones who came here first of all.
The ones with the wings and the golden things and wherewithal
Where are those angels? What do they think they're up to?
I'm looking. I'm searching. I'm marching. March Hup Two.
When life is gone
Candles guttered down
We'll say we didn't get as promised.
When will life be
The way I want it to be????????

(The music stops abruptly. The three face each other.)

BING: Hey, Bing, what are you going to do now?
ACTOR-ACTRESS: Hey, Bing, what are you going to do now?

(Bing very proudly and easily removes one cufflink and tosses it with great resolve in front of him. The other two follow suit. Bing tries to undo the other cufflink. It won't come loose. It's a struggle. It won't come out. He does not want to give it up. He can't give up that final cufflink. He lowers his hands in dismay. The other two follow suit. The lights fade on Bing.)

END OF PLAY

Frequently Asked Questions
On Playing Guare

1. "What have I just read?" Chances are it's a comedy. But it's like nothing you've ever read before. Accept the fact that you are working on something that is particularly original. It's like a Picasso painting, only it's not, it's a Guare play. Go with the originality of it.

2. "Have I experienced the likes of this?" Although it's funny and although it's original, the play should not frighten you just because it's not psychological realism or naturalism. The key is: The actor can find plenty to identify with in playing his or her character. You are playing a recognizable human being here on earth, a character whose problems and behavior are universal. Bing Ringling wants to be rich and famous, and we can all identify with that. He wants a meaningful relationship, we know what that is all about. He has parents he cannot connect with, and that is something many of us have unfortunately experienced. Find a bit of yourself in the character and find the character in you. (Guare permits that.)

3. You will be asking yourself, "How do I know I'm funny in this thing?" or "Why is everyone else in the play funny except me?" The answer to the first question is you will know you are funny when you are pursuing your intentions with enormous passion; when you are fighting to overcome obstacles. No one gives up in a Guare play. As for the second question, you should not feel you are funny. When you think you are funny you will be outside the moment, outside the play and not funny at all. Guare's actors have to risk being fools, zanies and madmen. These actors have to risk the chance of making the audience uncomfortable and terrified at the same time they're laughing. It's very dangerous as an actor not to settle, to keep your character spinning, twisting and experiencing the unexpected. It takes a lot of faith the audience will go along with you. (In my experience they do.)

4. Your biggest question is likely to be, "Is there anything I can hold on to when I'm working on this material? Sometimes I feel like I'm falling off a window ledge and I don't know if it's me the actor, or me the character." What you hold on to is Guare's use of Language. Like a musician you must be able to hear what you are seeing on the page. Diction, intonation, articulation... *how* your character speaks is *who* your character is. Look at the rhythms of speech, the length of the line, the syntax. Time your breath to the end of the line, especially if it's a joke. Make sure you don't take arbitrary pauses which have nothing to do with how the scene is building. Know your character may speak one way to another character, but differently to the audience. A John Guare character has a profound *need* to speak, *need* to sing, *need* to articulate even in silence. Need to be on stage

at that moment desperately needing what you need and speaking like you need to.

5. "And finally...?" Finally, originality, humanity, comedy, and very special language. An actor's dream.

—*Mel Shapiro*

PRODUCTION NOTES

Cop-Out was originally performed at the Eugene O'Neill Theater Center in Waterford, Connecticut in July 1968 with Ron Leibman and Linda Lavin and directed by Melvin Bernhardt and was subsequently produced at the Cort Theater in New York in April 1969 with the same cast and director and designed Fred Voelpel and Lit by John Gleason.

Home Fires was performed as a curtain raiser to *Cop-Out* at the Cort Theater in April 1969 with a cast that included Charles Kimbrough as Rudy, April Shawhan, Carrie Nye, Macintyre Dixon and George Bartenieff.

Marco Polo Sings A Solo was originally produced by the Nantucket Stage Company, Nantucket, Massachusetts in July 1973, produced by John Wulp and directed by Mel Shapiro with a cast that included Piper Laurie as Diane, Beeson Carroll as Stony, Kevin O'Connor as Tom, Paul Bendict as Frank, Diana Davila as Skippy, James Woods as Larry, Grayson Hall as Mrs. McBride and Joe Grifasi and Steve Roylance in various supporting parts. It was subsequently produced at the New York Shakespeare Festival in February 1977 with Joel Gray as Stony, Madeline Kahn as Diane, Sigourney Weaver as Skippy, Chris Sarandon as Tom, Anne Jackson as Mrs. McBride, Larry Bryggman as Frank, Chev Rodgers as Lusty, and James Jensen as Larry. John Wulp designed the scenery. Jennifer Tipton designed the lighting; Theoni V. Aldredge the costumes. Mel Shapiro directed.

Moon Under Miami was first produced as *Moon Over Miami* at the Williamstown Theater Festival, Williamstown, Massachusetts, in August 1987 with a cast that included Nathan Lane as Otis, Julie Hagerty as Corleen, Glenne Headley as Giselle, James Belushi as Shelley, Lewis J. Stadlen as Osvaldo, Max Wright as Wilcox, Laurel Cronin as Fran Farkus. The 3 Mermaids were Dana Reeve, Chandra Lee and Frances Barney. Larry Sloan directed, Scott Chambliss was the designer and Larry Yerman was musical director.

Moon Over Miami was produced by Yale Rep in April 1989 with a cast that included Oliver Pratt as Otis, Julie Hagerty as Corleen, Lewis J. Stadlen as Osvaldo, Stanley Tucci as Shelley, Susan Kellerman as

Giselle, Laurel Cronin as Fran Farkus, Sam Stoneburner as Bentine, Tony Shalhoub as the Sheik. Andrei Belgrader directed, Scott Zielinski lit it and Larry Yerman was the musical director.

Moon Under Miami was produced by the Remains Theater, Chicago, Illinois in April 1995 with Will Clinger as Otis, Matt deClaro as Shelley, Noe Cueller as Osvaldo, Larry McCauley as Wilcox, Krista Lally as Corleen, Kate Walsh as Giselle, Valorie Hubbard as Fran Farkus, Kevin Hurley as Belden, Jihad Haril as the Sheik, G. Knight Houghton as Bentine. The Mermaids were Jenna Ford, Cara Newman and Sara Rene Martin. Neel Keller directed. Red Grooms designed the scenery which was executed by Stephen Olsen. Allison Reeds designed the costumes and Adam Silverman the lighting. Jeremy Kahn was musical director.

Rich and Famous was originally produced by William Gardner at the Academy Festival Theater in Lake Forest, Illinois in August 1974 with Ron Leibman, Linda Lavin, Charles Kimbrough and William Jay. Mel Shapiro directed. It transferred to the Willimastown Theater Festival the same month with Ron Liebman now playing all the men except Bing. It was subsequently produced by the New York Shakespeare Festival in February, 1976 with Ron Liebman, Anita Gillette and William Atherton. Dan Snyder designed it, Arden Fingerhut lit it and Theoni V. Aldredge did the constumes. Mel Shapiro directed.

The music for all of the plays in this volume was written by John Guare and is available in the Dramatist Play Service acting edition for *Rich and Famous* and Samuel French acting edition of *Cop-Out* and *Home Fires*. The music for *Moon Under Miami* is available through R. Andrew Boose, 1 Dag Hammarskjold Plaza, NYC 10017.